Theory, (Post)Modernity, Opposition

PostModernPositions

A Series in Critical Cultural Studies — Robert Merrill, editor
Institute for Advanced Cultural Studies

Other books by Mas'ud Zavarzadeh

The Mythopoeic Reality: The Postwar American Nonfiction Novel
Seeing Films Politically
Pun(k)deconstruction and the Ludic Political Imaginary

Other books by Donald Morton

Vladimir Nabokov

Other books by Mas'ud Zavarzadeh and Donald Morton

Theory/Pedagogy/Politics: Texts for Change
*Theory (Un)Limited: Writings in (Post)modern Theory and Radical
    Pedagogy* (forthcoming)

Mas'ud Zavarzadeh

Donald Morton

Theory, (Post)Modernity, Opposition

An "Other" Introduction to
Literary and Cultural Theory

PostModernPositions, Volume 5

MAISONNEUVE PRESS

Publications of the Institute for Advanced Cultural Studies
Washington, D.C., 1991

Mas'ud Zavarzadeh and Donald Morton, *Theory, (Post)Modernity, Opposition: An "Other" Introduction to Literary and Cultural Theory*

Copyright © 1991 by Maisonneuve Press
P.O. Box 2980, Washington, D.C. 20013-2980

Maisonneuve Press is a division of the Institute for Advanced Cultural Studies, a non-profit collective of scholars concerned with the critical study of culture. Write to the Director for information about Institute programs.

Printed in the United States by BookCrafters, Fredricksburg, VA.
Manufactured to exceed the standards of the Committee on Production Guidelines for Book Longevity of the Council on Library Resources.

Library of Congress Cataloging-in-Publication Data

Zavarzadeh, Mas'ud, 1938 -
    Theory, (post)modernity, opposition : an "other" introduction to literary and cultural theory / Mas'ud Zavarzadeh, Donald Morton.
    p. 248, cm. (PostModernPositions ; v. 5)
  Includes bibliographical references and index.
  ISBN 0-944624-11-1 (cloth) : ISBN 0-944624-12-X (paper)
  1. Postmodernism (Literature) 2. Literature--History and criticism--Theory, etc. 3. Structuralism, (Literary Analysis) 4. Deconstruction. I. Morton, Donald E. II. Title. III. Series.

PN98.P67Z38 1991   91-13749
801'.95'09045--dc20   CIP

Contents

Pedagogy
of the Controversial—
A Foreword

1

This is an "other" introduction to literary and cultural theory. Its "otherness" lies, however, not only in its politics, but also in the implications of that politics for an "other" pedagogy.

Most "introductions" address themselves to an "innocent" subject of knowledge, a person innocent not only in relation to the issues being introduced (an unobjectionable assumption), but innocent also in relation to the process of understanding itself (not at all, we think, a justifiable assumption). The reader of an "introduction" is usually assumed to be unable to engage in contestation and comparative critical inquiry, and for this reason is always "protected" from the controversial. This "protective" pedagogy insists that the best way to teach is to provide the novice learner with established knowledges and to avoid disputes which may create "confusion" for him. This rule is broken, of course, only when the "controversial" itself has already been normalized and turned into a routine and canonical point of argument: an example in contemporary theory would be, say, the "controversy" between Foucault and Derrida over the question of "history." The institutional (power) move of erasing knowledge-as-contestatory by establishing knowledge-as-canonical (that is, of commodifying intellectual labor) is nowhere more clearly instanced than in a recent column by *PMLA* editor John Kronik, who observes that "[n]o academic heart swells so fully as when its owner becomes a citation" ("Editor's Column" 200). Although he deploys a ludic tone that is supposed to dissociate him from the practice of canonization, Kronik nevertheless reveals (in his statistical compliation of authorities most often quoted in the journal in the 1980's) that what is still at stake in the dominant academy is exactly the (careerist) desire for canonization and the containment of controversy.

Our assumptions (one of which is that culture is a site of struggle between various social groups conducted along the axes of class/ race/gender) and our goals (a principal one being to change existing social arrangements) have led us to a very different kind of pedagogy and thus to an "other" mode of representation of contemporary theory in this book. We inscribe the reader/subject of knowledge in the very process of writing theory as the contestation over cultural intelligibilities. To achieve this goal, we do not avoid polemic, but in fact make it part of the process of "knowing." Thus, instead of following the usual pattern of merely providing the reader with (neutral) accounts of theories, we try rather to place the reader in a position from which he cannot help but take a stand on the issues and go beyond the narrative of neutrality. In other words, instead of "teaching theory," we wish to engage and provoke the reader in the struggle over theory. Thus, we assume the reader to be not merely an "active" reader but a "partisan" one quite equal to engaging the issues. Ultimately, we want to encourage her to move away from the position of being only a theoretician (one well-versed in theories) toward being a theorist (one who conceptualizes and thus participates in the production of social meanings with urgency and as a partisan). Not a substitute for histories of or guides to contemporary critical theory, our book offers instead a politically positioned counter-discourse in the classroom that provokes and resituates students by raising pressing issues and by addressing them through "other" (non-dominant) concepts such as "critique," "the global," "ideology," "totality," and "resistance (post)modernism."

With this in mind, then, the reader should not expect this book to be "objective" (that is, "above" today's contestations) or "comprehensive" (in the sense of "covering" all the issues in contemporary theory): on the contrary, its chapters will neither "survey" the different "schools" of theory, nor evolve around the ideas of selected theorists. Instead this book articulates literary and cultural theory as an array of emergent issues on which it takes a stand and which it situates in broad conflicting frames of intelligibility.

In a preliminary way, we can designate these frames of intelligibility as the ethical frame, the rhetorical frame, and the political frame. We call on the reader to note that, in saying this, we have already situated our discourse in contemporary controversies and thus in a sense acted out the mode of articulation we intend to adopt: instead of "describing" the contemporary scene of theory, we have instead—by means of these very designations—entered the domain of contestation. For (what we call in this book) the dominant "ludic" (post)modern theory does not allow one to make the distinctions we have made among modes of contemporary intelligibilities (that is, does not allow one to assume that they are "identical" with themselves, and thus so clearly "locatable" as to be "nameable" as the ethical, the rhetorical, the political). The dominant theory insists instead that the ethical is inextricably involved in the rhetorical; the rhetorical, inscribed in the political; the political, rewritten in the ethical. . . . (Post)structuralism's differential logic—today's reigning logic—does not permit one to make the kinds of distinctions we believe it is urgently necessary to make for transformative political practices.

That, however, is exactly our point. From this sentence onward, the reader of this book, rather than simply "listening to" our narrative of these issues, must instead actively participate in the contest over which concepts and categories are needed for making sense of theory: for instance, the reader must engage with the issue of what is at stake in the collapsing of categories themselves into undecidable nonconcepts (differences). From now on, the reader must see theory not as an arena for investigating merely "local," "specialist," and "disciplinary" interests, but as part of a larger social discourse, the purpose of which is to produce concepts that articulate social priorities and to elaborate and justify a political agenda. In other words, as we deploy it here, theory is not just an academic subject: it is a critique of the social and the categories (the "ethical," the "political," . . .) that are deployed to make it intelligible. Again, we note that by articulating the social and situating the reader in relation to it, as we have just done, we are engaging in yet another contemporary controversy, the controversy over reading as a "private" act of pleasure as opposed to reading as the mapping of the space of the social and the public. We have, then, once more implicated the reader in another contested contemporary issue, to which he must respond. By responding to such a series of issues, the reader, we believe, will begin to constitute for herself (although not as a "private" act) a theoretical frame of understanding.

This teaching through controversy is all the more urgent now because some others who write and speak about literary and cultural theory, about politics and pedagogy today, seek to render "ideas" unthreatening by trying to cordon off the classroom from the contestations of the social and by seeking to make it a site of purely cognitive awareness. For instance, endorsing the segregation of the classroom from social struggles, Gayatri Spivak (who, by a judicious eclectic mixing of Marxism, deconstruction, feminism, and subaltern studies, has made a generic politics widely palatable and thus harmless in the academy) has recently suggested that it is foolish to suppose that institutions as they exist at present (as she puts it, those "within which one has signed a contract") can be the site of politics "from below" ("Interview" 97). According to her, politics is "very utopian in its articulation" and "cannot be taught in universities" (97). Putting aside her own ludic and populist occultation of "below" as a transconceptual experience, we would like to make it clear that unlike Spivak, we do not believe that the classroom has ever been or can ever become what she hopes to render it: a neutral, sanitized, and de-politicized space "safe" from political struggles, a "secure" space of merely professional and cognitive inquiries. It is in fact to demystify this safe pedagogy that we are writing this book, which produces "non-contracted" knowledges. To put it another way, the ambition of this book is not simply to teach self-reflexivity and cognitive vigilance (Spivak's aims): its goal is rather to hail the reader as an interventionist. For this is a book with a thesis, and the thesis is that theory is finally an apparatus of social transformation.

Spivak's subtle populism has become the current style of avoiding commitment; for in the arena of culture, commitment is read increasingly today as a form of crudeness. The political and social conservatism that is legitimated through the guise of analytical subtlety can perhaps best be seen in Terry Eagleton's *The Ideology of the Aesthetic* (the cover of which claims it as "his major work to date"). Eagleton's subtle leftism operates here under the sign of the aesthetic, understood as the site of the "shifting"/"slipping" relations of the general and the particular, the abstract and the concrete, the mind and the body, knowledge and experience. . . . As such, the book represents the absorption of mainstream conservative (post)structuralist "differential" textualism and its version of femininism. Instead of offering a *response* to (post)structuralism and (post)structuralist feminism, Eagleton's subtle eclecticism, like Spivak's sublte populism, simply *absorbs* the (supposed) "other."

It is not by chance that Spivak separates the classroom from the social world at large: like some others, she has elevated such separations to the level of a theoretical principle by arguing that "discontinuity"/"non-coherence" is required in order to avoid the spectre of totalizing ("Criticism, Feminism, and the Institution" 161). By means of this principle such pedagogues justify that theoretical eclecticism which, by never requiring that one series of theoretical inquires (feminism, for example) ever be made to confront to a conclusion another series of theoretical inquiries (Marxism, for example), simply underwrites once again—if at another level—the reigning pluralist politics. At the present historical juncture, this enthusiasm for the principle of incoherence (so urgently promoted in the discourses of the dominant academy's theorists) reproduces the same conservative ideological effect that is constructed in the supposedly "very different" arena of the "popular." For instance, the discourse of incoherence promoted by Spivak (whose views are not only widely circulated but indeed are represented as exemplary in a recently published book on *Intellectuals: Aesthetics, Politics, Academics* (Robbins, 1990)) is eagerly embraced in a recent issue of *Gentleman's Quarterly* as the informing discourse of George Bush's presidency. *GQ*'s commentator describes Bush's tenure in office as marked by the "episodic and peripatetic" and by the lack of "a unifying thread" (Blumenthal 101). Going much further than this, however, the same observer actually connects the social dynamics of the times to Bush's mode of enunciation as made up of "a series of self-interruptions, mental hiccups and arfs," (101)—in other words, as made up of that rhetoric so privileged in (post)-structuralist texts like *The Post Card*. The writer concludes that Bush (as compared with "humanist" Reagan) is emblematic of today's reigning ludic (post)modernism and emphasizes the pluralism of Bush's famous phrase "a thousand points of light": "If Reagan's great strength was his deep appeal to nostalgia," we are told, "then Bush's might be his incoherence, thus making him a man who captures the dominant mood of his time" (101). Incoherence, in other words, is the logic of dispersed, transnational capital which is produced "globally" on all levels of social practice—from the level of the consumption of fashion to the level of the presidency and to the level of the seemingly abstract philosophical discourses of the academy.

Spivak works hard to represent her endorsement of the principle of discontinuity (which she sees as involving her abandonment of theoretical "purity" ("Interview" 168)) as "daring" and even "brave": in the last analysis, however, it is only a "populist" (and therefore very "popular") ludic move. This principle of "discontinuity," which contributes to a "localizing" rather than a "globalizing" politics, is, as we shall argue throughout this book, a part of the ideological effects of the hegemonic intelligibilities underwritten by (post)-structuralism. Some (post)structuralists have even (predictably) given a moralistic twist to Spivak's notions: they argue that those who do not accept this principle of "discontinuity" and instead insist (for the sake of politics) on coherence as necessary for transformative practices (and we include ourselves in this group), are not "honest" (see Radhakrishnan, "Towards an Effective Intellectual" 94). We note, however, that they do so without ever problematizing "honesty" (letting it remain a moment of transparent plenitude outside history), an "odd" move for (post)structuralist theorists of the subject. We believe, on the contrary, that such eclecticism (which reproduces populist coalitionism) is quite "convenient" pro-fessionally to its proponents: not only does it reinforce the dominant ideology, but also because—on principle—it does not require that one connect the politics of the social world to the politics of the classroom as one teaches, it renders the pedagogue's relation to the institution to which she is attached quite safe and comfortably non-oppositional. Our book moves in the "other" direction.

In **Part I, "For Theory, But . . . ,"** we have engaged varieties of attacks on theory from traditional humanist scholars (Abrams, Steiner, Ellis . . .) as well as new traditionalists (Fish, Rorty, Knapp, and Michaels . . .). Chapter One deals with specific positions taken "against theory" and interrogates the politics of anti-theory. Chapter Two changes the perspective of discussion and focuses on the assumptions and presuppositions which enable these attacks on theory to acquire academic legitimacy and commonsensical appeal. It is, for example, by deploying a particular notion of history ("historicism") that the anti-theorists are enabled to argue for cultural history as the unfolding of a telos located in the ethical imagination. Furthermore, there is also a specific view of language that makes possible the semiotic instrumentalism behind anti-theory. It is important to bear in mind that we are not claiming that these assumptions and presuppositions are "consciously" adopted by anti-theorists. Quite to the contrary, we believe that dominant ideology works most effectively as a set of obviousnesses which are part of the anti-theory academy's cultural unconscious.

In **Part II, ". . . But For a Radical Theory,"** we have shifted our perspective and the level of analysis: here we no longer deal with the politics of anti-theory, but focus on the political consequences of what has been named as "theory" in the (post)modern academy. We open this section by a general discussion of (post)modernity in which we distinguish between ludic and resistance (post)modernisms: this distinction enables us to articulate the differences between, on the one hand, a discursive politics which decenters texts and evacuates the "obvious" meanings of culture's established categories, and, on the other hand, a radical politics which although it takes the decentering of texts as an inaugural moment in emancipatory political practices, by no means stops there. We believe that social change is ultimately brought about not by locating the aporias and slippages of texts of culture: such a practice at most leads to what we call a "semiotic" democracy in which people speak (only) for themselves, and read, write, and go to church "freely." This is merely a restating of the dominant bourgeois democracy under the sign of the (post)modern secured by the practices that Laclau and Mouffe have fetishized as a "hegemony" they promote as the foundation of "radical" democracy, which is actually a legitimization of a non-class, coalitionist, liberal politics. Social change will come about, we believe, not by emancipating signs from totalities (Lyotard's view), but by displacing the relations of production, for although the relations of production do not evade, they nevertheless always exceed, the fate of signs.

In Chapters Four and Five we unpack the implications of radical resistance (post)modernism for a reading of (post)structuralism in general and for deconstruction in particular as they are operating today in the ludic academy. It may be helpful to point out here that in Chapter Four we are "reading" the dominant narrative of changes in contemporary theory and are therefore less interested in the "primary" texts (which we have read in other sections of the book) than we are in the ways in which such "primary" texts (like those of Foucault, Derrida, Braudel . . .) are interpreted in order to construct the dominant narrative of change. In order to convey the interpretive differentials of this narrative, it is necessary that we quote the readers of these texts rather than the primary texts themselves.

Remembering Marx's observation not to offer the world a "doctrinaire . . . new principle . . . [as the] truth" but to "develop new principles" out of the existing ones (Marx and Engels, *Collected Works* 3: 142), we end the book not with a diagnosis and a blue print but with what will probably be seen as a manifesto. The manifesto (if that is what it is) aims not so much at prescribing a route to the truth of social practices but at a reading of the possibilities which are now suppressed under the tyranny of what is called the "real" and the "pragmatic": the manifesto is about how this pragmatic "is-ness" can be overturned and the boundaries of the possibilities inscribed in it overcome. In short, the manifesto concerns the removal of the economic and political closure which is naturalized under the name of the existent; it is the articulation of our view that things should not, and need not, be the way they are. This is the agenda of what we call "critical cultural studies," which we wish to mark as different from what is today being institutionalized in the United States as "cultural studies." Contrary to the views of proponents of the dominant cultural studies (such as John Fiske and Constance Penley), cultural studies is not a mere description of cultural emergents that aims to give voice to the "experience" of those who have been denied a space to talk. It is instead an articulation of the cultural real that will change the conditions which have blocked those voices from talking. Rather than producing an "explanation" of the social contradictions that suppress these "experiences," experiential cultural studies (the kind practiced, for instance, by Fiske and Penley) offers a "description" of the exotic "other" and thus provides the bourgeois reader with the pleasure of contact with "difference." In other words, critical cultural studies is not a description but an explanation, not a testimonial but an intervention: it does not simply "witness" cultural events, but takes a "position" regarding them. In this book we have not mapped out a program in cultural studies, but have instead enacted critical cultural studies by demonstrating how such a mode of reading the texts of culture (theory, for instance) produces spaces for transformative practices.

From its inception and through its various versions, several persons have given their sustained intellectual support to this project: Teresa Ebert; Robert Merrill; Benjamin, Karen, and Samantha Morton; and Scott Severance. For their editorial assistance, we want to thank Adam Katz, Jerry Leonard, and Mary Ellen O'Connell.

Some parts of this book were originally published in a very different form in *Syracuse Scholar*, and we would like to thank the editor of that journal for giving us permission to use material from the earlier version here.

Part I

For Theory, But . . .

Chapter One

Theory and the Politics of Pluralism "Against Theory"

1

More than two decades after the publication of Derrida's *De la grammatologie*, at a time when its impact has been institutionalized in the academy and contemporary theory has situated itself on new boundaries, it is embarrassing to encounter texts that still regard deconstruction as the latest theoretical position, texts that in fact equate deconstruction with theory itself: books such as John Ellis's *Against Deconstruction* (1989) and George Steiner's *Real Presences* (1989). In Peter Shaw's *The War Against the Intellect: Episodes in the Decline of Discourse* (1989), deconstruction is seen as the practice responsible for the loss of intellectual "objectivity" and "disinterestedness" and the "repudiation of strict rationality," which Shaw laments as "the decline of discourse" (xviii-xix). Meyer Abrams's collection, *Doing Things With Texts: Essays in Criticism and Critical Theory* (1989), ends with a set of essays on deconstruction, as if that theoretical position still marked the horizon for theory now. In concluding his investigation of the issues, Howard Felperin in *Beyond Deconstruction: The Uses and Abuses of Literary Theory* (1985), as if speaking for all of these theoretical limit-setters, expresses doubt that it is even possible to go "beyond deconstruction" (219-220). This pervasive identification of deconstruction as the outer limit of (post)modern thought rather than as an intellectual problematic of a historical moment—the late 1960's and early 1970's—represents the emptying of theoretical practices of their material specificity and a reduction of critical theory to a set of disembodied, free-floating "ideas." Such a move renders non-existent the more powerful and politically dangerous forms of post-deconstructive critical theory: deconstruction becomes the "generic" avant-garde theory, a marker beyond which one need not go.

Some of these critics further confuse matters by positing deconstruction not only as equivalent to theory itself (thus erasing, for example, Marxist theory), but as equivalent to politically-committed theory: Laurence Lerner, for instance, proposes that contemporary theory (comprised, according to him, of two strands, "structuralism" and "radicalism") culminates in deconstruction, "the form of criticism which sets out to analyze either a particular work or the very concept of literature so as to reveal its ideological basis" (*Reconstructing Literature* 3). Lerner goes on to divide the current critical scene between the "traditionalists," on the one hand, and "deconstructionists," on the other, and, lumping together writers he feels have overt political concerns, stretches the meaning of the latter designation to cover even Marxist critics (Lerner 15-18). While, as his editor suggests, Abrams appears in *Doing Things With Texts* to situate the boundaries somewhat differently, targeting the New Historicism for criticism because of its "ideological fixity" and deconstruction only because of its "predetermined results" (xi), he nevertheless ultimately joins ranks with Lerner by arguing that because it opens up what he calls "a cultural vacuum," deconstruction represents the greatest political challenge to the grounds and assumptions of liberal humanist culture (Abrams 268). Our aim in this chapter is to investigate the politics of this conflation of deconstruction with theory, indeed sometimes with politically interested theory, on the part of several generations of theorists.

By unwittingly providing sometimes glaring and sometimes less obvious instances of the trivialization of contemporary thought, some of these texts rob themselves of the possibility of being taken intellectually seriously. A prime example of embarrassing trivialization is Cedric Watts's essay (in Lerner) which recuperates the deconstructive notion of "play" by "playfully" suggesting that all the new understandings of language, reading, textuality . . . put forward in contemporary theory are already contained in classical texts, specifically in "A Midsummer Night's Dream": "Shakespeare's Bottom," he proclaims, "is the source of much recent literary theory" (20). To defend traditional thought from the impact of theory, he offers the proposition, which he represents as a conclusion drawn from empirical research rather than an ideological starting point of his inquiry, that "in so far as these doctrines [of contemporary theory] are sound, they are not new, and in so far as they are new, they are not sound" (Watts 22). Watts's situating of the problematic issues of (post)modern thought as "doctrines" (which he believes can be labelled as "fallacies" and thus rejected as simply "false"), not to mention his reinscription of the discourses of origins and empiricism, should not be read only as a sign of "ignorance" of his topic (although it is that), but more importantly as pointing emphatically to his own position of enunciation, that is, to the ideological position in culture from which he speaks.

In *Against Deconstruction* Ellis's trivialization takes a somewhat more sustained, and perhaps less immediately identifiable, form. Although Ellis claims to be inaugurating a "dialogue" with deconstruction (vii), he in fact systematically fails to engage deconstruction's most significant premises: by by-passing the particular question of the role of critique in deconstruction, Ellis evades the issue of critique-al inquiry which, we believe, is crucial to (post)modern oppositional practices. A critique (not to be confused with criticism) is an investigation of the enabling historical conditions and social contradictions of discursive practices. It subjects the grounds of the seemingly natural and self-evident discourse to an inspection and reveals that what appears to be natural and universal is actually a situated historical discourse, which is to say that it is produced to justify and maintain a particular set of relations of production, a regime of interested "Truth." It is a construct positioned in the economic and historical coordinates of a cultural institution, even though in blindness to its situationality, it presents itself as a panhistorical practice. The function of the (post)modern critique, therefore, unlike that of criticism, is to demystify the "authority" attributed to all the discourses and practices of culture.

Ignoring such elementary issues as the role of critique, Ellis, however, conducts his "debate" with deconstruction by means of Aristotelian identitarian logic, even though deconstruction has bracketed that model, and in the name of a "positive" program (41) for "progress" (81), while both "positivity" and "progress" are among the primary targets of deconstructive critique. (He, needless to say, does not reground the problematized concepts but continues to treat them as "obvious.") When he, furthermore, declares that the deconstructionist program is "inherently uninteresting" (80), Ellis is again not engaging intellectually with deconstruction, as he claims, but merely rejecting the fact that deconstructive and, more broadly, (post)structuralist discourses have thoroughly problematized the notion that any cultural phenomenon whatsoever is "inherently" anything. Ellis's text tries to shield itself against the charge of frivolity that Watts's text so readily invites. Yet while pretending to open up a "dialogue" with deconstruction, Ellis completely fails to realize that when the presuppositions behind different discourses are radically different, the discourses do not "meet" and there is no "dialogue." If one wants to change that situation, one cannot simply rehearse, as his book does, the established and familiar terms of the impasse, but must produce a different discourse at a different level, that is to say, theorize these differences. Intellectually serious texts do not "rehearse," but open up spaces beyond, the familiar. Serious theoretical investigations constantly enlarge the reader's frames of understanding, while Ellis's book shows little, if any, familiarity with the broader intellectual movements of the (post)modern moment, of which deconstruction is only one, if an important, part. With these contradictions in mind, then, the politics of Ellis's book (as of Watts's essay) becomes clearer: he is writing *not* to create a dialogue with deconstructionists (who, as he indicates, have little inclination to engage discourses like his), but—at one level—to raise the spirits of traditionalists who will "agree" automatically with his various "points." In other words, Ellis is addressing traditionalists, who he seems to be assuming want not a "thoughtful" book but a mere rehearsal of their already fixed views. Thus he offers them again the familiar discourses located wholly within the traditional humanist un-self-reflexive mode of "criticism," which has nothing to do with (post)modern critique. The limitations of Ellis's approach is something even Felperin indirectly recognizes when he remarks that any effective opposition set up against deconstruction will have to take seriously into account "the latter's own ground" (Felperin 219). If, in spite of their claims, books like Ellis's do not seriously take up deconstruction's premises, then what are they doing? As we shall argue more fully as this book proceeds, the ultimate political function of such texts as Watts's and Ellis's is not simply to buck up traditionalists' spirits, but rather to obscure the complicity well-established in the academy today between humanism and deconstruction that serves to block the political interrogation of contemporary culture. Indeed the ineffectivity of Ellis's book in not even touching deconstruction's presuppositions is a part of this complicity: he can cheer up traditionalists while not pressuring or threatening deconstruction at all.

This is why it is necessary to engage such trivial texts: because to ignore even one as simplistic as Watts's on the grounds that it is intellectually and philosophically empty is to confuse its "content" with its ideological "uses." The emptiness of the trivial text is not a matter of editorial or authorial neglect: its philosophical naivete and sheer vacuousness are as much historically constructed as are the theoretical sophistication and historical understanding of "serious" texts of culture. This, by the way, is why what is embarrassing on one level of discourse is illuminating on another: the embarrassing moment involves the sudden, unexpected, and rather violent removal of the rehearsed response, and it is in this unprotected moment that the embarrassing discourse is seen in its situationality in the economy of cultural signification. The naivete of the trivial text is constructed by the historical vectors of signification, since it is in the spaces of the trivial that the dominant ideology reproduces the reigning ideas and repairs the damage that commonsense discourse has suffered in its conflicts and clashes with the anti-hegemonic discourses of culture. Ideology proposes a way of seeing, and the author/editor/producer of the trivial text is ideologically situated at a position of intelligibility from which only that which is necessary for reproducing the existing social relations is seen. The trivial text, in other words, is unable to see what in fact it encounters and it is in this ideological blindness that its historical significance lies. The trivial text, in other words, opens up a textual/political space for the recycling of those discourses required to legitimate the practices that enable the existing set of representations to endure. In the cultural spaces articulated by the trivial text, the dominant ideology reproduces itself, constructs and maintains those subjectivities needed for the perpetuation of the status quo. Through such texts the dominant ideology offers the reader a position of intelligibility from which he can make sense of himself as a continuous subject in spite of the changing, conflictual, and discontinuous discourses of culture.

At times of crisis in intelligibilities like the present, when the continuity of the subject is threatened by the intervention of oppositional discourses, the trivial text acquires immense significance. By reproducing the traditional positions of intelligibility, such texts help secure the old subject-positions needed for prevailing social arrangements. This is why the trivial text cannot be ignored since its political uses in culture indicate the operations of larger frames of intelligibility and their connections within the dominant power/knowledge relations. To transform these relations, it is necessary to intervene in the circulation of the trivial text, since it is only through such an intervention that the speculary relation of people with the world may be changed and the continuation of the hegemonic representation interrupted. This speculary relation is what Lacan calls in *Speech and Language in Psychoanalysis* the "imaginary" and understands as a site of regressive plenitude (159-177). It is necessary, we maintain, to combat the dominant ideology because it foreshortens the horizon of historical possibilities by constructing the world in terms that legitimate the interests of one class by subjugating others. Only a sustained ideology critique of the trivial text can disclose the political function of its naivete and conceptual innocence.

As a prelude to articulating in Part Two of this book our position that theory must be understood as an act of political resistance, we will take up in the next chapter such a sustained ideology critique of the discourses circulated in "trivial" texts which are inscribed by the dominant ideology that represents itself in "resistance to theory." In this chapter, however, we want to inquire further into the various moves against critical theory being made in the academy today in order to articulate their political significance.

2

The texts of Abrams and Steiner are illuminating instances of different strategies for dealing with theory deployed by humanists who recognize the challenge of critique under changing historical conditions: the former's representation of deconstruction-as-theory-itself is exemplary of the cultural situation of the 1970's and early 1980's and the latter's, of the cultural situation of the late 1980's. Abrams's strategy is to abandon the project of trying to make the incompatible discourses meet, at the same time ensuring that the theoretical discourse is subordinated to commonsensical discourse. To achieve this end, Abrams calls deconstructionists (who may stand in for critique-al theorists at large) "double-dealers" (*Doing Things With Texts* 277), that is, writers who work simultaneously in both commonly understood (traditional) discourses (of "criticism") *and* the new counter-discourses (of "critique") they devise to resist and alter conventional meanings. This move relocates the tensions over contemporary thought as a relation not between theorists and non-theorists (the latter always being comfortably situated in the standard discourses), but as a relation of theorists *with themselves*. On this view, any new space opened by critique exists at best only fitfully and temporarily (perhaps even as the theorist's "fantasy") because, while they may deploy critique-al discourses, all speakers/writers/ readers must return to the standard and normative conventions of language and culture, that is, to the norms as they presently exist (the status quo). On this view, conventional codes form the "ground" of critique-al discourses, even if they are regarded by humanists as being "flexible" enough to permit plural interpretations (Abrams 237). Thus, if the existing norms change (and Abrams admits that they do), such change (which he sees as slow, continuous, evolutionary, and "consensual") can hardly be attributed to the pressure of critique. In trying to demonstrate the ultimately convention-bound nature of "meaning" as against the deconstructive notion that meaning is "undecidable," Abrams insists—using, like Watts, Shakespeare as his touchstone—that everyone would agree on the meaning of Lear's sentence, "Pray you undo this button" (246). The question for theory, however, is not the one traditionalism poses of whether everyone understands already the commonsensical interpretation of this sentence, but the very different question critique-al theory poses of whether it would be intellectually/socially/ . . . productive to imagine a different meaning for that sentence. Would a reconceptualization of the sign "button" be as productive, say, as the reconceptualization of the sign "phallus"? If the answer is no, this is not so much because such a reunderstanding cannot be accomplished as that such a reunderstanding would not produce a very significant conceptual/philosophical/social/political yield.

It is clear that if deconstructive "undecidability" troubles humanists like Abrams, the possibility of "precipitate" social or cultural change troubles them more. Since, as he understands it, linguistic norms (which he takes to be the core of social norms) are not finally authoritative once and for all but a set of consensual and changeable conventions, "our practice . . . must rely," he says, "not on rules, but on linguistic tact—a tact that is the emergent result of all our previous experience with speaking, hearing, writing, and reading the language" (294). Thus not only linguistic, but all social change is placed under the aegis of the virtue of "tact": tact, in other words, is what controls (or ought to control) change to keep it from getting "out of hand." By situating critique as a dependent second-order activity rather than as a distinct and effective mode of reading/writing/thinking, Abrams hopes to place it safely under "tactful" management.

By the late 1980's this charge of double-dealing had lost its force, for it is one that theorists—deconstructionists and others—routinely represent as an established feature of critique-al thought. Whereas when Abrams first used it, the charge of "double-dealing" carried an implied hint of "hypocrisy," it later came to be widely understood as indicating the very critique-al nature of the (post)modern theoretical enterprise. Early on it was pointed out that Derrida himself is in "the uncomfortable position of attempting to account for an error [that of logocentrism] by means of tools derived from that very error. For it is not possible to show that the belief in truth is an error without implicitly believing in the notion of Truth" (Derrida, *Dissemination* x). Only a few years later, however, such acknowledgments became routine: "My own language," says one writer ". . . exploits the resources of representation in order to discuss what I claim is antirepresentational" (Arac, *Critical Genealogies* 297). What is at stake here is the refusal of traditionalism to accept the possibility that theoretical inquiry, by means of critique, can open up alternative spaces for radically different (future) cultural practices. For the traditionalist, knowledge is, from beginning to end, thinking with and through established codes and conventions and pedagogy is the passing on of culture's required skills, whereas for the (post)modern theorist engaged in critique-al thought, knowledge is working against established codes and conventions and pedagogy is thinking beyond the required skills.

Given the widespread familiarity of academic and intellectual circles with the role of critique by the late 1980's, even a committed humanist like George Steiner in *Real Presences* is forced to acknowledge that, deconstructive "double-dealing," far from being a question of "hypocrisy," is rather a consequence of the seriousness and rigor of (post)modern thought: when he observes that "deconstruction privileges the discomforts of the theoretical" (117), his formulation does not suggest that the pressure of critique-al theory is felt by the theorist alone. Indeed, Steiner's text is a highly articulate record of the marks deconstruction has left on humanism. If, like Abrams, Steiner repeats the call for "tact" in negotiating the meanings of signs of culture (148), he is remarkably compromising and emphatic in his acceptance of deconstruction's critiques of humanist assumptions: according to him, "the challenge" of deconstruction not only "cannot be evaded" (134), but is furthermore "irrefutable" (132). Thus Steiner finds largely unanswerable deconstruction's critiques of humanist notions of the canon, intentionality, pluralism, consensualism, disinterestedness, the determinacy of meaning, and so on. So, whereas Abrams had tried to "ground" theory in linguistic and social codes and defied theorists to stray beyond the self-evident meaning of "Pray you undo this button" as a means of shoring up the liberal humanist view of reality, Steiner "frees" theory from linguistic and social codes by admitting that "*Anything* can be said and . . . written about anything" (53) and even goes on to question whether the "liberal, evolutionary model match[es] reality" (67) and to suggest that the answer is negative. Steiner, who carefully qualifies his "acceptance" of deconstruction by saying that it is "irrefutable" only "[o]n its own terms and planes of argument" (132), continually introduces, starting with his title, theological terms in order to point to the alternative, transcendentally grounded understanding of culture he prefers. If he "accepts" deconstruction's notion of the "indeterminacy" of meaning, he does so by rearticulating it as "an enigmatic enormity" that "inhabits" culture (53). If he "accepts" the critique of pluralism, it is only because he takes deconstruction to have undermined the "superficiality" of a mere "secular pluralism": for "secular pluralism" Steiner substitutes a radical conservative "sacred pluralism," a mark of which is what he calls "enigmatic enormity" (divine plenitude) which must be taken ultimately on faith. If he accepts "theory," it is a theory to which its now lost original "ritual" "meanings and connotations" have to be restored (69). This revival of theory's early ritual dimensions is necessary, according to Steiner, in order to combat the current "mutiny of theory . . . against the authority of the poetic" (116).

What becomes increasingly apparent is the accommodation Steiner's humanism manages to achieve with deconstruction. By reviving theory's connection with "rites performed" (60), Steiner uncannily brings his sacred notion of theory into adjacency with contemporary (post)structuralist understandings of theory as performance that are gaining increasing popularity today (Morton, "Texts of Limits"). Steiner's notion of theory again rejoins that of (post)structuralism in the endorsement of "humor" (what, for example, Gregory Ulmer in "The Puncept of Grammatology" regards as the playful, "punceptual" aspect of grammatology): as Steiner puts it, "[t]he deconstructive saturnalia, the carnival of dislocations, the masques of non-meaning need to be taken most seriously where they can be seen as a variant on merriment" (115). It is Steiner's overall effort to bridge the gap between deconstruction and humanism that ultimately makes *Real Presences* an exemplary text of the late 1980's, when it becomes politically important for humanists to abandon their earlier truculent tone so that deconstruction can be coaxed into a coalition for the sake of resisting a commonly perceived "enemy." Steiner gives a clue to what that "enemy" might be when, having given up trying to defend his own humanism as "disinterested," he characterizes deconstruction as marked by a higher "disinterestedness," which he calls an "abstention from preference" (118). The "enemy" are those forms of cultural understanding which take an oppositional stance towards the status quo. Humanism's strenuous attempt (as in *Real Presences*) to show that it can "comprehend" deconstructive "indeterminacy," "intertextuality," "différance" . . . is ultimately an effort to show that because its "radicalism" is purely "textual," deconstruction after all passes the tact test, which oppositional theories (those that do not abstain from preference and move beyond "the text") definitely fail. In the last instance, the ideological function of Oldhumanist texts, whether embarrassingly trivial ones like Watts's or intellectually elegant ones like Steiner's, is to propose—if under different historical conditions and at different levels of awareness—deconstruction as the ultimate theory in order to occlude theories more politically dangerous to the status quo.

To those willing to make "tactless" observations, it is no surprise that such adept defenders of humanist pluralism "against theory" as Steiner, Abrams, O. B. Hardison, Jr., Walter Jackson Bate, Wayne Booth . . . have become academic celebrities in a society that is dominated by a pluralist ideology that has, as Ellen Rooney puts it, a seemingly "infinite capacity to recuperate the potentially anti-pluralist discourses that have appeared" (*Seductive Reasoning* 1). It is also no surprise that since the discourses of these Oldhumanists (who basically repeat outworn positions) have come to be recognized as increasingly ineffective, their place has already been taken by another generation of Newhumanists, some of whom theorize "against theory" with an updated critical and theoretical vocabulary and make supposedly "new" moves in the contestations over literary and cultural studies, although the ideological effects remain pretty much the same. (In fact, such ideological reinscriptions reach quite beyond even Newhumanist positions: it is, for instance, this Oldhumanist "tactful" segregation of political critique from pedagogical practices that is being currently reaffirmed in the "advanced" (post)modern positions of celebrated critics like Gayatri Spivak, who—as we noted before—maintains that "the institution within which one has signed a contract" cannot be the site of political intervention ("Interview" 97)).

3

An exemplary instance of the Newhumanists's direct and unmistakable assault on theory, in order to buttress—in a "new" way—the dominant ideology of liberal pluralism, is found in the set of essays first published in the *Critical Inquiry* from 1982 to 1985 and republished in 1985 together under the title *Against Theory: Literary Studies and the New Pragmatism* (Mitchell, ed.). The essay that occasioned the volume is Steven Knapp and Walter Benn Michaels's "Against Theory." Whereas Oldhumanists like Steiner may represent deconstruction/theory as a "mutiny . . . against the authority of the poetic" (*Real Presences* 119), Newhumanists like Knapp and Michaels recognize the ineffectivity of such arguments because they understand that poetry has no authority of its own anyway, that in fact it achieves its "authority" to the degree that it reinscribes those structures of understanding recognized as "authoritative" at a particular time in a culture's history: it is thus not poetry per se, but those structures that must be defended. Moreover, the Newhumanists also "know," that to claim that deconstruction represents a mutiny against "the poetical" is an embarrassing misrecognition: after all, as arch-defenders of "metaphoricity" and "literarity," deconstructionists like Paul de Man and Barbara Johnson, not to mention Derrida himself, can—in spite of their critique of the ideology of the aesthetic—readily be seen as among the most vigorous defenders of "the poetical" writing today. Thus it is not deconstruction or other theories that "abstain from preference" that have to be attacked, but more specifically political oppositional theories.

Knapp and Michaels conduct their argument at two levels: at the level of the relation of theory to practice, and at the level of the relation of intention to meaning. Deploying their "wave-poem" example in order to reassert that the ground of argument is always ultimately that of common sense (in the same way Abrams's uses "Pray you undo this button"), they purport to demonstrate that there is no "intentionless" meaning. Their overall strategy is to identify meaning with intention and define theory as that mode of understanding which falsely separates the two elements: they are then in a position to deny that theory (which, they claim, is produced on the basis of a false distinction) has any effects or consequences. To put it another way, they argue that to separate meaning from intention, which is equivalent to opening a space for "theory," is to take the position that it is possible "to know without believing" (27)—that is, to acquire a knowledge that is not already completely encased in the standard conventions and codes of one's community (in its "beliefs"). Along the way, Knapp and Michaels criticize even some of their closest pragmatist allies like Stanley Fish, E. D. Hirsch, and John Searle, who also identify meaning with intention, for mistakenly allowing the separation between intention and meaning to creep back into their discourses and thus for becoming "theorists" themselves. This insistence on "intention" is a mark of Knapp and Michaels's complicity with capitalism, which needs "free" ("intending") subjects who provide the labor for "freely" intended "free" enterprise. From Knapp and Michaels's point of view, practice must be decisively and finally ridded of the taint of theory (practice, in other words, must not be seen as theory-inscribed): "[T]heory," they argue, "is not just another name for practice" (30). Why? Because theory is by definition that which has already abandoned practice: it is "nothing else but the attempt to escape practice" (30). Thus they urgently recommend that since "the whole enterprise of critical theory is misguided," it "should be abandoned" (12).

The aporia in the discourses of Knapp and Michaels's text, the aim of which is to show that theory "can have no practical consequences" (29) and thus no role in either legitimating or de-legitimating a culture's practices, appears in its contradictory assertion both of the necessity, and the impossibility, of getting rid of theory. While insisting again and again that theory is utterly different from practice (that is, theory is not inscribed in practice), they find it necessary also to assert that "it can never be *separated* from practice" (29) (that is, theory is inscribed in practice). This contradiction begins to make sense when we realize that Knapp and Michaels are—like other humanists—not really "against theory" *per se*, but against theories which claim to open up a space outside accepted conventions and codes, in other words, outside a given culture's established "beliefs." If they target allies like Fish, Hirsch, and Searle, it is not because their theories are really dangerous, but because they leave the door ajar for counter-speculation. Knapp and Michaels want to eradicate the radically "other" reading/writing/

thinking by insisting that all reading/writing/thinking is governed by "belief," which is produced by the prevailing codes of the community to which one belongs. Their assertion that "beliefs cannot be grounded in some deeper condition of knowledge" (26) can be rendered as "in some *other* condition of knowledge": thus to say that one is working in radically different conventions and codes is incoherent. Their goal is not to eradicate theory as such, but to render oppositional theory phantasmatic.

This line of argument which sees radical oppositional theory as a phantasm has recently been articulated more fully by one of the founders of American neopragmatism, Richard Rorty, in connection with a discussion of the political effects of the texts of Michel Foucault. Following Vincent Descombes, Rorty sees a tension in Foucault's texts that produces an "American" Foucault and a "French" Foucault. In "Foucault/Dewey/Nietzsche" he notes that the American Foucault is a liberal humanist, who is "an up-to-date version of John Dewey . . . who said that liberal democracies would work better if they stopped trying to give universalistic self-justifications, stopped appealing to notions like 'rationality' and 'human nature,' and instead viewed themselves as promising social experiments" (1). The French Foucault is the anarchistic, Nietzschean Foucault, who tries to achieve "autonomy" and to do so must "have 'inhuman thoughts'" and who urges us to have "no 'worries about sharing our beliefs with our fellow citizens'" (1). In Rorty's analysis, the American Foucault is the socially responsible citizen, concerned for his fellow human beings, while the French Foucault is "a knight of autonomy" (4) who, viewing all "power" as "bad," would not offer even "just once" "a positive evaluation of the liberal state" (3). In these terms, Foucault was overall too "French" for Rorty and not sufficiently "American," meaning that—to return to the terms we have introduced here—he was too persistently on the side of "critique." One can infer from Rorty's discourses (although he doesn't use the word) that to be "critique-al" means to open a space that is "inhuman", that is, a space beyond culture's established beliefs. This "French," critique-al Foucault, according to Rorty, was pursuing "[t]he Romantic intellectual's goal of self-overcoming and self-invention," which though it may be a "good model . . . for an individual human being" is "a very bad model for a society" (5). "The point of a liberal society," Rorty asserts, "is not to invent or create anything, but simply to make it as easy as possible for people to achieve their wildly different private ends without hurting each other" (5). If for the pragmatists, the model of the critique-al Foucault concerned with "overcoming" existing limitations is bad for "public purposes" but fine for "private identities" (5), this is because the "private" is the domain of the "dream" (5) or phantasm. It is only by evading any direct address to the question of critique that Rorty manages to render one of the century's strongest opponents of the subject-as-individual as himself an ardent "individualist."

We ourselves believe it is important to point out how and why Foucault's discourses—like those of deconstruction—have been so easily recuperated by the mainstream academy to support the status quo: it was not because Foucault was a Romantic "knight of autonomy," but because his discourses erased the possibility of ideology critique and thus the possibility of a global analysis of the systematic oppression and exploitation produced by multinational capital (Morton, "Texts of Limits"). Nevertheless, it has to be recognized that, as sustained investigations of the enabling conditions of the discourses of Western culture, his texts are exemplary instances of (post)modern *discursive* critique. Since this is difficult to overlook, Rorty's embrace of Foucault (although partial) would appear to be necessarily also an embrace of "critique": that this is not the case, however, is clear from Rorty's insistence ultimately on "positive evaluation." He cannot deny that Foucault practiced critique, nor can he deny that it is a "feasible, if difficult, project" (4): but by (in predictable humanist fashion) personalizing critique and situating it as the private project of "the Romantic intellectual's self-overcoming and self-invention" he rules it an inappropriate practice for the public sphere. It is a private practice for which "[w]e should not try to find a societal counterpart" because trying to do so only (and here he repeats the pieties of liberalism) "leads to Hitler-like and Mao-like fantasies about 'creating a new kind of human being'" (5). Critique may be good for creating a personal "inner autonomy" but not for outer public freedom. Rorty can only bring himself to discuss Foucault's form of critique at all because he understands it as Nietzschean and nihilistic and therefore no real threat to the liberal state: in this sense it is like deconstruction (as Steiner pointed out) in "abstaining from preference."

The difficulty with Rorty's claim is that the results of Foucault's critiques (investigations of the enabling conditions of discourses) of texts of culture were neither nihilistic nor anarchistic, as Rorty suggests. Although we shall take up the question of critique in more detail in Chapter Six, it may be helpful to elaborate on this question here in order to help clarify some differences between deconstructive (Derridean) critique, Foucauldian critique, and ideology critique. Foucauldian discourse analysis is different from classical literary analysis in that the latter is conducted in terms of the form, content, and style of a text, of which they are regarded as inherent parts. Foucault's discourse analysis concerns what might be called the mode of meaning-production in a text because what it discovers are the rules of formation of a given discourse or set of discourses which are external to and not the same as the "essential" (truth of the) discourses themselves: thus like other forms of critique, Foucauldian critique is a speculative articulation that opens a different space of understanding. Derridean critique likewise is a speculative form of thought that opens an "other" space of understanding (through the invention of new terms such as "logocentrism," "the pharmakon," "hymen," "the supplement," "différance," . . .) but the Derridean space is "peculiar" in that it is a space of terms that are, as Derrida says of "différance," neither "word[s] or concept[s]" (*Margins* 11).

The classic contestation we referred to in our introduction between Derrida and Foucault concerning the status of history has to do precisely with their disagreement about the status of the rules of discourse in relation to the texts which those rules produce. Derrida takes the position that the rules of discourse are not external to the discourses themselves but immanent in the very processes of signification by which those discourses are constructed. Foucault claims that in *Madness and Civilization* his goal is to produce a history of madness by speaking for "madness," by articulating what reason has suppressed and excluded, by giving voice to reason's "outside," so to speak. Yet Derrida critiques Foucault's project by arguing that such a goal is impossible since the discourse of madness can never be separated from the discourse of reason, both being a part of a logos that "preceded the split of reason and madness, a logos which within itself permitted dialogue between what were later called reason and madness" (*Writing and Difference* 38). In Derrida's view, "[a]s always, the dissension is internal. The exterior (is) the interior, is the fission that produces and divides . . . " (39). In other words, Foucault's project of getting "outside" of "reason," and thus of writing anything like a history from "outside" is what Derrida calls a logocentric project, which demands to be read deconstructively, as Derrida proceeds to read it in his well-known essay on Foucault. Yet Derrida does not reject an "outside" altogether, for Derridean critique moves from the closural space of logocentric representation into a non-representational space outside "words" and outside "concepts" and thus outside "power," "history," and "practice" (which are themselves words and concepts that Foucault wants not simply to preserve, but to exploit). (By way of bringing this "classic" contestation a little into the present, we wish to note parenthetically that Derrida's attack on conceptuality and its role in the operations of the cultural "system" is continually being rearticulated and recirculated in academic and intellectual circles today: notably by Lyotard, who in "Sensus Communis" denies, for instance, that the public sphere—the arena of politics—should be understood "through the mediation of the concept" (1)). In contrast to Derrida, Foucault, in the interests of politics, argues that

> [Discourse] has its own rules of appearance, but also its own conditions of appropriation and operation: an asset that consequently, from the moment of its existence . . . poses the question of power; an asset that is by its nature the object of struggle, a political struggle.
>
> *(Archaeology of Knowledge* 120)

In other words, the production of discourses is governed not strictly by operations internal to texts, as Derrida insists, but by the forces of history external to texts. Foucault himself has marked this effort to move beyond textuality and beyond discourse, from the discursive to the non-discursive by connecting it to a shift in his own thinking from the mode of "archaeology," with its stress on "epistemes" and on "knowledge," to the mode of "genealogy," with its stress on "apparatuses" and on "power" *(Power/Knowledge* 196-197).

What Derrida appears to be attacking in *Madness and Civilization* is what one commentator has called its "rhetoric of crisis" (Megill 271). When toward the end of his essay, Derrida remarks—with evident "admiration"—that "nowhere else and never before has the concept of *crisis* been able to enrich and reassemble all its potentialities, all the energy of its meaning, as much, perhaps, as in Michel Foucault's book" *(Writing and Difference* 62), he is nevertheless pressuring the very political force of Foucault's writing: he is, we might say, "de-crisis-ifying" it. In the last analysis, what this famous "contestation" articulates is, in our view, the differing effectivities of the two politically limited kinds of "critique" represented by "deconstruction" and "genealogy." The conclusion some draw from these considerations is that by comparison with

Derridean deconstruction, Foucault's work is in some sense more "political" because it appears to work at creating cultural crisis. In the end, however, it seems to us that even Foucauldian "genealogy" remains thoroughgoingly "discursive" and that its operations, like those of Derridean deconstruction, remain debilitatingly "local." The "extra-discursive" does not ultimately play much of a role in Foucault's account of culture, nor finally does ideology. For, as we have already suggested, Foucault also theorizes the rules of discourse formation in such a way as to localize those rules: in other words, his theory suggests that at a certain "micro" level of analysis, ideology (recognized as systematically cutting across all discourses) does not operate, so that the politics he defends against Derrida (who renders critique a rhetorical and textual matter) remains a purely local and localizing politics. Ideology critique moves beyond both deconstruction and discourse analysis to open the space of a global political analytics, as we will elaborate in Chapter Six. To return to Rorty's characterization of Foucault, the rules of discourse formation that Foucauldian critique discovers are "regularities" and thus by no means nihilistic or anarchistic as Rorty insists. Rorty's defense of humanism thus forces him to take the rather fragile position of (implicitly) opposing critique as if all critique were nihilistic, just as Knapp and Michaels, in one broad swipe, oppose all theory as if it were critique-al.

To return to the latter: in the last analysis, Knapp and Michaels transform Abrams's narrower linguistic and literary pragmatism into a philosophy of culture which says that theory cannot "ground" anything, what ground there is is whatever we are doing now (our present practice): without denying the possibility of resistance or opposition to established conventions (the status quo can be "criticized"), they nevertheless maintain that it is incoherent and non-sensical to try to ground such efforts outside established codes. Such is the political effect of pragmatism: not to deny that culture has a fringe but to deny that this fringe can ever transform itself into a politically effective margin opposing the dominant center by grounding its efforts in critique-al theory. If change must be admitted to occur, it must be robbed of any "disruptiveness" it may contain. It is humanism's need to block critique which informs the strategies of the texts we have been investigating: if these strategies change as we move, say, from Abrams and Steiner to Knapp and Michaels, it is because the latter (whom we have nominated Newhumanists) recognize that, in the current stage of culture's crisis, the

Oldhumanist principle of "tact" has utterly failed to tame the opposition. In the face of this failure, the insistence on the inescapability of the status quo (culture's codes and conventions) becomes less and less "tactful" as the stakes become clearer. The damaging thing about theory, according to Knapp and Michaels, is that it "creates the illusion of a choice between alternative methods of interpreting" (18)—that is to say, the choice between the prevailing understanding of the real and a radically different understanding.

The editor of *Against Theory*, W. J. T. Mitchell, who is also chief editor of *Critical Inquiry*, insists that the book "might as well be entitled *A Defense of Theory* as *Against Theory*" because "[m]ost of the contributors defend some version of literary theory" and that the choice of the latter title was dictated by the fact that the exchanges were stimulated by the appearance of Knapp and Michaels's article bearing that title (1). Mitchell's treatment of the issues, however, simply reconfirms the anti-critique-al, neo-pragmatist position of Knapp and Michaels, even while claiming (as we saw Ellis claim) to open up a "dialogue" and engage in "dialectical pluralism" (3). The claim Mitchell makes here is a rehearsal of the position he articulated earlier (1982) in an essay, "*Critical Inquiry* and the Ideology of Pluralism," situating the editorial policies and practices of the influential mainstream journal he edits. In this text, Mitchell renders the political, "taming" function of liberalism quite clear: he laments the current tendency to engage in what he calls "position mongering" (610) and goes on to indicate that the function of *Critical Inquiry* is to help "cure the feverish internal warfare which threatens to tear [the structure of critical institutions] apart" (611) by "airing" the debates. According to Mitchell, while some other journals, such as "*New Literary History* or *Glyph* . . . have dedicated themselves to the task of importing European critical traditions . . . into the Anglo-American critical scene" (613), "*Critical Inquiry's* function has been, at least in part, to stage encounters of these ideas with the native tradition, to bring European and Anglo-American criticism into debate and dialogue" (613).

With Mitchell's notions of the role of his journal in mind, we can better understand why and how the discourses of his introduction to the volume, *Against Theory*, do little more than repeat, with a slightly different accent, Knapp and Michaels's moves first, by pointing to and then dismissing the claims of critique-al thought and then by concluding that all thought has a "pragmatic" function anyway. When in the preface to *Against Theory* Mitchell declares that "[a]ll the defenses of theory in this collection of essays would have to be called 'pragmatic'" (3), even the presumably "deconstructive" one (1), he in effect closes the door on any non-pragmatic theory (any critique-al theory not working within prevailing codes), thus repeating in his own idiom Abrams's insistence that the commonsensical, the pragmatic, the normative is the inescapable "ground" of all cultural activities. To preserve the "critical" of *Critical Inquiry* as "criticism" (that is the "business-as-usual" kind of inquiry) Mitchell has to suppress all hints of the importance of critique that appear in one or two of the texts in *Against Theory*. While not rejecting theory as such, Mitchell emphatically rejects theory-as-critique-al-openness-and-otherness, for in his view this kind of theory is too "pure," on the one hand, because, he claims, theory actually has an ineradicable element of the "empirical" in it (7), while too "dangerous," on the other, because what theory (which he claims is "monotheistic, in love with simplicity, scope, and coherence" (7)) actually "seeks" is—and here one must note the loaded phrase—"a final solution" (7). Thus, for the Newhumanist, critique-al theory must be opposed because it is fascist, indeed Nazi: so much for (Oldhumanist) tact.

As *Against Theory* suggests, the Newhumanists don't really bother to take on deconstruction, at least not in the point-by-point manner of Steiner: this is not because they "like" it, but because so many of deconstruction's premises have already become an ineradicable part of the academic commonsense of new pluralism. This new pluralism is in fact the very foundation of the ruling North Atlantic community that Rorty so ardently defends (Rorty, 1985). If deconstruction cannot be displaced, an at least tacit alliance against a common enemy can be formed with it. After all, (post)structuralist lines of argument against the political have taken a new turn which Newhumanists can exploit to their advantage. Whereas Steiner addresses (post)structuralism more or less in terms of Derrida's texts, Knapp and Michaels address it (albeit indirectly—they discuss particularly a text by de Man) more in the form it has subsequently taken in those of Lyotard, for whom—like Knapp and Michaels themselves—the arena of investigation has shifted away from questions of "textualism" and "indeterminacy" to larger questions of the operations of discourses and narratives. When neopragmatists like Knapp and Michaels or Fish insist that their theories "have no consequences," they can find support for this view in Lyotard's understanding of (post)modern discourses as autonomous language games with no relevance to each other (*Just Gaming* 45). In rejecting the possibility of a reader/writer/thinker reaching an "outside" of the beliefs of a community, they meet up again with (post)structuralism, which has devoted considerable energy to erasing the difference between "inside" and "outside." Indeed the deconstructive idea of the indeterminacy of meaning can be used to shore up the neopragmatist notion that some discourses, specifically theoretical ones, have no consequences. Such claims about the inconsequentiality of theory do not occur in a vacuum: they are a response to calls heard increasingly now for taking seriously the political effects of theoretical, pedagogical, professional and other cultural practices. Thus Knapp and Michaels find it necessary to state vigorously that "[n]othing in 'Against Theory' tells you whether programs in women's studies are a good thing, whether teachers should be tenured, or whether graduate programs should be maintained or cut back . . . " (105). As the pressure continued to build in the period after the publication of their essay, one of their allies, Stanley Fish, found it necessary to repeat the formula that "nothing else follows" from theoretical analyses ("Reply" 220). Claims like these, along with Lyotard's assault on "grand" narratives in *The Postmodern Condition* (31ff) and his declaration of war on totality (82), which are echoed in what we have quoted from Mitchell above, work together to "localize" all inquiries (especially political ones) and help to block any investigation of oppression and exploitation in systematic and global terms. These are questions we shall investigate more fully later.

Avoiding Steiner's direct appeal to the transcendent (theirs is a "secular" humanism), Knapp and Michaels's strategy of assimilating meaning to intention produces a radical reinscription of the subject-as-individual and of liberal pluralism as key elements in the understanding of the real. Since everyone has "intentions," everyone produces "meaning": in this sense, everyone is an "author" and has "authority." If some have more "authority" than others, this is not the result of transpersonal structural and systematic features of culture (not the result of ideology), but merely the "consensual" result of the widespread recognition in the community of the "merit" of their meanings/intentions/authority. As the origin of intention, the subject is the origin of meaning in culture: "Meaning is just another name for expressed intention" (Knapp and Michaels 30). In order to save the subject, they deny the (post)structuralist effort to shift the level of cultural investigation from the subject-as-individual to the level of the systematic operations of signification in culture: in particular they reject the (post)modern claim that language is an autonomous system which helps to construct the subject and is not constructed by him or her, by arguing that "because language consists of speech acts, which are also always intentional," then "language has intention already built into it" (24). The effect of this denial is to prevent the analysis of culture and its politics from reaching beyond the local arena of the "individual" to the global arena of the systematic operations of ideology in culture.

4

What *Against Theory* shows, among other things, is that for a new generation of humanists, who have seen how (in order to defend the status quo) they can form a coalition against the political with deconstruction and (post)structuralism (especially after the weakening of deconstruction in the wake of the de Man affair), it has become less important to posit deconstruction as the "outer limits" of theory. For Newhumanists, the struggle is no longer (as Ellis, Abrams, Steiner, Hirsch, and others propose) that over the determinacy vs. the indeterminacy of meaning or even over "positive" (humanist) vs. "negative" (deconstructive) theory (which Knapp and Michaels themselves discuss): the struggle today is that over conservative/liberal *vs.* marginal/radical political theories/practices/positions. And at a time like the present, when the crisis has reached new proportions and the lines of contestation have been redrawn, one can expect to find attacks "against (critique-al) theory" even in the most conservative and centrist of professional organs.

As an exemplary case in point, we take David Kaufmann's "The Profession of Theory," published in a special issue of *PMLA* (1990) on "The Politics of Critical Language." We choose to address this text, among other reasons, because its discursive horizon is articulated not only with reference to some of the texts we have already discussed but also with reference to some oppositional writers. Most importantly, however, we choose it because it shows that the effort to broaden and strengthen the Newhumanist attack on the political requires an explicit address to the status of "critique," "crisis," "theory," and "opposition" in literary and cultural studies today. In fact Kaufmann opens his text by directly raising the question of how "literary theory that is wedded to radical politics" can expect "to intervene in the power structures of the academy and the state" (519).

Although the vocabulary has changed, nevertheless the issue here is the same we have been addressing all along in this chapter: the humanist concern to contain radical social and cultural change by insisting that critique can produce no alternative space for "difference." Kaufmann begins with the reminder that "[t]he word *crisis*, like *critique* . . . harks back etymologically to the notion of choice; a crisis calls for important discriminations and decisions" (519). He next rejects Knapp and Michaels's contention that theory is a "flight from practice," arguing that, on the contrary, "American theory" has tried to introduce "a degree of rationality" into the practice of literary studies (520). But the results, he claims, have been "paradoxical" (520) because this effort at rationality (and coherence) has not produced "coherence": on the contrary, "the explosion of theory has made literature departments larger and more unwieldy and the field more fragmented" (521). It is the aim of his essay to offer a narrative that helps us "understand the reason that guides this paradox" (522). His representation of the history of the American academy purports to show that literary studies, as a result of the development of modern universities, has been a site of perennial conflict between generalist (anti-professional) and specialist (professional) rationales for literary studies. In spite of the recurrent calls for a general and coherent rationale (the call he offers as paradigmatic is Matthew Arnold's), "the most popular justification for the study of literature seems to have had little structural effect on the departments designed for that study. It has led neither to the abolition of national literature departments nor to the amalgamation of departments within the humanities. At most, it has led to the creation of literature programs and courses that have supplemented, not superseded, departmental divisions" (521-522). Thus the history of literary studies, according to Kaufmann, produces a "constant instability" that is produced by the "double imperatives of professionalization and anti-professionalization" (522). He proposes that the best way to understand the operations of this "permanent crisis" is to adopt "a functionalist point of view" (522).

At this point the superficial differences between his approach and that of Knapp and Michaels (whom he begins by criticizing) give way as his functionalist approach rejoins their pragmatic approach in producing an operational description of the processes involved in literary studies, of what people do when they "function" or "practice" in that domain. Like the pragmatist model, the functionalist model—both, we should remember, are the foundation-stones of Abrams' humanism (*Doing Things With Texts* 239)—is unable to comprehend decisive historical breaks, but only historical continuity: it does not (fore)see gaps between the present and the future but rather envisions that the presently functioning system will "evolve" into whatever "follows" it. Indeed "function" itself is defined as that self-identical principle by which things "go on." In other words, built into the pragmatist and functionalist approaches are presuppositions which "tame" historical "crises" so that—while permitting reform—they can never, under any circumstances, be seen as producing radical change. Kaufmann's text is thus an exemplary instance of how the contestation over literary theory has shifted conceptually and discursively: whereas earlier in the decade Knapp and Michaels found it politically effective to mount an attack "against theory," by the decade's end, Kaufmann—who builds upon, if superficially athwart, their position—must mount an argument "against crisis" by taming it.

What Kaufmann's functional analysis predictably reveals is that the "perennial crisis" in literary studies is a result of the tension between professionalism and anti-professionalism that is "built into" the discipline itself. By the time Kaufmann is writing, the struggle cannot be formulated as one against deconstruction (theory), since— as he hints in a footnote reference to the "classic" confrontation between Meyer Abrams and Hillis Miller over the (in)determinacy of meaning in literary texts—deconstruction has been thoroughly institutionalized and professionalized by the academy. Today the humanist fight is explicitly against the radical understanding of "crisis" and "critique": toward this end, the crisis in the academy must be shown to be no crisis at all. In order to bolster his view that the present crisis in literary and cultural studies produced by oppositional and marginal groups (he identifies them specifically as feminists and Marxists) is just more of the same, he must show furthermore that the critiques launched by these groups have been "ineffective." To do this, Kaufmann then reads texts by Fredric Jameson, Toril Moi, and Margaret Homans to show that although each helps create the sense of crisis in literary studies by envisioning a space of "radical difference," each in various ways "defers," "cancels," or "puts" that difference "in quotation marks" and thus remains within the space of "the same." In this way, each writer lives up to Arnold's view that literature "is socially integrative and socially critical at the same time" (524). Thus, Jameson is, "[f]or all his dislike of immanent criticism . . . a high formalist" (525), one who argues "within, not against the logic of institutional specialization" (525). Moi "can foresee the revolution but has to keep it in the anterooms of utopian hope," and she, "like Jameson, must defer the dream while anchoring it firmly in the literary academy" (526). At critical moments in her analysis, Homans reveals her "tentativeness" by switching "from the present to the conditional [tense] . . . and follows Arnold as much as Moi and Jameson do, by predicting radical change and then deferring it" (527). Explaining these critics's "deferral" of politics, Kaufmann observes further: "If there were an easy passage from the academic to the public sphere, if a Marxist reading of Balzac could generate strikes or a revolution, surely no Marxist readings would be allowed" (527). In Kaufmann's view, these critics work finally in the interests of humanist values: "Moi and Homans entertain ideals . . . that in fact point to a humane and general humanism. Jameson's critical practice . . . is predominantly ethical" (527). While we do not wish either to defend the critics he reads (and have indeed marked the radical inadequacy of their work, (see Zavarzadeh, *Pun(k)deconstruction*)) or take up the details of his readings, we would like to point out that Kaufmann's strategy of assimilating oppositional writers to the Arnoldian paradigm of the eternal conflict between the categories of the general and the particular depends on his completely unwarranted and intellectually naive assumption that those categories "function" in the same way in Arnold's, Moi's, Jameson's, Homans's . . . frames of intelligibility. Categories then become "reversible" in the sense that they will fit into any frame or mode of understanding. It is this pragmatist and functionalist dehistoricizing and universalizing of such categories that allow him, for instance, to read Jameson pretty much as Rorty reads the "good American" Foucault: as concerned basically with his ethical relation to his fellow citizens in the liberal state rather than as concerned with the transformation of the liberal state.

In Kaufmann's reading, oppositional critics and theorists "pull their punches," so to speak, and in doing so fulfill the pragmatist and functionalist thesis that they are as much guardians of academic professionalism as are the staunchest conservatives. In other words, Kaufmann answers his opening question about how radical theory can expect to "intervene" in the academy by suggesting that it does so by making itself "comfortable" there. Of course, the functionalist paradigm does not permit any other outcome. Like Mitchell and others before him, Kaufmann charges that theory is "utopian"; in fact, he offers the general proposition that "contemporary theoretical presentation" at large has a "utopian structure" (527). Like Mitchell (who insists that theory has an ineradicable element of the "empirical" in it), Kaufmann also argues that theory is not so pure after all, because all its practitioners work comfortably within established institutions. "[P]olitical commitment," he suggests, "far from being a liability, has become a desideratum for contemporary literary theory" (527): thus political commitment itself has been "professionalized." In other words, whereas Knapp and Michaels ask us to conclude that theory has no "effects," Kaufmann repeats a version of Abrams's "double-dealer" argument and Rorty's "knight of autonomy" argument and asks us to conclude that oppositional theorists and critics themselves cancel the very effects they "hope" their theories will have. (Again, one finds this conservative reading of politics in the academy as "utopian" reinforced by some of those who claim most strenuously to be politically committed: as by Gayatri Spivak, for instance, who endorses Kaufmann's reading by arguing for a feminism that "is very utopian" and "cannot be taught in universities" ("Interview" 97)).

What we, on the contrary, conclude from his text is that Kaufmann has absorbed from deconstruction the practice of constructing "reverse" readings so that opponents of the status quo are turned into its staunch supporters. Indeed, functionalist analysis works hand-in-hand with deconstructive "reversals," since from the functionalist point of view, all elements (even those from other frames of intelligibility) introduced within the system will be shown to "function" (to be "reversible") within it. Functionalist analysis lines up with deconstruction again by representing all elements of culture (the social, the institutional, the professional . . .) as operating autotelically, just as deconstruction understands language and signification to operate: in both, then, "intervention" is nonsensical. Like all humanists, Kaufmann misrecognizes (by an act of projection) oppositional theory and writing (especially Marxism) as aiming at tyrannical *closure* (which actually characterizes the humanist paradigm) whereas in fact it aims at *openness*. The closedness of his own position is revealed by the fact that he represents the space critique opens up as nothing more than nostalgia for the future, which is merely a reflection of his own directly expressed yearning to become "truly political and truly central" (529). He seems utterly unaware that radical and oppositional critics put enormous pressure on anything that claims to be "truly political" (that is, to be doctrinaire) and harbor no ambitions at all to be "truly central" (that is, to leave the margin). If "radical" theory has been "remarkably successful" in the academy, as he claims it has been, then this is only the result (he goes on to observe) of its "invoking and then bracketing the promise of extramural political practice" (527): but the changes he points to in "hiring and teaching practices" are actually reformist changes in the institution and the profession and are, by definition, what radical theory understands as "failure," not "success."

Kaufmann's text is blind to one of its own most important insights when, at the outset, it labels "paradoxical" the condition by which the explosion of theory as the introduction of rationality into literary studies results not in coherence but in fragmentation: in his understanding of it the introduction of rationality would mean submission "to a unitary methodological reason" (521). What, however, he idealistically calls a philosophical "paradox" is actually a contradiction that marks the politicality of reason and knowledge. The introduction of social idealism into any community may bring with it an awareness that reason is not "unitary," an acknowledgment that reason is political. The ideological blindnesses we have marked in Kaufmann's text are the result of humanism's need to equate philosophical idealism with social idealism: the latter does not necessarily commit one to the former, but social idealism does commit one to an understanding of reason which incorporates social justice into its presuppositions, operations and goals.

This concern for social justice requires a commitment to history and deeply conditions the radical understanding of history and distinguishes it from the humanist understanding in general and in particular the pragmatist and functionalist understanding that Kaufmann invokes (we will elaborate on the question of history at length in the chapters that follow). From what we have said about the sense of continuity and evolution that is built into the functionalist model, one might assume that functionalism has a sense of the future. Yet, as we have already suggested, functionalists like Kaufmann write the future as "nostalgic" yearning because their presuppositions enmire them in an eternal self-perpetuating present. For radical understandings of history (and here we take Marx as exemplary) "[h]istory is . . . constructed backwards—not just, as many would agree, from the present, but from a calculable future of that present, which may or may not arrive" (Eagleton, "Marxism and the Future of Criticism" 177). This is where misunderstandings about "utopia" are likely to arise and the role of critique needs to be clarified, for as the same writer points out, if this assertion that the radical understanding of history must be future-oriented seems an "odd assertion," it is because it appears to take the bearings of history from "a non-space, an impossibly non-existent vantage point" (177). If, as he goes on to suggest, Marx rejects the "utopian" effort "to posit a replete future and then deduce political activity in the present from that" (177), it is because such "positivism" (which is after all what Rorty, among others, insistently calls for) plays into the hands of the guardians of the status quo. Radical theory deploys critique to investigate the conditions of what exists now in the name of a non-oppressive and non-exploitative future and thereby opens up a productive social space beyond the oppressive present without measuring all "directions" towards that future in terms of a doctrinaire "utopian" blueprint.

It is important to note that Kaufmann's reading of contemporary radical theorists like Jameson and Moi is part of a larger attack on radical theory that is under way in the academy today. Critics such as Gerald Graff and William Cain, who find their own claims to "radicality" questioned by the politically transformative practices of Marxists, have recently launched an attack on Marxism in the name of American liberal democracy in such places as the MLA convention and the volume *Criticism in the University*. This positing of America and Marxism as utterly disjunctive categories has become by now a reflex of the liberal mainstream: the readers of the *New York Times Magazine* were recently reminded of (and consoled with) the unthinkability of this pairing by one of the contributors to *Criticism in the University*, Frank Lentricchia, who in an anecdotal vein remarked that he is "too American to be a Marxist" (qtd. in Atlas, "Battle of the Books" 27). Another contributor to the volume mentioned above, William Cain, in his essay, "English in America Reconsidered: Theory, Criticism, Marxism, and Social Change" (in Graff and Gibbons, eds.) articulates this supposed disjunction by observing that while "'Marxism' comprises a potent and complex body of texts" of "importance and interest" (98) and while it "[f]rom time to time" rouses the interest of American intellectuals (99), "it almost certainly is not going to win the endorsement and affirmation of the students and public constituencies" that Marxists want to reach (98). Like other pragmatists, Cain can represent Marxism as "impractical" because it is "out-of-phase with American political realities" (99) only because he assumes an unproblematic notion of political realities." As a consequence, he betrays, like other pragmatists, considerable cynicism regarding social justice when he observes that "Marxism is primarily a refuge for academics who seek reassurance about their social conscience and commitment" (99). Such unthoughtfulness and its accompanying cynicism seem to us doubly inscribed in his charge that Marxism is a position for people who are eager "for conversion, for an instantaneous movement from critical questioning and doubt to certainty" (99). After all, as we have argued, radical opposition in general and Marxist opposition in particular are the sites of a relentless practice of critique: it is this oppositional critique-al practice and not the opposition's "certainty" that so disturbs those positioned in the academy like Kaufmann, Lentricchia, and Cain.

Doing his part to block such critique, Gerald Graff responded to a paper (delivered at the annual convention of the Modern Language Association in December 1989) on contemporary changes in the curriculum in the American academy, "'Class Wars' at the Limits and the Containment of Politics" (Morton) by labelling the paper's position as "radical Marxism" of the Althusserian wing and as "leftist purity" ("Response to Papers" 3). He furthermore tried to reduce its critique of the liberal academic reformism he himself champions to a simple call for a "politically correct" curriculum, ignoring the fact that the paper to which he responded offered no "blueprint" for the "right" curriculum. In his response, Graff repeated the phrase "politically correct" several times, rendering it an equivalent to Cain's term "certainty," but in the end it was neither the opposition's "certainty" nor its "political correctness" that troubled Graff (who operates on a notion of liberal "political correctness" that no amount of "debate" could possibly shake), but the mode of critique itself which exposed the conservatism of his discourses.

Graff's discourses actually provide evidence of the fact that humanists like himself "know" that they occupy the same epistemological and contemplative space as deconstructionists. There is, for instance, a notable change in the rhetoric of Graff's discourses about deconstruction from his early essay (1976-77) in *American Scholar*, "Fear and Trembling at Yale," in which he attacks deconstruction, to his recently published "Editor's Foreword" to Derrida's *Limited Inc.* (1988), in which he is very friendly to what he had formerly attacked. The ease with which Graff can suture the two ("hostile" and "friendly") rhetorics together indicates finally the absence of any deep discrepancies between the discourses of his two texts. In its ideological canniness, then, institutionalized humanism (exemplified by Graff) recognizes its sameness with deconstruction, realizes that while deconstructive theory bears the mark of radicalness, it is ultimately a conservative form of understanding. Humanism thus "sees" that the semantic order is threatened far less by a "rhetorical" (that is, deconstructive), than by a "political," reading. Thus although the proponents of the dominant humanism may represent deconstruction as the "radical" *other* of the humanities, it is actually the radical political modes of interrogation that are the target of their attack. While ostensibly rejecting deconstruction, humanists like Hazard Adams, Frederick Crews (*Skeptical Engagements* 115-178), and Gerald Graff soon put aside the question of deconstructive theory and get down to the business of pushing the real "threat," the political, to the fringe.

Adams is quite explicit in his "recognition" of the real enemy of the academy, that is, those who—unlike deconstructionists— posit a "true" knowledge. In his essay, "The Dizziness of Freedom; or Why I Read William Blake," he suddenly breaks his narrative and announces, "Now I come to expressions of concern which go beyond Blake and his time," and the "concern" is "events that have recently occurred in my own discipline of literary criticism and theory" (440). The "events" are the quarrels between those who believe in the possibility of the "interpretation" of texts and those who by regarding texts to be a mere instance of tropological playfulness deny such a possibility. In other words, Adams is initially concerned about the contestation between the humanists and the deconstructionists. However, it soon becomes clear that this concern is overshadowed by a far more urgent and radical problem:

> The quarrel is sometimes seen as one between old style interpreters and new style poststructuralist theories known as deconstruction. But what I am concerned about here is a third force apparent in much contemporary critical theory that claims liberation from the stranglehold of the repression of textual possibilities, from epistemology, aesthetics, hermeneutics, philology, psychology. It is to be liberation

into, or more accurately, the triumph of a reborn sociology. So complete has this triumph been prophesied to be that the term 'literary theory' is completely smothered by the term 'critical theory' which in turn means only sociological analysis. Before this triumph has its way completely, we should ask what *it* represses. In the questioning we may yet rescue what must always be rescued from abstraction and generalization in order to maintain *sanity*: the unique and *individual*. (441, emphasis added)

What Adams "knows" here is that the important contest in the discourses of the human sciences over the meanings of culture is not that between humanism (the "ethical"/the "moral") and deconstruction (the "rhetorical"), but that between Marxism (the "political," codenamed in his text as the "sociological") and deconstruction. Adams's deep agitation about the shifts in contemporary discourses is caused by the "political"'s' displacement of the "moral," an ideological apparatus for interpellating the petty-bourgeoisie and for articulating the neoconservatism which that class supports.

The main project of such an interpellation is—as we shall elaborate later—what we call saving the subject, or as Adams explicitly states, "rescuing" the "unique and individual." The kind of "freedom" that Adams wishes to preserve for and through the "individual" is exactly the one that Marxism denies him. In a letter to Pavel V. Annenkov, Marx points up the dilemmas of the petty-bourgeoisie by first formulating the pervasive question: "Is man free to choose this or that form of society?" His answer is "by no means" (*Collected Works* 38: 96), and his reasons are fairly clear: "Man is not free to choose his productive forces—upon which his whole history is based—for every productive force is an acquired force, the product of previous activity" (96). Man, in other words, is produced by history, and it is the confines of this history that the petty-bourgeois attempts to break through by an appeal to moral and ethical conduct that asserts the autonomy of the individual from the collective. The mark of this ethical freedom is, of course, the bourgeois democratic principle of free speech: a principle that is fetishized in the legal code and theorized—as we shall argue later—in (post)structualist theory. In short, in contrast to Marx's materialist mode of production, (post)structuralist theory privileges the ludic norm of the mode of signification. By gaining control of the mode of signification, through interpretive practices that provide "variable" (different from individual to individual) but recognizably "obvious" readings of the texts of culture, the petty-bourgeoisie is enabled to dismiss "history" and non-empirical intelligibilities that posit knowledge and knowing as the effect of history (and the mode of production) and, in contrast, seek knowledges that are presumably true for all ages and classes. It is the promise of this cultural obviousness and transparent political intelligibility that lies at the "heart" of various (neo)conservative movements to which the petty-bourgeois is attached. The political triumph of these (neo)-conservatisms always depends, in bourgeois democracies, on the electoral support of the petty-bourgeois: hence the political importance of the "moral" and the "ethical" (and their allied planks in today's neo-conservative political platforms on such issues as the sanctity of the family, anti-abortionism, patriotism, the deregulation of commerce, the rejection of other sexualities . . .).

Support for particularistic modes of interpretation like that put forth by Adams acquires enormous political significance during periods of crisis in intelligibility such as the one we are now witnessing. The narrative of interpretation produced in Adams's text and its consequent pedagogy, like all the discourses of ideology, provide for the petty-bourgeois what Hodge, Kress, and Jones in "The Ideology of Middle Management" call "categorical security" (93). By condemning radical political intelligibility that denies empiricism and transhistorical cognitivism and therefore cancels the "eternal truth" of culture, Adams's text offers "categorical security" to the petty-bourgeois by placing him/her in a position of intelligibility from which the world makes clear sense in terms of a realistic theory of knowledge and interpretation (by reasserting the theory which posits a relation of equivalence between the signifier and the signified). In spite of (because of) its theoretical naivete, Adams's text serves an important and vital ideological purpose: it opens up a politico-textual space in which the traditional practices of the petty bourgeoisie are re-legitimated and given new life in a period when their very premises are put in question by new theories of reading the texts of culture. By postulating "obviousness" through straightforward reading and interpretation, Adams's text renders impossible the very modes of economic and political "reading" (analysis) that inquire into the powerlessness of the petty-bourgeoisie and other exploited classes. Moral and ethical modes of intelligibility naturalize the political and economic plight of the petty-bourgeoisie

and thus render support to (renders them supportive of) the reproduction of the dominant relations of production. The moral
narratives produced by centered interpretations of social texts are
indeed "varied," but their variety is only a variation of the same
allegory: the economic and political powerlessness of the petty-
bourgeoisie in these narratives is represented in fact as a form of
superior moral power. "Lack," on one level, in these narratives is
represented as a higher form of "non-lack" on a more "permanent"
and "authentic" level. Since the petty-bourgeoisie does not have
the intellectual skills (because they lack the economic means and
the educational opportunities such means provide) to read in a non-
straightforward, non-centered, and symptomatic manner, they then
reject all decentering interpretations as "nihilistic" (i. e., immoral)
and thus not worthy of the attention of "serious" readers. They are
encouraged, especially by humanists, to reject deconstructive reading
or the inquiry into the political economy of signification in a Marxist
mode, and to regard this rejection as a form of superior moral force.

It is in support of this (petty-bourgeois) program of straightforward reading and interpretation of texts that the works of Frederick
Crews and Gerald Graff are also directed. For example, in such essays
as "Textual Leftism," what Graff attacks is not so much the
economic and political consequences of deconstruction but its
interpretive program (here he is continuing the dissertation on "The
Politics of Anti-Realism" he offered in *Literature Against Itself*, 1979).
This latter essay is of particular significance in our discussion because
in it Graff advocates what might be called "moral" leftism against
the irresponsible politics of what he calls textual leftists. In this
double move (advocating a right-wing theory of realistic reading and
a left-wing morally committed coalitionism), Graff exemplifies what
Marx, in his critique of Proudhon ("Letter to Annenkov"), describes
as the plight of petty-bourgeois intellectuals:

> In an advanced society and because of his situation, *a petty
> bourgeois* becomes a socialist on the one hand, and an
> economist on the other, i. e., he is dazzled by the magnificence
> of the upper classes and feels compassion for the sufferings
> of the people. He is at one and the same time bourgeois and
> man of the people. In his heart of hearts he prides himself
> on his impartiality, on having found the correct balance,
> allegedly distinct from the happy medium.
>
> (*Collected Works* 32: 105)

The historical situation of the petty-bourgeois intellectual places him/her in a contradictory position. This contradiction manifests itself in the "moral" *leftism* and "textual" *rightism* of Adams, Crews, Graff, and the majority of those in the dominant academy who have adopted a "generic" notion of "politics" and, like these authors, defend "historicism" and social awareness, but not "historicizing" or political commitment. They naturalize this contradiction as just a mark of the "complexity" of real life, a mode of "moral ambiguity": humanists have always insisted that life is not a matter of black and white, left and right, but a vast, pervasive, middle-ground grayness—an ensemble of contradictory middle-discourses. Economic and political contradictions are thus fetishized by Graff and others as inherent qualities of the morally superior (i.e., complex) life which they contrast sharply with the moral reductiveness of the committed intellectual who, according to them, regards life in "simple" terms. Thus the dominant academy dehistoricizes economic and political contradictions: they are not seen as conditions of a specific class at a given historical moment, but as inescapable transhistorical verities. Marx's critique of Proudhon is exemplary in its insights into this fetishization of contradictions (i.e., the naturalization and dehistoricization of class conflicts in petty-bourgeois practices):

> the petty bourgeois of this kind deifies *contradiction*, for contradiction is the very basis of his being. He is nothing but social contradiction in action. He must justify by means of theory what he is in practice, and Mr. Proudhon has the merit of being the scientific exponent of the French petty bourgeoisie, which is the real merit since the petty bourgeoisie will be an integral part of all the impending social revolutions.
> (*Collected Works* 32: 105)

Kaufmann, Cain, Graff, Lentricchia, Adams . . . all repeat the basic argument we have seen at work in the texts of Abrams and others: they construct Marxism as "useless" in discussions of American culture, by arguing, as Cain does, that if Marxism acts from within the academy and is thus a part of the discourses of the academy, it has the same effectivity as any other position "within." Whatever the differences that may exist between the kinds of pressure exerted on the academy from different positions, none can have radical significance, since all are said finally to come from the same space. By such appeals to American liberalism, which works to homogenize all differences, critics like Cain can legitimize their claim to be doing "urgent" work. The trouble is that Cain, Kaufmann and others fail to realize that political "urgency" itself is the subject of contestation: the question is what is most "urgent" finally—to reform a curriculum (as at Carnegie-Mellon, Syracuse . . . (see our essay "(Post)Modern Critical Theory and the Articulations of Critical Pedagogies")) in such a way that the old gets relegitimated, or to produce discourses that read these reformist acts and show their seeming urgency to be part of a long-term operation of continual conservation of the status quo by means of renovation?

The problem with our critique of positions like those of Kaufmann and Cain is that, on a commonsensical level, it may be thought that we are defending the positions of persons like Jameson and Moi, when that is not the case (see Zavarzadeh, *Pun(k)decon-struction*). These latter critics are designated simultaneously by the academy as its "radicals" and its "celebrities"; however, in order to become a celebrity, one has to accommodate to the needs of institutions; that is, one becomes a "property" of the center. Transformative radicalism in the academy is not to be found in the texts and classes of such celebrities (Spivak—the celebrity—argues, as we have already noted, against the idea of radicalism in the classroom), but in the margins of academic institutions, margins whose texts and practices are suppressed by the very people who complain of radicalism's inadequacy to the present circumstances. The fate of the academy's radicals is actually traced in an invisible record, an unacknowledged archive comprised of letters of rejection to them, firings of them, and other acts of suppression undertaken by the very people who at the same time gladly call attention to "radical" celebrities (who, must we say, hardly need defending). This double move of suppressing the margins while foregrounding celebrities is a key maneuver that helps keep the machinery of exploitation running smoothly.

5

A historical understanding of the contestation now going on over the way in which the cultural "real" is to be understood and over the discourses deployed to produce and maintain dominant understandings will reveal that what may at first appear to be a quarrel among academics over how to read literary texts is indeed a struggle over a global problem: in other words the struggle over "meaningfulness" (the status of knowledge in culture) involves much more than disputes between English professors. At this moment in the history of the West, there is underway an interrogation of the practices in the production and dissemination of knowledge in "cultural studies." From anthropology and ethnography to law and zoosemiotics existing modes of knowing are currently being questioned.[1] It might be helpful to mention the configuration of issues and their institutional context in one such case, a case in which the outcome will have deep and direct consequences for the relationship between knowledge and material daily practices.

One of the most significant challenges to established forms of inquiry in the field of law has been launched by what is known as "Critical Legal Studies," a mode of inquiry that questions dominant legal discourses and regards existing legal practices and legal institutions as instruments of social control.[2] This development has affected both pedagogical and research practices in almost all major law schools, but we will instance here the case of the Harvard Law School, which has "the world's largest and best collection" of practitioners of Critical Legal Studies (*Critical Times,*" 67). Putting under erasure liberal legalism which conceives of law as a set of neutral principles derived from justice, Critical Legal Studies contests the dominant view that when these principles are applied in daily practices to various cases, they produce a consistent result.[3] Instead it holds that the result varies because of the highly complex effects of power produced by acts of interpretation, by textual indeterminacy, by semantic incoherence, and by ideological control. In this view, law is seen as a state apparatus whose purpose is to preserve the dominant social order by reproducing and maintaining the subjectivities necessary for perpetuating the prevailing order. In short, the "rule of law" is a fiction required for the operation of liberal

---

1. See for example, Clifford and Marcus, *Writing Culture* (1985); Sebeok, *How Animals Communicate* (1977); and Sebeok and Umiker-Sebeok, *Speaking of Apes* (1980).

2. See for example Kennedy, *Legal Education and the Reproduction of Hierarchy* (1983); Kirby, *The Politics of Law* (1982); Black, *Radical Lawyers* (1971); and Norris, "Suspended Sentences" (1985).

3. See also Dalton, "An Essay in the Deconstruction of Contract Doctrine" (1985); Peller, "The Metaphysics of American Law" (1985); and Boyle, "The Politics of Reason: Critical Legal Theory and Local Social Thought" (1985).

capitalism, as suggested by Kennedy in "The Political Significance of the Structure of the Law School Curriculum" (1983). At Harvard this new mode of inquiry has exposed deep divisions among the faculty, forced the postponement of some tenure decisions, and raised questions about the school's ability to attract faculty (*Critical Times* 67-68). But the horror of humanists and their allies in university central administrations—who speak as if the termination of their particular mode of domination is the end of civilization itself—is not the horror of finding tensions among faculty (this is merely a thin naturalization), but the horror of discovering that the myths of neutral knowledge and disinterested inquiry upon which the liberal academy is founded are collapsing upon themselves under the weight of the contradictions in the capitalist regime of truth.

Texts like the ones we have examined in this chapter must therefore be addressed, and in a manner that can account for their ideological uses in culture. It is part of the ideological operation of these texts that they "regionalize" the "global" contestation over signification in contemporary knowledges as a squabble among various factions in English departments or law schools or other sectors of Anglo-American universities. In this way they divert attention from the politics of cognition and from the ideological struggles over the "real" in culture to provincial debates, petty personalizations, and gossip—all cultural devices for trivializing the discourses of society and thus rendering them safe for the status quo. We are addressing these texts because we are committed to the political contestation of the "real"—to the struggle over the constitution of "meaning" in (post)modern culture—and because we believe that the "meaning of meaning" in society is the outcome of such political contestations that are carried out, among other places, in social texts such as those we are examining and our own. This means that we are not writing as impartial subjects, but are rather articulating the crisis of signification in (post)modern discourses from a given historical post of intelligibility. This is another way of saying that we are not writing to reveal the Truth and then use that Truth to expose the Untruth of the texts we investigate. We find such a pursuit of Truth philosophically and politically uninteresting, historically obsolete, and more of an amusement for liberal humanists than a serious endeavor for committed intellectuals. Liberal humanists, who believe that they have access to Truth (or at least can discover it) engage in "debates" whose function is not merely to reveal the Truth, but also to indicate who owns it, an activity that reproduces the relations of private property. Their texts, far from being the embodiment of Untruth, are in fact representations of (Absolute) Truth for many of their readers, especially certain kinds of contemporary academics. These readers find the subject positions and systems of intelligibility offered in such texts quite illuminating of their own class positions and of the imaginary relations to the world that such positions produce. Such texts thus become "Truth" for those academics because they offer them a discourse that ideologically justifies their pedagogical practices in support of their (social) class position and their political views. Denouncing deconstruction while often incorporating its strategies, these texts legitimate the dominant interpretive and reading operations through which these academics situate texts in culture and assign meanings to them.

Instead of addressing the traditional question, what is Truth?, we have focused on why a set of statements is regarded as "true" by a circle of readers. This critique-al procedure requires that we not simply (as in the traditional manner) criticize or offer counter-arguments to dislodge the statements made by other texts (a strategy that would presuppose that we have access to an absolute transdiscursive "truth"), but that we show how statements in these other texts acquire "truthfulness" among certain readers with particular class affiliations. In order to follow the trajectory of those statements to the moment when they become intelligible as "true," we have had to situate them in the archives of contemporary knowledges (as we shall do in the next chapter) so that we can point up the discourses that are involved in their construction. It does not make sense to us simply to "argue" against dominant views on the status of textuality, for instance; we think it more important to indicate why such a position on textuality is attractive ("truthful") and to indicate, when a reader nods in agreement with that position, what ideological series lies behind that nod.

Chapter Two

Making (Common)
Sense
of the World

By producing a set of cultural "obviousnesses," ideology assures the continuation of the dominant representations of the real in a culture, without the requirement of "proof." That, for example, "experience" is obviously the ultimate test of "truth" or that all phenomena in the world are obviously made intelligible by the logic of "cause and effect" are among such ideological "obviousnesses." By establishing uncontestable (because obvious) truths, ideology postulates a world that has always already been there and will always already be there, a world of unalterable truths and unchangeable verities to which the individual must consent since these truths and verities are the effects of "laws of nature." To show how humanist writings inscribe these "laws of nature" in texts of culture we need to articulate the system of assumptions that enable their "readability." The "un-said" of these texts can be articulated by an inquiry into their presuppositions about history, meaningfulness, science, representation, language, textuality, subjectivity, and politics.

1

The idea that history has an "inner essence" expressed in different "periods" through various outer phenomena is, of course, the hallmark of a mode of historiography that postulates history as a teleological movement of events through "diverse" "periods" which nevertheless share an underlying continuity and unfold according to a transcendental plan. This humanist theory of history (based on a notion of causality usually designated as "expressive causality") appeals to the conservative mind because it constructs history as a closed narrative, thus becoming a stable and stabilizing force amid the chaos of diverse and confusing events. Though its philosophical underpinings are in Leibnitz's notion of "expression," it was of course most powerfully elaborated by Hegel. In Hegelian historiography, the "inner essence" of history, of which all outer phenomena are mere "expressions," is absolute Idea—"the logical power of the divine" (*Reason in History* ix). This Idea develops both in Space (becoming Nature) and in Time (becoming Spirit). Spirit's movement towards self-consciousness (Freedom, for Hegel) is the course of history, whose trajectory is projected by Reason, "the *substance* of the Universe; viz., that by which and in which all reality has its being and subsistence" (*The Philosophy of History* 9). Reason is the "energizing power" of the "Spiritual Universe"—"The History of the World" (9). And since Reason "is the law of the world," therefore "in world history, things have come about rationally" (*Reason in History* 11). Reason for Hegel works in the adjacency of "religious truth" (*Philosophy of History* 12). Hegel postulated the stages of the progress of what he called Spirit (Idea as unfolding in Time) as "periods" in history, each with its own unique *Geist* so that human history not only "expresses" the grand design in its totality, but also is a manifestation of that "purpose" in its smaller moves (*Phenomenology of the Spirit* 12). The concept of "period" as a monolithic space within which different and apparently various events can all be seen as manifestations of one single purposive force has indeed been a most useful tool for popular historiography. Through the notion of "period" a form of historical thought that Althusser calls "historicism" represents history as a set of relations between men and thus suppresses the relations of production in order to postulate a history in which an ahistorical telos and an equally ahistorical subject are privileged in the linear organization of periods (*Phenomenology of the Spirit* 180; see also 119-144).

Humanist historiography renders the "various" periods of history as fundamentally homogeneous, transparent, rational, coherent, and teleological, as Hegel himself did, by representing the "different" aspects of each period as an expression of a "spirit of the times." Hegel's concept of Reason as the "law of the world" is an implied premise of this kind of historiography and makes it possible to equate "reason" with the "real" and thus for humanist historiographers to designate any oppositional reality that is politically and ideologically threatening to its hegemony as "un-reason" and to place it on the fringes of history as the "unreal" of culture. Since the "unreal" is the absence of reason, it has mere existence but not reality and as such it is a "contingent" but not "necessary" part of history which will soon perish. By understanding history as purely rational, by removing from the scene of history as unreal all that is opposed to the dominant order, such a historiography actually produces a history of exclusions. In other words, the narrative of each period produced by humanist historiographers, operates by a process of "exclusions"; for in order to produce history as purely "rational," such historiography must systematically remove from the scene of history all that does not "fit" into the coherent narrative it is trying to construct. Since "rationality" is assumed to be a property of the human person as subject, humanist historiography, following Hegel, represents "rationality" as the agency by which human beings acquire what they call "freedom." Of course, while offered as standing beyond the coordinates of culture as an absolute norm of being, such "freedom" is actually a historically specific construct. In Hegel's case, freedom is actually a formulation of the political ambitions and desires of the bourgeoisie of his time, who were betrayed by Frederick William III, who reneged on his promise for a constitution. Hegel's free state resembles uncannily the political agenda of the liberal bourgeoisie of his time and the notion that a constitutional monarch would indeed change the situation of oppression in Prussia after the Napoleonic wars.

Humanist "historicism" finds its most political form in a type of "activism" which is, interestingly enough, more "moral" than "political." Such moral activism, however, ultimately relegitimates the dominant power by producing a moral subject who effectively withdraws from the "chaos" of the threatening and unintelligible present into the "harmony" of a luminous past which it then uses as the model for the future. This humanist moral activism is merely an articulation of the class position of the petty-bourgeois who is effectively denied all access to material power within capital. "Moralism"—which we shall later see rearticulated as "ethics" in Foucault and other (post)structuralists—turns the petty-bourgeois's powerlessness into a "specialness" or "unworldly virtue," that is to say, into a mark of his "superiority"—an ideological effect which pacifies that class.

The goal of discourses of ideology has always been to provide the subject with what Hodge in "The Ideology of Middle Management" calls "categorical security," a sense of "order" which in effect shields the subject from any awareness of the actual "disorder" (contradictoriness) of his life. Today, by regarding the moment of the (post)modern as "existing" but not "real," humanist historicism promises the petty-bourgeois a "real" history that will unfold with (an ethical) telos and liberate him from his present constraints as a reward (to come in the future) for his moral superiority. In other words, what the petty-bourgeois does not have in the present is constructed as a sign of his moral virtue: for instance, his lack of access to advanced modes of reading such as deconstruction or such literacies as the high-tech languages of computers is seen as a mark of a moral "righteousness" that places him in a privileged space beyond such "decadent" practices.

The ideological outcome of humanist moral activism (seen not only in the texts of academic writers like Ellis, Shaw, Bloom, Hirsch, and Booth but also in those of para-academic writers like Bennett, Cheney, and Bellow) is that it turns the "lack" in petty-bourgeois life into an "authentic" mark of rightness and thus provides this class with a "categorical security." One of the major ideological functions of the trivial text—which passes itself off as non-political and thus non-ideological and as able to speak for the ethical truth of all the ages—is to open up this space of moral and ethical activism for the petty-bourgeois—a space in which the traditional practices of the petty-bourgeoisie are relegitimized and given new life. They are located in a space which renders impossible the very modes of economic and political analysis that can inquire into the power-lessness of the petty-bourgeoisie and thus offer ways to empower that class. This moralization of the plight of the petty-bourgeoisie and its permanent economic and political subjugation is necessary for the reproduction of the dominant relations of production. At the present time, the interests of the hegemonic economic powers are in fact represented around the world by the conservative ideologies that have found their political power through the administrations of George Bush, Helmut Kohl, Margaret Thatcher, Brian Mulroney, Toshiki Kaifu, Giulio Andreotti. These conservatives will not last in power without the support of the petty-bourgeoisie, whose votes they need. To get those votes, conservative ideologues have to represent the traditional ideologies and views of the petty-bourgeois as eternal moral truths and offer the conservative administration as the only legitimate moral force available at the present time. (That many conservative leaders—e. g., Reagan, Thatcher—have come from the petty-bourgeois class is significant but not directly relevant here. For a rather interesting account of allegiance to petty-bourgeois ideologies, even when the petty-bourgeois as a person has moved into the upper classes, see the autobiographies, *Making It* and *Breaking Ranks: A Political Autobiography* of Norman Podhoretz, one of today's chief neoconservative ideologues and editor of *Commentary*.)

The political function of moralizing texts is to make sure that the vote of the petty-bourgeoisie is delivered and that conservative administrations remain in power to protect the economic interests of the ruling classes. The vote will not be available without the creation and maintenance of a permanent petty-bourgeois underclass. Moralizing texts aid that permanent subjugation: rather than encouraging petty-bourgeois youth to acquire the knowledges of (post)modernity, moralizing texts provide them instead with a categorical security through which they can renounce computers and deconstruction as signs of moral evil and thus withdraw from their own historical conditions. Such a withdrawal will do nothing but widen the gap between the two classes (petty-bourgeoisie and bourgeoisie) and thus keep the former always a powerless class with strong moral views—views which are exploited by ideological texts like those we examined earlier. It is by privileging the moral in social practices that the status quo is enabled to reproduce itself by, for example, substituting moral measures for economic sanctions against South Africa (witness the slogan, "Using Morals, Not Money, On Pretoria," in the *New York Times*, August 3, 1986). One can see very clearly the political and economic effects of such religiously sanctioned moralism, for instance, in the petty-bourgeois who takes up a "morally superior" position against the practice of usury, following what he understands to be Biblical "injunctions," while simultaneously supporting capitalism, which is based on the production of surplus value.

This moral approach to life is given official approval in the academy under the sign of "humanism" in the traditional practices of the humanities. Humanism, in its contemporary manifestation, is, in the last analysis, an ideological discourse the purpose of which is to reify petty-bourgeois values and attitudes in the guise of timeless truths. As a mode of aggressive reading, deconstruction, for instance, is rejected by humanists as simply a manifestation of contemporary inhumanity, violence, and nihilism; but much more than this is at stake in such a dismissal. Used as a reading strategy by the petty-bourgeoisie, deconstruction will dismantle the moral explanations given of the plight of that class and will detect the violent hierarchies and elaborate textual schemes at work to represent the ideological interests of political conservatism as the moral ideals of the petty-bourgeoisie. Humanist narratives tend to represent the (post)modern moment in terms of a negative narrative that sees the "essence" of the times in "unfortunate" phenomena such as deconstruction, computers. . . . Yet what humanists represent as the coherent moment of history is not coherent at all since the purported essence of the time is really a set of historical series. If one chooses other phenomena as part of the "essence" of the times, one can construct a counter-narrative of the present that is politically "positive," rather than "negative." One such counter-narrative will relate deconstruction to feminism (which, like deconstruction, is based on dismantling the patriarchal hierarchies of society), to the emergence of the Green party in Germany (which aims at rendering the contestation of the superpowers for global domination through nuclear superiority as an ideological binarism that should not be imposed, through the narrative of freedom, upon the rest of the world), and to the opposition of the African National Congress to apartheid (from the late 1960's to the present) in order to delegitimize the official narrative of sameness (racial purity) in South Africa and the prevailing inscription of difference (white, black, colored, Indian, and so on). Both the "negative" humanist narrative of the (post)-modern and the positive counter-narrative are "coherent," but both are also "ideological," their enabling conditions being an essentialized history that allows closure. History, nevertheless, is actually the effect of struggles between these and many other contesting narratives and cannot be contained in any one of them. It gives the humanist nightmares to realize that there is no empirically available history, that history is always already textualized and narrativized, and that the attempt to move beyond the textualization in order to get to history's core is also one of the texts that cultures write about themselves, one of the discourses of ideology. History—and here is what the conservative mind fears—is not a "solid" thing, but a contestation of diverse textualizations. To recognize that history is not an empirical thing, but a set of contesting narratives, is to recognize that that narrative which gets installed as history does so not because it is an embodiment of Truth in some general and abstract sense, but because its "political" truth legitimizes the existing power structures. It is, in other words, not the selfsame and self-evident truth of eternal verities that informs history, but the truth of the contradictions of the material forces and the relations of production. These truths cannot be turned into a linear progression of periods towards some moment of transparency as the goal of history. If one has to think about history in terms of causality, then causality has to be reunderstood and theorized in terms of what Althusser has designated as an absent cause: contrary to the humanist view, history is a process without a telos or a subject. Such a reunderstanding of cause-effect is ideologically impossible for humanist texts, since in such a reformulation of these laws of intelligibility, those texts would lose their grip upon a reality that they need to understand as "solid" and "out there." A theory of history based on expressive causality makes it possible for the text to postulate an essence that is always behind phenomena and that as such always anchors random events in the lawfulness of order.

The humanist theory of history, which controlled historiography in the 19th century and has found in various forms a place of privilege among conservative historians in the 20th, has become popular again recently (in the mid-70's to the late-80's) as the political climate in Western Europe and North America has taken on a decidedly neoconservative cast. For instance, the re-reading of the French Revolution by Francois Furet, *Interpreting the French Revolution* (1981) and *Marx and the French Revolution* (1989), is one mark of this re-turn. According to another revisionist historian, Richard Andrews, the conclusion of this re-reading is that "Old Regime justice was more lenient and humanistic than Revolutionary justice" ("Revolution Brought Cruel Justice" 1). Of course, a vulgarized version of the humanist view of history informs not only almost all the editorials and many of the essays regularly published in such neoconservative organs as *The Public Interest, The New Criterion, The New York Review of Books, The New Republic,* and *Commentary,* but also the innumerable books which are dutifully reviewed in their pages.

The pervasiveness of this notion of history, in spite of its frequently cited "outmodedness," is easily documented. For example, the writer of another "trivial" text—"Save Us, Batman, It's the P-M Word!"—for a popular magazine recently offered to his readers "a map . . . to the *Zeitgeist*" (spirit of the times) of the present period in history, in other words, a map of the "(post)modern" (Maddocks 11). As he describes it, (post)modernity is marked precisely by being a time which fails to recognize the teleological movement of history according to a "plan": this is what, in his view, makes the (post)modern merely a "detour," an understanding of culture "with no destination of its own," in other words, a time to be "gotten through" as quickly as possible so that history can be put back on its tracks. This is because, as the writer concludes, with an obvious sense of annoyance, that in the end, the (post)modern takes "a distinctly casual view toward rigorous thinking or passionate sensibility" (12), that is, it betrays both of those traditional anchoring elements of "human nature," reason and passion. This rational and passionate "human nature," which according to humanist ideology, undergoes a "progressive" development, is the force behind the progress of history through its various "periods." The (post)modern, according to this reader of culture, appears to defy categorization because it is a mode of culture which just lets things "go to pieces" (12): such an "incoherent" mode would appear to have no "spirit." Yet the transparent effect of this text is to "periodize" even that which seems to resist "periodization"—the (post)modern—in order to reaffirm the humanist notion of history. What is missed in such an account of history and of the "(post)modern," which trivializes the issues through its unthoughtful and unproblematic defense of its understanding of the "truth" of history, is the recognition that what is called history is itself a domain of struggle where the very notion of the "(post)modern" is being strongly contested, as we argue throughout this book.

Nearly two decades ago a well-known humanist scholar and historian of literature remarked that "[t]he whole concept of the *Zeitgeist* [the spirit of the age] which was basic to German *Geistesgeschichte* [intellectual history] has been called in doubt" (Wellek, *The Attack on Literature* 69). However that may be, as the popular text quoted above suggests, these doubts have not prevented such an essentialist conception of history from remaining a pervasive part of contemporary discourses, not only in the domain of the popular but also in the area of academic and scholarly writing. A literary critic, for example, recently argued that contemporary (post)modern theory has robbed us of the "pleasure of reading" and describes the "unpleasure" supposedly produced by (post)modern theory as the mark of our "ideological age": it is, he says, "a discouraging sign of the times" (Alter, *The Pleasure of Reading in an Ideological Age* 12). Thus, "shaky" or not, the essentialist notion of history is continually and pervasively reinscribed in contemporary texts of culture and in the pedagogical practices of the academy.

Nothing more powerfully reinscribes American students today

as subjects of essentialist historiography than Oldhumanist textbooks like the two-volume *Norton Anthology of English Literature* (published for close to thirty years under the general editorship of Meyer Abrams), which divides its objects of study ("the major works in prose and verse from *Beowulf* to the present," Abrams, 1986, xxxix) into seven distinct but continuously developing "periods" (namely, "The Middle Ages," "The Sixteenth Century," "The Early Seventeenth Century," "The Restoration and the Eighteenth Century," "The Romantic Period," "The Victorian Age," and "The Twentieth Century"). In his preface to the latest (the fifth) edition, Abrams rehearses the humanist position on history and its "changes" that we saw at work in the previous chapter. If culture "never stands still," as he declares here, it can only be conceived as changing "gradually," and thus the updating of the anthology (which takes place every five or six years) is represented as necessary if it is to "stay in touch with scholarly discoveries, new developments in criticism, and the altering interests of readers": the goal is to keep "the anthology within the mainstream of contemporary cultural and intellectual concerns" (xxxix). Such language indicates quite clearly that those who edited it regard the anthology as merely "reflecting" (and not as producing) cultural trends and developments; and this notion of "reflection" is what enables not only the humanist notions of the subject, language, signification (as we will go on to elaborate them shortly), but also of historiography, in which the surface phenomena of a given period, while they may exhibit a certain "variety," are ultimately taken to be a reflection of that period's "core truth."

A sustained genealogical inquiry would investigate the *Norton Anthology's* relation to an array of its pretexts which put forward the same theory of history as a string of essentialized periods, that is, for example, to other well-known compendia of knowledge comprised of texts selected for the education of earlier generations of Americans. We will take time here only to point to one exemplary "pretext" which, like the *Norton Anthology,* uses "literature" as its organizing category: Charles W. Eliot's fifty-volume collection (first published in 1910), *The Harvard Classics,* which "covers" something called "The History of Civilization" from "Ancient Egypt" to "Modern Europe" by drawing on "literary materials" (Eliot, 1917, 1). In the introduction to the second edition of his collection (1917), Eliot is pleased to note that "The Harvard Classics have demonstrated their fitness for the special work they were intended to do," which was "to provide from famous literature, ancient and modern, an ample record of 'the stream of the world's thought'" in order that the student may not only attain "the standing of a cultivated man or woman, making up through this long course of reading any deficiencies which might have existed in [his or her] early education" but also acquire "a new power to enjoy" (Eliot 13). When we bring this goal of "cultivating" the human person as individual into relation with the other stated goal of giving the "careful and persistent reader" "a fair view of the progress of man observing, recording, inventing, and imagining from the earliest historical times to the close of the nineteenth century" (1), we can see the conjuncture of the essentialist theory of the subject and the essentialist theory of history, that is, see their collaboration with each other: the attainment of "the standing of a cultivated man or woman" (13) is to be achieved not only by absorbing the "content" of the historical narrative offered by *The Harvard Classics* but also by absorbing the theory of history inscribed in that narrative.

We should not think that in this age of attention to "difference," the idea of the classic is on its way to extinction. Far from it. As a part of the neoconservative political agenda in the arena of "culture," the reproduction and promotion of the "classics" goes on apace: a group of writers and scholars (including such persons as William F. Buckley, Jr., and Gertrude Himmelfarb) held a symposium at the Library of Congress in October, 1990, to celebrate the publication of the sixty *Great Books of the Western World*. It is important to note that the latest version of this set of "classics" includes works by four women and no persons of color. When asked about the latter omission, the series editor-in-chief, Mortimer Adler, replied: "No black American has written a great book" (qtd. in Alterman, "Not So Great" 585).

To go back to the question of history: in addition to the kind of historical revisionism noted above regarding the French Revolution, bourgeois writers and ideologues are currently using several other strategies to protect and defend the dominant view of history which has been problematized and politicized by (post)modernity. One is to produce texts that reassure the dominant class by striving to contain the damage done to the their historical narratives by what we have just articulated as the (post)modern textualization of history; another is to declare that history itself has finally come to an end, which is to say that it has been "frozen" so that the class struggles, which are an ongoing part of culture's contestations, can be represented as permanently over. As an example of the former we will take a lecture delivered by Robert Berkhofer which was the principal address for a showcase session of the American Studies Association's 1988 annual meeting: the session was titled "From Demystification to Deconstruction: The Challenge of the New Scholarship to American Studies." One mark of the significance which the sponsoring organization attaches to Berkhofer's lecture is that it has made the lecture available to its members (and others) on videotape (see American Studies Association, 1988). Like Ellis, Berkhofer purports to take up "deconstruction" and "the new scholarship" in his lecture: however, the session title frames the presentations in the mode of "survey"— and Berkhofer's is a "surveying" lecture—and thus, from the start, the session's discourses have been firmly inscribed in the pedagogical modality of "surveying knowledge," a practice on which the traditional humanities disciplines strongly rely. After all, if history is an essentialized set of periods, then producing knowledge about history amounts to the descriptive act of "surveying" the features of a given period's (in Berkhofer's case, the (post)modern period's) "essence."

Part of Berkhofer's strategy is to produce a text that "mocks" the modalities of (post)modern writing. To identify Berkhofer's text, "Poetics and Politics in and of a New American Studies," as an "uncertain" text is not to suggest that it participates in (post)-structuralist "undecidability," any more than saying that it is undoubtedly a parody of scholarly synthesis assures its installation in the pantheon of the (post)modern, for both its uncertainty and its parodicity are conventions, familiar elements of the significatory modality that governs all texts belonging to the knowingly naive "What-Are-We-To-Make-Of-It-All?" genre (in abbreviated form, this is one of the opening phrases of the paper; and the emphasis on "all" is underscored by the 12 pages of 81 footnotes that accompany the 23-page lecture text). The text's uncertainty derives not from the writing subject's resituation in the discourses of (post)modernity, but from the rhetorical maneuver of the "feint," that is, momentarily "giving up control" (admitting the challenges to, if not the inadequacy of, its own ruling categories) in order ultimately to restore control once again (and thus reassure its liberal humanist audience of the survival of the dominant academy's cherished premises).

In order to mobilize the discourse of abandonment-to-the-new Berkhofer deploys several devices. One is to engage in tongue-in-cheek neologistic play, for instance: " . . . the current tendencies to denaturalization, demystification, deconstruction and, if I may coin some words to continue the alliterature and rhyme, dehierarchicalization and dereferentialization . . ." (6). Another is to pose questions as indicators of a faux-(post)modern interrogative, rather than traditionalist declarative, enunciative stance (sometimes in a seme-by-seme dispersal that mistakes interrogation for query: "in their larger [that is, their proper?] context" (2); "in academic discourse [texts?] (7); "but that reduction [degradation?]" (8); "interpretation [constitution, derivation?]" (12), but sometimes in cascades and barrages (1, 13, 14-15, and 23). Indeed the most general effect of Berkhofer's technique of "questioning" is to render (post)modern interrogation as mere conundrum. More important, however, are the workings of the text's peculiar analytic strategy, which involves —at the level of pre-text—the ASA's recruitment of a historian to address the crisis creating the pressure for what he calls "a New American Studies." It was not for reasons of relative "distance," "objectivity," and "non-implication," as Berkhofer himself makes quite clear, that a historian was asked to "mediate" what has basically been understood as a disciplinary contest between philosophers and theorists of literature over the tension between conceptuality and textuality, but because, as Berkhofer remarks, "the linguistic turn . . . appears more devastating to historians and social scientists than [to] literary and other humanistic scholars" (11). The consequences of (post)modern theory are, of course, *not at all* less devastating to literary and other humanists: what is true is that other humanists have been able to take for granted (and thus avoid accounting for) the concept of history on which their practices rely somewhat more easily than have historians themselves.

Historian Berkhofer's strategy is to renarrate the tale of textuality vs. *con-cept-uality* as instead the story of textuality vs. *con-text-uality* by proposing that what all the contending parties and claimants to American Studies have in common is a concern for "context" (2)—that is, bringing their intellectual practices into relation with that "Great Story" which is "America" itself (what else "unifies" the disparate academic enterprises falling under the American Studies disciplinary rubric?). The litmus-test for truth in American Studies will then be whether "context" is understood as anything that can possibly be called "historical" at all, and when that distinction is firmly set, serious political (as opposed to merely poetic) engagement will be seen to depend, in turn, on this test of "the historical." Thus how the lines of battle over American Studies are drawn rests on the particular sets of binaries that constitute Berkhofer's categories and the trajectory of exclusions derived from them; and indeed as it develops, Berkhofer's text becomes a definitional essay in the specific sense of "setting limits."

As Berkhofer sees it, three conflicting definitions of "context" are at work in the academy today in the wake of the "linguistic turn"; but in the definitional phase of his essay, the feigned rhetorical "uncertainty" mentioned before becomes in fact a conceptual muddle, for the only clear distinction he is able to draw is the traditional one that recognizes "context" (his "context$_3$") as "the extra-textual(ist) world" (13), that is, what he calls a "(truly) (properly) contextualist" one that reintroduces "history" in its quite familiar guise as relying on the notions of "reference" and "realism." What he identifies as "contexts$_1$ and $_2$" are products of that troublesomely "self-referential" and "solipsistic" post-Saussurean understanding of meaning. Here Berkhofer's analysis (with its insistence on context rather than concept) collapses upon itself when he is unable to distinguish between context$_1$ and context$_2$ except to imply that the first is restricted to the single text, while the second is intertextual. All such a tautological analysis as the one Berkhofer builds can finally suggest is that contexts$_1$ and $_2$ are mere "textualities" anyway and have no right to be referred to as "contexts" in the first place. Such a denial is the point not only of his text's "feint" maneuver, but also of the peculiar oscillation of its verb tenses: the odd tense shifts (for example, on pp. 6 and 7) in his narrative suggest the unacceptable "was-ness" of the traditionalist past and therefore the unacceptable "is-ness" of the (post)modern present. Berkhofer's staging of the question of "context" adds up in the end to a revalorization of traditional views, for the upshot is that his account has the effect of representing as patently impossible a contextualist position that would take history seriously at the same time that it takes (post)-modernist textualism seriously (for an understanding of history that accepts "the linguistic turn" *and* stresses the urgency of the political, see T. Bennett, *Outside Literature*). Thus even someone aware of and responsive to (post)modern thought (presumably like Berkhofer himself, who was called on by the American Studies Association to account for it) must finally defend "realism" and "referentialism" once again. Hence the received idea of "history" is saved—without any sustained inquiry into that notion (the focus of Berkhofer's lecture has been ostensibly, if confusedly, on the "new" notions), as are all disciplines—including American Studies—which rely on that "history."

In all texts of the "What-Are-We-To-Make-Of-It-All?" genre, after a rather tedious journey (this one a de/tour through what are to the writer some of the more amusing and accessible parts of the (post)-modern terrain), we arrive right back at our point of departure. This is, after all, the underlying message of Berkhofer's performance, for it begins with the (predictive) observation that although "[p]ro-ponents of both poetics and politics seek to constitute the conceptual framework(s) of a new American Studies . . . they basically . . . de-construct each other" (1)—that is, cancel each other out—and concludes with the (confirming) rhetorical question: "Must all who would mediate between the polar positions remystify as they de-mystify, reconstruct as they deconstruct, reify as they rematerialize, politicize as they poeticize?" (23). Berkhofer merely reassures his audience that the "new" thought is just a contradictory mishmash which while answering some questions, just manages—a signal inconvenience to non-thinkers—to raise new ones. An audience sympathetic to Berkhofer's ideological goals will not notice how much of this presumed "confusion" is *produced* by Berkhofer's text: when, for example, he grossly distorts (post)modern discourses to suggest that they deny that there is such a thing as biology (7) (that is to say, *deny* the existence of an "actual" as well as a culturally produced "real"), or when he charges that they transform "strata or groups into class(es)" and convert "sex into gender and peoples or races into racism" (7), as if (post)modern discourses do not know that there is "sex" as well as "gender," "peoples" or "races" as well as "racism." Such distortions are exemplary instances of the intellectual and political anxiety in the face of the radical potential of (post)modern thought that produces the "demand" for the kind of lecture Berkhofer gave: that is, a lecture in which the speaker apparently does not take a position regarding the issues involved, but rather from a safe and "objective" distance "surveys" the battleground, noting an advance here by one army, an advance there by the other, but no decisive victory for either side and thus no need yet for academic careerist "fence-sitters" (who always, before committing themselves, wait to see who is winning) to move. Ultimately, what Berkhofer "found" is what he was expected to find: since things are thus still so much "up in the air" (here one notes a thoroughly commonsensical recuperation of "undecidability"), any serious concern about the new thought can be safely deferred.

Whatever the intellectual deficiencies of Berkhofer's treatment of the various understandings of context, his text has nevertheless a definite ideological effectivity. What Berkhofer identifies (at the beginning and the end of his paper) as the boundary-point of the political is rather telling, as is the manner in which he represents it: twice he quotes in full (5, 20) a passage from the introduction of Sacvan Bercovitch's *Reconstructing American Literary History* setting forth some general premises shared by contributors to that volume:

> that race, class, and gender are formal principles of art, and therefore integral to textual analysis; that language has the capacity to break free of social restrictions and through its own dynamics to undermine the power structures it seems to reflect; that political norms are inscribed in aesthetic judgment and therefore inherent in the process of inter-pretation; that aesthetic structures shape the way we understand history, so that tropes and narrative devices may be said to use historians to enforce certain views of the past; that the task of literary historians is not just to show how art transcends culture, but also to identify and explore the ideological limits of their time, and then to bring these to bear upon literary analysis in such a way as to make use of the categories of culture, rather than being used by them.

This passage "surveyor" Berkhofer might easily have read as itself a "survey," but instead he treats it as a dangerous political manifesto—a move that can only be made by ignoring the fact that Bercovitch's catalog is a rather innocuous mixture of traditionalist premises with (post)modernist ones that introduces the idea of the "material" while simultaneously robbing it of its force (for instance, "art" is "ideological" but still nevertheless "transcends culture," and furthermore in Bercovitch's catalog it isn't historical agents that work to produce social and political change, but language itself that "has the capacity to break free of social restrictions"). In other words, what is for Berkhofer the absolute "outer limits" of the political (that is, Bercovitch's text) is—conveniently—not in fact very "far out." Berkhofer's text thus sets up a "false" danger that is, in his mind, easily "overcome." He reads the passage ultimately as the very emblem of the "incompatibilities" in the basic premises in the discourses of (post)modernity at large and concludes that their presence, far from being a stimulus to further intellectual labor, robs them of their force: the fundamental message here is that any intellectual undertaking based on what Berkhofer identifies as the (post)modern concept of the "problematic" (as opposed to the traditionalist concept of the "problem") is, from the beginning, incompatible with anything like "rigor." A mere "problem," after all, can be "solved," whereas a "problematic," Berkhofer laments again and again, just leads to other "problematics." Thus, traditional historicism (and by implication a dominant historicist American Studies)—which in Berkhofer's view evidently doesn't suffer from any such "incompatibilities"—is saved by the academic trouble-shooter, though (not incidentally) at the expense of intellectual inquiry.

Another bourgeois strategy deployed to defend humanist historicism is to declare, as Francis Fukuyama (an official of the U. S. State Department and former student not only of the academic conservative, Allan Bloom, but of the deconstructionist, Paul de Man) has recently done, that history itself is now over, an interpretation of culture that "freezes" history by rendering irrelevant current struggles against exploitative power relations under late capitalism and represents the prevailing social relations as permanent. Fukuyama's argument, which draws on Alexander Kojève's reading of Hegel, is in fact that history has been over for quite some time now: it came to an end (as Hegel thought) in 1806 at the Battle of Jena with the triumph of liberal democracy when the "*vanguard of humanity . . .* actualized the principles of the French Revolution" ("The End of History" 5). For Hegel, this "actualization" was the Prussian state. If we have been unable to see this "triumph" until recently, that is only because—according to Fukuyama—the opposition produced by liberal democracy's last resistant ideological "others" (fascism and communism) had to play themselves out, a process the conclusion of which is now in view. What we are witnessing, he says "is not just the end of the Cold War, or the passing of a particular period of postwar history, but the end of history as such: that is, the end point of mankind's ideological evolution and the universalization of Western liberal democracy as the final form of human government" (4). As one who has watched "the flow of events over the past decade or so," Fukuyama proposes as the primary symptom of the "end of history," the notion that "'peace' seems to be breaking out in many regions of the world" (3). In other words the thesis is not so much the "end of ideology," but the triumph of liberal ideology.

The goal of Fukuyama's essay is to provide a "larger conceptual framework for distinguishing between what is essential and what is contingent or accidental in world history" (3), or in his terms to get beyond the surface of history to its governing core "ideas." Therefore, in constructing this "larger" narrative of contemporary culture as a reconfirmation for today's readers of Hegel's bourgeois politics, Fukuyama must also recover and rearticulate the "radical idealist" (8) philosophical presuppositions which enable Hegel's bold declaration. Such a recovery of Hegelian idealism requires that Hegel be saved from the "distortions" of Marx, who turned Hegel on his head and gave a materialist rather than idealist reading to the social. Following Hegel, Fukuyama proposes once again that the meaning of history is to be found in "ideas," not "events": as he puts it, "the ideal . . . will govern the material world *in the long run*" (4). Thus while we can expect that conflicts will still be produced by differences of race/class/gender . . . these struggles are merely "residual" and will exhaust themselves sooner or later since the vanguard of human consciousness (the "essence" in which meaning resides) has not only arrived at, but begun the worldwide consolidation of, that state of awareness he names as "economic and political liberalism" (3). As final fulfillment of the development of the Hegelian World-Spirit, this "unabashed victory" (3) of the liberal state of human consciousness thus spells the end of history.

Such idealism constructs the end of history as basically a "state of mind" which has already found in many nations (and will eventually find in all) its appropriate correspondence in what Fukuyama (after Kojève) calls "the universal homogenous state" (8) constituted by "liberal democracy in the political sphere combined with easy access of VCRs and stereos in the economic" (8). The economics does not "cause" the politics, he argues, for both "presuppose an autonomous prior state of consciousness that makes them possible" (8). Whereas Hegel put forward the Prussian state as the "actualization" of liberalism in his day, Fukuyama proposes that "the egalitarianism of modern America represents the essential achievement of the classless society envisioned by Marx" (9). On this point he hastens to add: "This is not to say that there are not rich people and poor people in the United States, or that the gap between them has not grown in recent years. But the root causes of economic inequality do not have to do with the underlying legal and social structures of our society, which remain fundamentally egalitarian and moderately redistributionist, so much as with the cultural and social characteristics of the groups that make it up, which are in turn the historical legacy of premodern conditions. Thus black poverty in the United States is not the product of liberalism, but is rather the legacy of slavery and racism which persisted long after the formal abolition of slavery" (9). What we are asked by such statements to believe is that no connections are to be drawn between liberalism, America society's "moderately redistributionist" character, and economic inequality. Inequality is, it would appear, simply the result of an "unfortunate lag" between the achievement of liberal consciousness and the diminishment of inequality, between the "ideal" and the "material." Evidently the way to overcome the problem of "lag" is to bracket the question of the "material" by theorizing ideas as more important than events, thoughts as more important than practices, and to throw the emphasis not on changing society but on achieving a liberal state of mind, which, if—from the idealist perspective of Fukuyama—is not, in a purely technical or formal sense, quite the same thing is *"in the long run"* just as good. Given the strong emphasis he places here on "ideas," Fukuyama's response to a journalist who inquired about the time he had spent "in Paris, sitting in on classes with Roland Barthes and Jacques Derrida" is rather telling: "I developed," he said, "such an aversion to that whole over-intellectual approach that I turned to nuclear weapons instead" (Atlas, "What Is Fukuyama Saying" 38-40).

Fukuyama's text is among the clearest recent examples of the strategy of defending humanist historicism by a direct appeal to those views of Hegel which we articulated earlier: history as a succession of homogeneous periods each containing its own "essence" (idea), a movement which unfolds teleologically toward a final fulfillment. This is history as a univocal narrative of mastery. In the light of contemporary thought, what is most striking in this vision of the end of history is that it is specifically a vision of the end of otherness and resistant difference. It not only posits "the total exhaustion of viable systematic alternatives to Western liberalism" (Fukuyama 3), but when it runs into counter-evidence conveniently declares that "it matters very little what strange thoughts occur to people in Albania or Burkina Faso" (9). Such statements indicate that the "outbreak of peace" / "disappearance of violence" which Fukuyama posits as a mark of the triumph of liberalism is a mystification: what he presumes to be "objectively" marking as the "exhaustion" of discourses oppositional to liberalism (the foundation of capitalist entrepreneurship), is actually a "suppression." Indeed he goes on to argue that the spirit of liberal tolerance does not demand that "difference" be eradicated altogether and become "the same." It must simply give up its demands for power and recognize its "master": for "at the end of history it is not necessary that all societies become successful liberal societies, merely that they end their ideological pretensions of representing different and higher forms of human society" (13). In the end, Fukuyama is aware that what he proposes as the "highest" form of society, the homogenous liberal state, is comprised basically of citizen-consumers who are offered nothing more than the "boring" "prospect" (18) of an endless supply of VCRs. Again, so much for ideas. Ultimately the same nostalgia for history which we saw marking Kaufmann's text as the longing to be "truly political," reappears at the end of Fukuyama's as a yearning to see "history started once again" (18).

2

Humanism's representation of the world as a lawful, rule-governed and authoritative check on our conception of "reality" is reinforced by the theory of knowledge to which it adheres: empiricism as the mode of knowing the world. In the name of empiricism, humanism rejects the (post)modern view that data is always already an interpretation situated in ideology, for fear that such a view destabilizes "knowledge" and threatens not only its authority but Authority itself. Hardly a purely scientific or philosophical issue concerning the reliability of knowledge, empiricism is also implicated in political and ideological questions. Jerome Bruner in *Actual Minds, Possible Worlds* points to the involvement of politics in the development of empiricism as a theory of knowledge when he remarks that "[t]o be sure, *Locke* did not invent empiricism: it had flourished before him in Hobbes and grew afterwards in the writings of Bishop Berkeley and David Hume. Note that all four of them lived in a period of rising mercantilism when prospering merchants were seeking an equal footing with king and church, or at least freedom from exploitation" (137; see also Brinton, *Anatomy of Revolution*). Empiricism, in other words, is the scientific and philosophical ideology of a rising class—a class that is attempting to dislodge the "authority" of Divine Rights and Divine Revelation by postulating Nature itself as the source of knowledge and that furthermore theorizes that access to Nature as direct, free, and open to all. Having by our own time succeeded in obtaining power, however, the bourgeoisie is now attempting to maintain that power by transferring "authority" from Divine Right to Nature so that Nature in itself becomes the source of incontestable knowledge, indeed replacing Divine Revelation. Freedom for one class then becomes suppression of others, and it is this suppressive, authoritarian aspect of empiricism that is institutionalized in various forms of modern positivism.

Because of the very "success" in our day of what is popularly understood as the "scientific" (that is, the "empirical") view of things, it seems at first implausible to link empiricism to idealism and theology. Althusser, however, has persuasively emphasized this connection: for him, empiricism is a secular transcription of a religious mode of knowing. In theological theories of knowledge, true knowledge is obtained at the moment that the opacity of the material world is transformed into an epiphanic transparency by means of an "expressive reading," that is to say, "an open and bare-faced reading of the essence of existence" (*Reading Capital* 35). This "expressive reading" regards "meaning" to be not the effect of the act of reading, which is historically situated in the discursive practices of culture, but the inherent quality of the texts of the world, which is "revealed" in them by a direct reference of the text to the master code of the logos. Underneath all their variety, empiricist theories of knowledge also postulate a similar untroubled passage of "meaning" from the "object" to the consciousness of the "subject." They are based on the notion of "knowledge" as an unmediated moment of lucidity and plenitude that transcends the processes that in fact engender it. Empiricism is an idealistic mode of knowing that dematerializes and depoliticizes knowledge. This idealism is inscribed in the specific procedures and assumptions about reality that are supposed to be involved in the emergence of knowledge. Knowledge, it is assumed, is the outcome of an abstraction of the true essence of the "object" by the "subject," which means knowledge is primarily regarded to be part of the "object" itself regardless of the situation of the subject and the knowledge processes involved. Empiricism conceives of the object (data/fact) as originary and immutable. It is originary in the sense that it embodies knowledge in itself; and this knowledge being self-evident, no interpretation is necessary to attain it since the object yields its essence (knowledge) to the senses of the perceiving subject directly through experience. This knowledge, transferred immediately from the object to the subject is also beyond the reach of history and thus always "true." It is in fact its changelessness that makes knowledge acquired in this manner appealing (reliable) since if objects and data change with time there will be no unvarying origin for knowledge— no fixed point of reference against which the accuracy of knowledge can directly and certainly be measured without culturally-conditioned interpretations. "Change" creates an epistemological anarchy because without the security of uncontested facts, one has to accept the relativism of interpretations, accept the historical determination of discursive practices in culture. The politics of empiricism becomes clearer if one follows the implications of such a view of knowledge.

If the object is meaningful in itself, independent of the subject and the cultural practices that produce significance, then by extension the reality "out there" in its entirety is also a free-standing reality whose meaning is in itself—its inner essence. Such an essentializing closure which anchors meaning (knowledge) in the object politically postulates the world "as it is" as the world "as it ought to be" and thus obstructs the reconstitution of the real by any intervention.

Empiricism accepts the world in its present form (the status quo) as the only natural and thus inevitable form of organization of the real and thus unchangeable: hence its deep appeal to the conservative mind. By proposing nature as the authority on reality, the empiricist theory of knowledge fulfills its ideological function, which is the naturalization of authority. For empiricists reality resides outside the significatory activities of culture in the world of physical objects and relationships, in "things" rather than "words." Since "words" are used conventionally and convention can change, thus destabilizing meaning, things, it is assumed, belong to nature and are thus outside the interventions of conventions and therefore are stable forever. It is the ideological program of empiricism to establish a reality whose meaning is self-evident and does not lie in the conventions of intelligibility of a culture, but derives directly from properties of nature. Yet intelligibility, which is culture's way of knowing reality, is not the effect of nature (as it is understood in empiricist problematics) but the outcome of the political, economic, and theoretical practices of a society. By rejecting the cultural, empiricism locates truth in what it regards to be the bedrock of reality—nature.

By assuming that knowledge is the effect of an abstraction of the essence of the object by a subject, empiricism posits a self-identical and self-present subject: in fact, knowledge is, from its perspective, a correspondence between the object and the subject. Such a view of the subject, as the place in which knowledge is created, has close affinity with another idealistic theory of knowledge which is dominant in contemporary critical theory, that is to say, "cognitivism." If in empiricism, the object is the locus of knowledge, in "cognitivism" that locus is the "mind." In fact cognitivism is a form of empiricism of the subject. Both mind and object in these two theories are reified as the ultimate grounds of knowing and both are conceived to be beyond the interpretive practices of culture.

Both cognitivism and empiricism fulfill the demand of bourgeois epistemologies that require knowing the world as an act that takes place in isolation from political and social practices; both, in other words, segregate knowledge from the discursive activities of culture. Knowledge, however, is neither the effect of cognitive processes alone nor the outcome of unchanging objects/facts. Contrary to these two views of knowledge and modes of explanation that dominate contemporary theories, neither mind nor the object is a free-standing entity anterior to knowledge processes. To be more specific, knowledge is not simply abstracted from the object (that is, it is not already there) as empiricist theories propose, but is produced (that is, brought to the world) and this production, like all productive acts, is historically determined in the sense that it depends on the economic, political, ideological, legal as well as theoretical and scientific-philosophical practices and systems of signification available at a given moment in culture. In fact the perception of an object as an object is a function of these systems: "facts" are, in other words, always already interpreted and are therefore part of the conceptual schemes of a society. A culture that has a vast inventory of abstract concepts and advanced theoretical practices understands an object quite differently from the one in which what Lévi-Strauss has called the "science of the concrete" dominates. In Althusser's words, "There is a great difference between the raw material (i. e., the object) on which Aristotle worked and the raw material on which Galileo, Newton, Einstein worked" (*Reading Capital* 42-43). But no matter how "concrete" the systems of signification through which an object is conceived in a culture, it is never a pure instance of sensuousness—a moment of unmediated intuition and epiphanic cognition. The object is always already "represented" (that is to say, constructed through the signifying activities of culture) and is, as such, a complex and impure entity.

The world/reality that emerges from the empiricist and cognitivist theories of knowledge exists outside the discourses of culture in a pure state of objecthood and cognition. The "there-ness" that empiricism attributes to the world and the "here-ness" that cognitivism inscribes in the world are both, in the last analysis, a reification of the status quo and consequently a view of understanding that depends on the notion that the world is always already constituted (in the mind or in the equally closural space of the interior of objects) and as such is beyond intervention and negotiation: all that one can do, it is assumed in these modes of understanding, is to adjust oneself to this pre-existing world.

Empiricism, then, regards the world of experience as the incontestable site of knowledge and furthermore assumes that the materials upon which experience is founded are in a pure state, that they form an ensemble of uninterpreted phenomena (facts and objects). It is not a world which is always already processed and ideologized by the very process of knowing, by the frames of intelligibility that are used in order to make sense of it. To make sure that knowledge is always tied to experience and sense data, empiricism requires that all theories and statements about the world produce evidence of their truth and thus be tested. In the empiricist research program, theory is verified (confirmed or justified in the phase of acceptance) by designing research projects that provide evidence and thus make sure that the theory "fits the facts," that it corresponds with "reality." The theory, in other words, is tested against a set of incorrigible data acquired from immediate (and thus non-interpreted) experience so that knowledge is built upon a core of certainty. The aporia of the empiricist program of verification is that although it postulates the principle of verification as the condition of truth, this principle itself is not empirically verifiable. It is a mark of philosophical and theoretical naivete to ask for a "test" of theory, for any test of theory is, at the same time, itself a theory of testing and thus in need of a test which will be subject to the same condition of theoreticity: that is to say, there is no end to the chain.

The search for certainty is represented as an effort to discover the uncontaminated truth, but in fact it has an ideological function in the empiricist problematic. It attempts to place knowledge and theories of knowledge beyond the reach of social and political frames of intelligibility and claim a universal truth for them, a claim that severs knowledge's ties from the practices of the community which in fact makes knowledge knowledge, which make it a body of significant (meaningful) statements. In requiring positivistic evidence, proof, and testability (as part of its search for an idealistic and thus apolitical certainty provided by facts beyond change), empiricism joins its ostensible opponent, cognitivism, the theory of science which holds that reason rather than experience is the source of knowledge. Both empiricism and cognitivism, on this level, search for an uncontestable certainty through protocols that, by designing formal procedures, ensure the internal coherence of theory and thus postulate it as a self-sustaining system whose truth is not in danger of being destabilized by external factors. These criteria of verifiability are summed up in a rather clear and precise form by one of the most influential contemporary cognitivists, Karl Popper. In his *The Logic of Scientific Discovery*, Popper argues for what he calls a scientifically respectable belief. Such a belief is rationally grounded and thus scientifically acceptable if and only if it has been subjected to a "crucial experiment" designed to falsify it. Taking a different route from those verification procedures that attempt to test the theory in a direct and "positive" manner by evaluating its predictive power, Popper's method uses the test of falsifiability. If a theory fails this test, it is declared unscientific and marked as unintelligible, as non-sense.

This positivistic testing of theory that promises "certainty" about an uncontestable truth was eagerly embraced by traditional scholars in cultural studies (the humanities and the social sciences) because, by instituting such tests, they could guarantee that the only work in cultural studies which would be recognized as knowledge would be their own dominant and on-going piecemeal empirical research. The same desire to place this mode of inquiry at the center of the academy and thus to acquire power for its practitioners accounts for the enthusiastic support that is part of the common sense of the dominant humanities today for a research program based on evidence, experiment, and other forms of empirical proof.

Such enthusiasm, however, is blind to the fact that the use and function of theory in critical theory and cultural studies are very different from its use and function in the sciences. In critical theory and cultural studies theory is an "intelligibility effect"—a historical understanding of the material processes and contradictory relations through which the discourses of culture make sense. No cultural act that produces "meaning effects" could be outside such historical mediations and the workings of social intelligibilities and be atheoretical. To produce and to understand meaning effects is always already theoretical. Poetry, for instance (to use the discourse that humanists deploy as the paradigm of the non-theoretical understanding of experience in the world), is as much a theory of reality as any other discourse; it produces intelligibility/knowledge, and knowledge is always an effect of cultural and political institutions. To say, as humanists do, that poetry is by nature atheoretical amounts to saying that poetry is a transdiscursive act which is auto-intelligible—that it makes sense and is meaningful in and of itself outside all cultural mediations and without being entangled in the materiality of the signifying practices of society. Poetry, in short, is declared to be a transcendental moment of self-identity, panhistorical plenitude, and nonmaterial transparency. To say that poetry is atheoretical is a partisan political statement and not, as such humanists as Helen Gardner (*In Defense of the Imagination*, 1982) and Frank Kermode (*An Appetite for Poetry*, 1989) seem to think, a disinterested defense of the human imagination against the totalitarianism of theory, because what they are actually stating is that (poetry as the synecdoche of) desire is outside ideology. That this is a political program becomes clearer when one considers that it is aimed, among other things, at producing a particular type of subject. Reading poetry as an atheoretical and transhistorical discourse produces the reader as a nonconstrained, self-same (speaking) subject who is marked by autonomy and a direct, unmediated access to the plenitude of the imagination: this theory produces the subject as an instance of presence free from all social contradictions. This notion of the subject is necessary for the maintenance of the existing exploitative social arrangements.

Sense-full-ness is the effect of cultural assumptions or frames of intelligibility and historical practices of knowing—in other words, a "theory." Such an understanding of theory makes it impossible to comprehend how anything could be "by nature" anything—poetry or nonpoetry. Nothing is inherently ("by nature") anything. Things become "somethings" when they are used in a culturally senseful way, that is to say, when they are situated on a cultural grid of intelligibility in a social location. It is the process of such situating—the use of discourses to enunciate them—that produces a "thing" as (socially) "something." There are, of course, modes of representation that suppress the material processes involved in producing this cultural something and consequently attribute the "something" to the "thing itself" (that is, to the "nature of things"), but this suppressing is itself a mode of cultural behavior and a consequence of the social situating of discourses. It is, in other words, the effect of a theory of the real. The traditional notion of theory (as predictive and verifiable by empirical testing) is questioned by the sciences themselves.

The more recent views of theory in science in fact move towards the kind of understanding of theory that prevails in cultural studies: theory as intelligibility effect and not as apparatus of prediction and verification in the traditional sense. In his *The Structure of Scientific Revolutions*, Thomas Kuhn has demonstrated that the positivistic theories of philosophers like Popper are indeed unable to account for the most characteristic aspect of the production of knowledge in science: the existence of a culture of science—a community of agreements, assumptions, presuppositions, procedures, and protocols that come together under a paradigm (1970). Kuhn's work is of great significance in other respects, two of which are important to our own argument: his critique of the notion of fact as used in the empiricist research program and his questioning of the idea of the scientist as a rational and unitary subject in cognitive theories of science.

Kuhn's most basic contention is that the reason why the sciences do not and cannot emulate a Popperian account of their practice is that our access to the facts in the light of which we test our beliefs is always filtered by our existing "paradigms" or frameworks of understanding. He therefore not only critiques the rationalist models used in evaluating the "truth" of the scientific theories but also puts in question the foundation of empiricism, which is—as we have seen—the notion of the fact that embodies knowledge and is accessible to the senses without any interpretation. To put the point more clearly: according to Kuhn, there are no facts independent of our theories; far from being free-standing, self-evident entities, "facts" are produced by paradigms of knowledge; the facthood of a "fact" is established by the means through which it is recognized as a fact. One other implication of Kuhn's ideas for theory in cultural studies is that he questions the notion of the "rational person" (the individual scientist) as the originator and determiner of scientific knowledge. In Kuhn's theory of knowledge, in other words, the "subject" is problematized and this interrogation of the subject brings the domains of scientific theory and cultural theory closer to each other by situating the scientist in the daily ideological contestations of culture.

The problematization of "theory," "fact" and "subject" in the writings of Kuhn and other contemporary philosophers of science who have argued against the dominant empiricist and cognitivist views, is to a very large extent in line with research in the new physics itself. If we insist on the idea of verification, evidence and testing in the traditional empiricist manner, we are forced to rule out as "non-scientific" the most important and scientifically significant part of (post)modern physics: we refer here to the "superstring" theory of current physics. The world, according to superstring theory, is not, at its most simple level, made of sub-atomic particles, but of tiny, one-dimensional elongations of energy called "superstrings." The superstring theory has created a theoretical crisis in (post)modern physics because superstrings are so tiny—the difference of scale between a superstring and an atom is roughly equivalent to that between an atom and the solar system—that they are not accessible to any experimental, verifying procedure that contemporary physics can design. To "test" the theory, experimental physics will have to build an accelerator more than a billion times as powerful as anything that can be conceived with modern technology. There is, in other words, no way to "verify" the theory in a traditional empirical sense. This lack of verification has not only been no bar to the development of the theory, but in fact the theory has become so powerful and scientifically interesting that, it is said, most promising graduate students at major universities are focusing on this new area of understanding (much as the most rigorous thinkers in the field of literary studies are gravitating towards critical theory). Innumerable consequences of the superstring theory are already threatening the normal—"empirical"—view of the world. According to it, for instance, the world is comprised of ten, not four, dimensions and it furthermore contains what is called "shadow matter" composed of invisible particles of all the elementary particles that make up matter and force in the universe. Theory, in short, has put in question the empiricist research program and posed new questions about the very status of theory, verifiability, and proof in (post)modern physics.

The superstring theory is, of course, not non-controversial: there are many physicists who are doubtful about its validity. Their doubts, however, have not prevented the increasing appeal and growing scientific sophistication of the theory. It is interesting that at a time when physics is itself encountering a crisis in its very notion of experiment, evidence, and verification, some humanities scholars are attempting for ideological reasons to impose an inadequate notion of theory on cultural studies. For them, the appeal of empiricism—as we have argued—is the promise that through it the world will be established as uncontestably "out there" in pure phenomena and this "out-there-ness" can then be used as the anchoring point for a "solid" authority, an authority that legitimizes law and order as the condition of possibility of reality and thus of life itself and in doing so will help resecure the petty-bourgeois life-world while allowing conservative politics to continue its exploitation of this class by constantly using its fear of "chaos" and "anarchy" in order to keep itself in power.

3

The old empiricist/cognitivist human sciences regard language to be a transparent medium through which the already determined meaning of the world is reflected. Language, in other words, is a means of transferring meaning from one sovereign subject (the independent and separate individual) to another. Since meaning is prior to language and signifying activities, then one is only obliged to make sure that one handles language as clearly, precisely, and unobtrusively as possible: hence the privileging of "clarity" in traditional theories of writing. This is an instrumental view of language, and its ideological necessity derives from the cultural position of intelligibility offered to the petty-bourgeoisie, a class whose cultural formation leads them—as we shall indicate more fully in the next chapter—to espouse a theory of interpretation that valorizes "things" rather than "words," *inexpressible* and unspoken emotions rather than articulated ideas. The petty-bourgeois in fact takes inarticulateness to be the mark of the authenticity, simplicity and the depth of one's feelings. He associates the mastery of an opaque style and complicated uses of language with fraudulence, clever articulateness, and a seeming ease and intelligence that is attributed to the upper classes and to professionals. This position of understanding requires that the petty-bourgeoisie mistrust any communication that moves beyond the norm of referentiality—beyond simple parallels between language and "reality"—and that this group condemn any such writing as an indication of decadence and unethical conduct.

The referential view of language draws upon a theory of representation that has dominated Western thinking about language, reality, and the subject for many centuries, a view only problematized for the first time in a "strong" way by ludic (post)modern critical theory. The far-reaching implications of this challenge are partially manifested in the contestation over the constitution of knowledge itself now taking place between ludic theory and institutionalized philosophy. One of the outcomes of this interrogation is the placing under erasure of the very possibility of "philosophy" as anything other than a generalized mode of textuality or, in Richard Rorty's words, "a form of writing" (*Consequences of Pragmatism* 90-109). The signs of this institutional battle are visible in the daily discussions in universities in which, for example, the philosophy department rejects the most exciting and provocative theoretical activities of the literature department as non-knowledge, a bracketing enabled by a curiously contradictory "argument" in which the theoretical undertakings in literary studies are seen as the effect of adopting language theories that are, at the same time, "merely fashionable" (that is, do not have real intellectual merit and thus are deprived of that most envied placed in academia—the place of the "permanent") and "superseded" (no longer valid because their time has come and gone). This confused rejection of (post)modern theory because it is supposedly simultaneously over-up-to-date and not-quite-up-to-date points up not so much an inability on the part of philosophers to offer a clear argument. It indicates rather the existence of a historical misrecognition, which is itself a sign of crisis in the institutional organization of knowledge which is, in the last instance, nothing other than a struggle over "representation," over the relation between discursive practices and truth, over the unsaid of these discursive practices, and over who (which segment of the academy) speaks on truth's behalf (posits the "correct" intelligibility).

Broadly speaking, the contestation over representation evolves around two theories of meaning: meaning as *reference* and meaning as the effect of *difference*. Referential theories have, of course, many different articulations in the long history of philosophy, linguistics, and textuality; but their basic tenet can be summed up in Foucault's words from "Politics and the Study of Discourse." For referentialists, "discourse . . . is but a slight addition which adds an almost impalpable fringe to things and to the mind; a surplus which *goes without saying*, since it does nothing else except to say what is said" (17-18). Although the theory of representation based on a referential view of language has received various emphases, one can see its basic paradigm very early when in the *Phaedo* Socrates announces: "I decided to take refuge in language, and study the truth of things by means of it." Here language is regarded to be a reliable substitute for reality, a more or less faithful reflection of the world. This essentially referential view of language has dominated Western thought from Plato through Locke and Kant and the Wittgenstein of the *Tractatus* to the present time. In Kant the theory is given an epistemological twist that reveals its underlying master concepts, for he regards language to be not so much a reflection of reality (because he believes reality is not accessible to human beings) as it is a reflection of our thoughts about reality. Kant thus foregrounds two major issues in referential theories: first, that the source of meaning in language is outside it; and second, that the relation between language and that which is outside it is secured by the subject. The assumption here is that the world is reflected in the mind of the subject (in ideas) who then organizes words in a fashion to guarantee their correct reference to ideas. In other words, ideas in the mind of the subject reflect the world; and by the agency of the subject words reflect those ideas. Communication, then, is an exchange of meaning (produced in the consciousness of the subject non-discursively) through language (which is controlled by the subject) between two sovereign subjects. The twentieth century-version of the referential theory of language has been widely disseminated through analytical philosophy, which is a form of empiricism that acquires "certainty" by obtaining knowledge from a mode of referentialism often called the "picture theory of language" and associated with Russell and the Wittgenstein of the *Tractatus*. Although analytical philosophy (with its attendant theory of language) is no longer "dominant" as a mode of intelligibility in the academy today, it still forms a kind of general common sense in the philosophy departments of Anglo-American universities.

Referential theories of representation are problematized in the writings of Saussure. His *Course in General Linguistics* is itself a mixed set of discourses, containing very conservative views and quite innovative theories. His most important contribution to the theory of meaning is his postulation of the concepts of "value" and "significance" (111-119) and his demonstration that significance is the effect of value: meaning in language is engendered by the differential relationships that signs acquire by virtue of their membership in a system, in short, "differences carry signification" (118). In a famous passage, Saussure states that "[i]n language there are only differences *without positive terms*. Whether we take the signified or signifier, language has neither ideas nor sounds that existed before the linguistic system" (120). The radical conclusions he draws from such a view are that, contrary to the referential theories of language, meaning in language is not caused by entities outside of it (empirical reality), but by the operation of the system of the language itself: language does not reflect or refer to empirical reality as such. This also means that meaning is the effect of a *systematic* relationship (no individual entity is inherently meaningful) and that *difference* is the enabling condition of meaningfulness. Saussure's revolutionary view of meaning also decenters the Cartesian *subject*, who in referential theories is the agency of securing the relationship between reality and language.

This radicalization of anti-representationalism finds its most powerful articulation in the texts of Jacques Derrida, who criticized Saussure for his residual logocentrism (*Of Grammatology* 27-73) and who in his "Sending: On Representation" argues that the traditional program of representation should be given up. In Derrida's theories, the text is seen as unable to refer to anything outside itself, to represent an idea, a message, or any other form of "reality." Rather than a point of "reference," texts have—in Frege's word—a "sense" (see "On Sense and Reference"): they acquire their "meaning" by pointing to the processes of signification in other texts. If all that language can do is represent the processes of signification, then what has seemed to be "truth" outside language and represented by it is, in the last instance, merely a textual mirage, since truth is nothing other than the effect of intertextuality. Texts are thus understood to acquire meaning through their "reference" to the processes of signification (other texts). The contestation of academic philosophers with (post)modern theorists is partly in the space of this theory of representation, since if language cannot refer to a truth outside itself, then the traditional claim that philosophy is the guardian of (the discourse) of truth and the judge of legitimate intelligibilities breaks down, and philosophy becomes a form of textuality, a narrative of "truth" that competes with other fictions engendered by other textualities. If philosophy is to preserve its institutional power as owner of the discourses of truth, then it must rescue some form of referential theory of language: such a rescue is exactly what current academic philosophy is undertaking in its attacks on (post)modern theory.

As we have already mentioned, traditional analytic philosophy (which has as its main focus linguistic analysis) is still the commonsense of academic philosophy in the Anglo-American world (or, as some put it, "the dominant philosophy in capitalist countries today," Rajchman and West x). However, in its traditional mode analytic philosophy has actually collapsed upon itself. In order to return to some form of referentiality, it has become necessary then to move (along with the new form of pragmatism put forth by Rorty or the view of representation put forth by Cavell) towards a "post-analytic philosophy" or adopt other modes of referentiality by drawing upon the writings of Austin (and through him on Wittgenstein's ideas on "rule") and Searle (who through "speech acts" attempts to point language towards empirical "reality" by offering a grammar of conventions of reference) in what might be called a form of "neo-analytic philosophy." The new referentialism of post/neo-analytical philosophy has had, as might be expected, a great influence on recent philosophical writings and on new theory itself. We are not thinking of those who have championed philosophers like Searle in order to offer some "defense" of the humanities against deconstruction, but of the rigorous writings of theorists like Charles Altieri, who, by a re-reading of Wittgenstein, has attempted to offer a new mode of textual interpretation (see *Act and Quality*).

It should be added that the desire of contemporary philosophy to formulate a calculus of references and to rescue language from "nihilistic" theories has a great deal to do with research in artificial intelligence studies and the research funds that are (through defense contracts) made available for research in these areas. The intelligibility posited, in other words, is not a mere matter of the pursuit of truth. As Lyotard puts it: "No money, no proof—and that means no verification of statements and no truth" (*The Postmodern Condition* 45). Our point here is that the current interest of philosophers in language and their rejection of deconstruction is related to the form of power/knowledge relations that these funds and grants make available.

The contestation between university philosophy and contemporary literary theory should be understood in the space we have just described. New theory is over-up-to-date, from philosophy's point of view because it puts in question the basic tenets of academic philosophy; and it is not-quite-up-to-date because it does not pay attention to the revival of referentialism and regards it as merely a last grasp at institutional power in the name of "genuine" philosophy that has suspended "fashionable" notions about language and reality. The contestation over intelligibility between the traditional humanities and ludic (post)modern theory, as exemplified in deconstruction, is, from a radical political point of view, the struggle between two versions of empiricism and cognitivism: the empiricism of objects and the cognitivism of the consciousness of the subject of experience in the old theory and the empiricism of language itself and the cognitivism of the "speaking" subject in the new theory. A radical theory of representation and knowledge must be global: it must place language and the subject in the historical material series of culture. We shall return to this question at the end of this section by focussing briefly on the notion of the sign in Marxist theories of language.

4

We have undertaken this excursus on representation because the full implications of the traditional human sciences for the reproduction of the dominant ideology in the spaces of language, textuality, and subjectivity can only be comprehended by such a situating of it. The desire of the established humanities to anchor language, text, and the subject in the actual through the concept of reference and thus to obtain a coherent and stable world of representation is particularly evident when it commonly (mis)reads (as somehow crucially untenable) the Saussurean view of the relation between the world and language. What Saussure is saying is that, in a social and cultural but not ontological sense, language precedes the world and makes it intelligible through concepts that it provides for producing differences, whereas conservatives frequently misread Saussure to be proposing that "language" *makes* the world. Such a misrecognition of Saussure derives from the ideological imperative of the humanist program of intelligibility to confuse "the actual" with "the real" and thus to bypass the politics of meaningfulness. Saussure's theory is about the constitution of the "real" and not about the ontological status of the "actual" (the nature of "being"). Therefore, when he states that language practices in culture produce the real, he is not saying that language produces the actual in the sense of creating trees, snakes, tables, and male and female persons in their actual physicality. For instance, as long as they are part of the continuum of nature only, the male and the female are not culturally "different" and therefore have no cultural reality since they do not play a role in the organization of the political economy of life: they play no part in social arrangements. They have, in other words, no meaning, nor reality since reality is a cultural and not a natural matter. However, as soon as the actual male and female enter the domain of culture, which is—as Althusser makes clear in *Lenin and Philosophy* (127-186)—before they are even born, and are differentiated by its symbolic order, its codes of gender, they acquire meaning as "masculine" or "feminine" persons and become culturally "real." From that point on, they participate in cultural negotiations and in the organization of the economy of culture's symbolic systems. The transformation of the actual into the real takes place through the various languages of culture which produce differences from the continuum of nature. Without language (differences) there is no (cultural) reality: the question in Saussure is that of *the constitution* of the real and not that of *the existence of the actual.*

When Marx observes in the *Economic and Philosophic Manuscripts of 1844* that *"the entire so-called history of the world is nothing but the creation of man through human labour"* (100), he like Saussure is addressing the problematics of the construction of the real in culture. History (the real) is produced by human labor (the economic practice which is articulated with the political, ideological-significatory, and theoretical practices of the social formation). The site of meaning is not nature, but nature transformed into a social product—the real. To substitute the actual for the real and tie language to the actual is precisely to postulate meaning as natural, given, and thus inevitable—a move that is in fact a strategy of containment. In fact it is a part of the ideology of the dominant humanities studies to mystify culture by representing it as nature and to offer the real as actual so that culturally constructed values are put forth as natural givens and as such are placed beyond interrogation and contestation.

The assumption here is that we have to adjust to these given values and not attempt to change them since they are, like the laws of nature, unchangeable and sacred. They are, in other words, part of "the order of things." However, intelligibility is produced by specific historical and material practices through which a culture codifies the "actual" (nature) as the "real" (the culturally meaningful and thus the intelligible). In *Critical Essays*, Roland Barthes gives a rather clear and interesting account of the dialectic of nature and culture and of the role of signifying practices in mediating the actual:

> According to Hegel, the ancient Greek was amazed by the natural in nature; he constantly listened to it, questioned the meaning of mountains, springs, forests, storms; without knowing what all these objects were telling him by name, he perceived in the vegetal or cosmic order a tremendous shudder of meaning, to which he gave the name of a god: *Pan*. Subsequently, nature has changed, has become social: everything given to man is already human, down to the forest and the river which we cross when we travel. But confronted with this social nature, which is quite simply culture, structural man is no different from the ancient Greek: he too listens for the natural in culture, and constantly perceives in it not so much stable, finites, "true" meanings as the shudder of an enormous machine which is humanity tirelessly undertaking to create meaning, without which it would no longer be human. (218-219)

Employing some of the concepts that Saussure and Hjelmslev (*Prolegomena to a Theory of Language*) have provided, we can conceptualize the processes through which language transforms the actual into the real, the same into a set of differences, a process which makes the world intelligible. The new theory regards each signifying system as having been composed of two planes: the plane of the signifier (expression) and the plane of the signified (content). These two planes themselves are constituted by two strata: the stratum of "substance" and that of "form." These two terms are easily misunderstood since, as Roland Barthes warns us in *Elements of Semiology*, "each of them has a weighty lexical past" (40). "The form," according to Barthes, is "what can be described exhaustively, simply and coherently (epistemological criteria) by linguistics without resorting to any extralinguistic premise." The "substance," to continue Barthes's exposition, "is the whole set of aspects of linguistic phenomena which cannot be described without resorting to extralinguistic premises" (40). Since both "form" and "substance" exist on the plane of expression as well as the plane of content, a four-term analytical scheme emerges which can be diagrammed in the following manner:

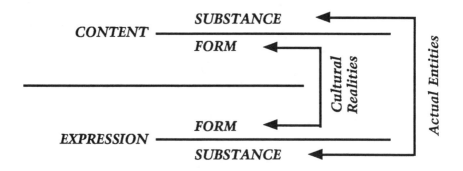

SIGNIFYING SYSTEM

On the plane of expression, substance (in a language) is all the sounds that the human speech organs can produce; using the International Phonetic Alphabet, some are transcribed as:

$$\Theta \quad d \quad b \quad \vartheta \quad s \quad t \quad x$$

These "phones" are physical events, and as such non-linguistic (non-cultural) entities that belong to nature, to acoustic actuality. They acquire cultural "reality" if and only after they have been given a form by the phonological system of a language. The "phone" (an actuality of sound) becomes a "phoneme" (a culturally meaningful part of language) and in being en-formed by the phonological laws of a language constitutes a part of the cultural reality. In English [s] [b] [θ] are real sounds (phonemes) in the language, while as far as the English sound system is concerned [x] is nonexistent, while it is real (a phoneme) in modern Persian.

While the features of substance and form on the expression plane are fairly easy to determine and demonstrate, their characteristics on the plane of content are much more complex. The substance of the content is described by Saussure as "the whole mass of thoughts and emotions common to mankind independently of the language they speak—a kind of nebulous and undifferentiated conceptual medium out of which meanings are formed in particular languages by the conventional association of a certain complex of sounds with a certain part of the conceptual medium" (qtd. in Lyons, *Introduction to Theoretical Linguistics* 56; Saussure, *Course in General Linguistics* 111-112). Such a description of substance, as we have already mentioned, is psychologically and theoretically conservative.

We can reduce the psychologism of Saussure's idea of the substance of content by theorizing it as the undifferentiated continuum of all perceptual, conceptual, and physical "events" that the human sensory system is capable of producing and or responding to. Like the substance of expression in language, which is composed of all the sounds that human speech organs can produce, the substance of content is an effect of the materiality of the human sensory system (always already situated in society) and as such an actual entity. In perceiving a cardinal flying against the sky, in responding to the darkness after sunset, the human person responds to an actual event through the nervous system. This event is then made intelligible by being situated on the historically specific set of cultural grids that differentiate the entity "cardinal" from all other birds and also from the "sky." Depending on the occasion, the intelligibility of the event can be increased by describing it as "beautiful." We might observe, however, that "cardinal" has a more or less clear "referent," while "beautiful" derives its "sense" from belonging to the semantic field that in English also includes "lovely," "attractive," "pretty," and so on. The meaning of "beautiful," in other words, is the effect of a sense relationship in this particular semantic field in English. The substance of such terms as "beautiful" then is more a sense-relation among various members of a semantic field in a given language than it is a referable physicality. This, however, does not mean that terms such as "cardinal" (which have a physical "referent") are any more in themselves accessible to us through "reference" rather than "sense" than is "beautiful," which is more obviously a cultural term. Both terms acquire intelligibility from the cultural grid on which they are placed: both are, in other words, intelligible as cultural terms rather than as actual or natural categories.

To make this last point about entities like "cardinal" a little clearer, it might be helpful to examine color terms in various languages and to investigate their differences. Like "cardinal," color terms seem to have a clear referent: they are assumed common-sensically to be physical phenomena and, as such, directly accessible to the viewer without cultural mediation. Research in modern linguistics, however, proves otherwise. Color terms in various languages are not merely different labels for the "same thing" (language is not a mere nomenclature), but are signifiers that enform the color spectrum and thus make it culturally intelligible.

Since colors have physical existence, it is convenient to think that language merely reflects that existence and that what is actually "out there" is present in its plenitude by the mere act of reporting/reflection "in here" (that is, in language). However, this is far from being the case: we understand colors not because we respond to them directly by our sensory organs, but because the responses of our sensory organs are made intelligible for us by the language we speak. Different languages make sense of this physical continuum in startlingly different and dissimilar ways, thus putting in question the commonsensical view that nature is in itself intelligible. The English word *brown* "has no equivalent in French (it would be translated as *brun*, *marron*, or even *jaun*, according to the particular shade and the kind of noun it qualifies . . . there's no equivalent to blue in Russian—the words *goluboj* and *sinij* (usually translated as 'light blue' and 'dark blue' respectively), refer to what are in Russian distinct colours, not different shades of the same colour, as their translation into English might suggest" (Lyons, 56-57). The role of culture in turning the actual into the real is made even more clear when we examine the color terms in a language like Hanunoo that has a system of color terms which—unlike those of Western languages—are not based entirely on hue, luminosity, and saturation, often considered to be the three-dimensional substances that underlie color terms. In his essay, "Hanunoo Color Terms," H. C. Conklin has demonstrated that the four main terms of the Hanunoo color system are based on lightness, darkness, wetness, and dryness. That the distinction between "wetness" and "dryness" is not simply a matter of hue (green versus red) is clear from the fact that "a shiny, wet, *brown* section of newly cut bamboo" is described by the term which is often used for light green. According to Conklin, not only is color in its technical sense not a universal, "natural" category, but the very oppositions in terms by which the substance of color is determined depend on culturally important features (qtd. in Lyons 431).

In his book *Pertinence et pratique*—which forms the basis of Umberto Eco's interesting essay, "How Culture Conditions the Colours We See"—Luis Prieto calls these culturally important features "pertinent" points according to which a signifying system makes the world intelligible. These points of pertinence are themselves effects of the daily material practices in culture, not nature. In his exposition of Prieto, Eco provides a simple example of how the practical purposes (daily practices determined by social arrangements and not by the actual) produce pertinent categories according to which we endow meaning and significance to our world (make sense of it). "If," Eco writes,

> I have on a table before me a large crystal ashtray, a paper cup and a hammer, I can organize these pieces of furniture of my limited world into a twofold system of pertinences. If my practical purpose is to collect some liquid, I then isolate a positive class whose members are the paper cup and the ashtray, and a negative class whose only member is the hammer. If, on the contrary, my purpose is to throw a missile at an enemy, then the heavy ashtray and the hammer will belong to the same class, in opposition to the light and useless paper cup. Practices select pertinences. The practical purpose does not, however, depend on a free decision on my part: material constraints are in play, since I cannot decide that the hammer can act as a container and the paper cup as a missile. Thus practical purposes, decisions about pertinences and material constraints will interact in leading a culture to segment the continuum of its own experience into a given form of the content. To say that a signification system makes communication processes possible means that one can usually communicate only about those cultural units that a given signification system has made pertinent. It is, then, reasonable to suppose now that one can better perceive that which a signification system has isolated and outlined as pertinent.
>
> ("How Culture Conditions the Colours We See" 163)

The form of content segmentizes the substance according to the principles of pertinence that are established by material practices, whic] are tied to the obtaining and maintaining of power in a culture, the power to own and operate the means of production. The content of a language, then, is more an effect of the pertinences that a culture accepts as necessary coordinates for differentiation rather than a space in language through which the actuality of nature shines through. "What is content?" asks Eco in response to the problems that are involved in inquiring into the relation between substance and form, actuality and culture. His answer is helpful and should be quoted in full here. "Content," according to Eco,

> . . . is not the external world. Expressions do not *signify* things or states of the world. At most, they are *used* to communicate with somebody about states of the world. If I say that ravens are black and unicorns white, I am undoubtedly uttering a statement about a state of the world. (In the first instance, I am speaking of the world of our experience, in the second I am speaking about a possible world of which unicorns are inhabitants—the fact that they are white is part of the state of affairs of that world.) However, a term like 'raven' or 'unicorn' does not necessarily refer to a 'thing': it refers instead to a cultural unit, to an aspect of our organization of the world. (162)

For the traditional humanities, a text (like language itself) acquires its meaning because of the entities which are located outside it and which it faithfully "represents." In a sense, as a language construct, the text is the reflection of a reflection, a mimesis of a mimesis. Since in empiricist theories supporting the traditional humanities research programs the text is given its meaning by nature and the actual, it is always already "full"—it is determined and as such is, fundamentally, a non-negotiable entity. In its fullness, the text is an instance of presence and plenitude which humanist interpretation designates as the unity of the text and which it defends as a unity from the decentering reading strategies of (post)modern theory. These strategies reveal the "absence," which is in fact the condition of possibility of this "presence," by exposing the "lacunae" (the points of referential and representational vulnerability) of the text. A full text is seen as already occupied by the actual, and thus comes to the reader as a meaning-full entity. In empiricist and cognitivist programs of intelligibility, the function of the reader is also predetermined: she is supposed to recover the meaning that is put in the text by the originary agent, the author. We shall later examine some of the implications of such a monological mode of straightforward reading, in particular its obliteration of all markers of the productivity of the text.

The process of reading then in the empiricist proposal of intelligibility, especially in its version in literary studies, is merely the act of abstracting the essence (meaning) from the text, without violating the text's aesthetic integrity. A reader who reads transgressively is a "careless" reader, a "disrespectful" reader. Aesthetic integrity is the critical assumption by which the borders of the text are protected; by means of such protection, the text is isolated from the larger series of culture, cut off from the politics of signification, and thus reduced to a mere cognitive entity. One appreciates the text and does not subvert it.

New critical theory, from ludic (post)structuralism to radical Marxism, puts the representationalist notion of the full text and of reading-as-receiving in question by theorizing the text as constituted not by elements that are present to themselves and "refer" to the outside of the text (signs corresponding to the actual) but by "traces" of absent signs (Derrida, *Positions*, 26). "Brown" is understood to mean what it does to a person familiar with the system of signs called the English language, not because it "corresponds" to an extra-textual entity (the essence of a color), but because it is *not* "yellow," "red," or "green." The meaning of "brown" thus derives not from its positive "identity" but from its difference from these other signs and its difference is produced by "traces" of all these "absent" signs. The Derridean version of (post)modern theories argues that the text, rather than being a full entity that simply refers to the world "out there" is instead the scene of the "playfulness" of signs: the meaning of a text is a constant drift of *différance*, a semantic chase, an unresting referral of one sign to other signs. "Brown," in order to be marked as an intelligible entity, is differentiated by reference to "red," and "red," by reference to "green," and "green" by reference to . . . In the humanist view, once signs have performed their function, they disappear in their "meaning." For Derrida, however, since there is no ultimate sign (a sign that is, in and of itself, "meaningful," a "transcendental signified"), then signs never disappear in the "meaning" but always remain a material entity. Since they do not have any meaning in themselves and acquire their meaning from their difference from other equally slipping signs, the play of signs in the text never ends. In fact, this is what the text is regarded to be: the scene of differential "playfulness" (of significatory activities). As we shall see later, Derrida calls this notion of textuality and meaning "dissemination" and distinguishes it from controlled polysemy.

5

(Post)modern radical theories of textuality and meaning politicize this notion of the materiality of the sign and the productivity of the text. Although the Derridean mode of reading and its theory of textuality breaks from traditional common sense and proposes intelligibility as the effect not of mimesis, but of the very process of signification itself, it, like other modes of ludic theory, finally situates the signifying process as a formalist program.

Radical (post)modern theories of language and textuality not only contest the empiricist/cognitivist views of the traditional humanities, but also the new formalism of (post)structuralist theories and propose intelligibility to be, in the last instance, the product of social struggle. This notion is, to a considerable extent, developed in (post)modern marxisms, which take as their point of departure the works of Marx and such Marxist linguists as Bakhtin/Voloshinov. In *The German Ideology*, Marx and Engels write that "Language is the immediate actuality of thought" (446) and thus point up that the actuality of the world "out there" is mediated to consciousness through language, which is itself a material entity. However, what is significant in Marx's notion of language, textuality, and signification for our own purposes here, is his emphasis on language as social—a point which although hinted at in Saussure's *Course* (14, 113) is rarely brought up in deconstructive (post)modernism. In the same book, Marx and Engels also write that "language . . . is a product of species" (426) and, most importantly, elaborate the idea that "language is practical, real consciousness that exists for other men as well and only therefore does it exist for me; language like consciousness, only arrives from the need, the necessity, of social intercourse with other men" (44). In *The German Ideology*, which offers the first recognizably materialist theory of reading/writing texts of culture, Marx and Engels situate the sign in all the complexity of the social.

The notion of the sign as a site of restlessness and semantic agitation is one that Marxism and deconstruction share, but their understandings of this linguistic agitation are radically different. For Derrida, as we have seen, this semiotic stirring and excitement is the very characterization of textuality. For Marx, the sign is a scene of semantic disturbance because it is the site of class struggle: various social groups attempt to contest the established and assigned meanings of the sign to obtain hegemony. The notion of the sign as the site of social contestation is further developed by Bakhtin/Voloshinov in *Marxism and the Philosophy of Language*:

> Class does not coincide with the sign community, i. e., with the community which is the totality of users of the same set of signs for ideological communication. Thus various different classes will use one and the same language. As a result, differently oriented accents intersect in every ideological sign. *Sign becomes an arena of class struggle.* (22, emphasis added)

In short, (post)modern theories of text and meaning, in their different articulations dismantle the humanist model of communication as an unproblematic process of the flow of knowledge from one "subject" (i. e., the author) to another (i. e., the reader) through a dematerialized and transparent "language." For deconstruction as well as for radical marxism, the text, in Pierre Macherey's words, is "a dense fabric which obeys its own logic" (*Theory of Literary Production* 55). The reader reads this text from a historically specific situation and depending on her reading strategies (themselves historically determined), "produces" meaning in the text. Text, author, reader, language—all are thus historical: there is no inherent meaning in the text and no stable text to guarantee an inherent, determinable "intelligibility." The concept of "(post)modernism," for example, which we will investigate much more fully in the second part of this book, is not an empirically verifiable one, nor is it an essence which can be contemplated by the subject in his consciousness so that he may grasp its plenitude of "truthfulness." It is a cultural construct which attempts to explain certain material and discursive practices. Explanations of what "(post)modernism" is, however, are themselves problematized by the fact that they are produced by contesting "readers" from various social classes that are interested in legitimating as intelligible one set of practices over other alternative practices as "(post)modern." For Foucault, Derrida, Lacan, Kuhn, and Rorty, the term is employed to make sense of practices they regard to be "radical": Fredric Jameson, on the other hand, contests the intelligibility achieved by these writers and regards (post)modernism to be the notion through which the "logic" of late capitalism is naturalized. These two intelligibilities, then, are forms of knowledge over which two classes of readers are struggling. By trying to legitimate its "truth" of the "(post)modern," each class is offerin g its own political, economic, and ideological practices as the "obvious" (natural) ones. What "(post)modernism" means, in other words, is in no way "certain" or ascertainable in "its own terms" (inherently). This means, above all, that intelligibility is a social and political category through which practices of the class in power will be recognized as the norm of culture and addressed as the "real." Our attempt in writing this book is part of this struggle over intelligibility: we write in order to argue for a radical theory that supports certain practices as opposed to others.

The most important result of the understanding of language and textuality as non-representational is that the new theory proposes cultural intelligibility as produced by processes of mediation and signification, rather than simply as the "reflection" of the actual itself. Having de-actualized intelligibility, (post)modern theory opens it up to textual and/or political contestation and thus indicates the "arbitrariness" (in the sense of "historicity") of knowledge and its produced intelligibilities.

In the new theory, culture is regarded as an ensemble of contesting claims to knowledge. The outcome of these contestations determine which of these claims are recognized as "knowledge" and thus have the authority to designate the intelligible (the "real") of a culture and its "values." Although what is put forward as knowledges in the old empiricist/cognitivist program are represented as direct and unmediated embodiments of "truth," what is put forward as knowledges in the new theory is viewed as highly textualized (i. e., mediated) through their articulation in various texts of culture, whether in the form of novels, anthropological treatises, films, or scientific papers. It should be kept in mind that from the viewpoint of the new theory, laboratory procedures in the sciences, field work in anthropology, literary conventions for composing novels, cameras and other technical apparatuses and procedures in film-making are all part of the "textualization" of knowledges. Texts, in other words, do not merely reflect or simply "represent" knowledges that are "found" outside them. Rather—as Derrida (in *Of Grammatology*), de Man (in *Allegories of Reading*), and Foucault (in *The Archaeology of Knowledge*, *The Order of Things*, and *Discipline and Punish*), among other contemporary philosophers, literary theorists and historians of ideas have shown—texts actually intervene in the truth of the knowledges they are purportedly representing. The "truths" of knowledges, in other words, are "constructed" through the very means that are supposed simply to "represent" them.

From among all the textualized knowledges that have claims upon the intelligible and thus upon the values of a culture, only a few are recognized by that culture as "genuine" knowledge, and the rest are rejected as merely pseudo-knowledges. Those that are designated as "genuine" knowledge, however, are so designated not because they inherently, unequivocally, and powerfully embody "the truth," but because their claimed truth conforms with the codes and conventions that are at the time dominant in the scientific and scholarly institutions and communities that have the final say in such matters. As Thomas Kuhn has demonstrated in *The Structure of Scientific Revolutions*, these codes and conventions of knowledge amount to a kind of culture of texts in themselves, the culture of science, which is composed of all the texts of customs, procedures and established habits that form what he calls a "paradigm." Furthermore, it is the dominant "paradigm" and not the inherent "truth" of knowledges, that ultimately determines "genuine" knowledges and separates them from "fake" and "pseudo" knowledges. Through these codes and conventions then, the dominant culture of science controls what is "knowledge." All that we know about the world "out there," in others words, is the effect of the mediations of the paradigm, of the codes and conventions of our modes of inquiry, and not the direct reflection of empirical "nature" or consciousness or "actuality" in themselves. Even "facts" in science are not self-evident, empirical givens, but are determined by the means that we use to know them: there are, in short, no such things as unmediated, nontextualized facts. All facts are facts because our process of knowing designates certain phenomena as "facts," while rejecting others as "non-facts." The determination of "facts" (and consequently the judgment about what is "true" knowledge and what is merely a pretense to knowledge) depends finally not on the inherent "factuality" of facts or the "truth" of knowledges but, on the circumstances of knowing codified in the dominant paradigms.

"Truth" is, in other words, a convention. However, ludic (post)modern theory treats these conventions as a matter of "form," as an agreement among members of an organic community. We would like to point out, nevertheless, that positing the intelligible as the effect of cultural conventions does not in itself make a significant political difference in the theory of intelligibility between the old empiricist/cognitivist project and the new theory. In ludic theory, convention is itself a form of empiricism of forms. It is here that the intervention of radical marxism becomes significant since it argues that these conventions of intelligibility are, in the last analysis, economic, political, and ideological: the effect of social contradictions. Today those modes of intelligibility that "naturalize" the reproduction of the relations of production in late capitalism are the ones which are designated as modes of "authentic" intelligibility. That is to say, the theory of codes and conventions that ludic (post)modern theory puts forth in itself merely replaces an old mode of conservative intelligibility (the empiricism of the senses) with another (the empiricism of forms). It is the uses of codes, how they enable certain practices and prevent others, that are the final determining factors. By putting emphasis on *practice* rather than merely on the *codes*, radical marxism therefore offers a new understanding of cultural intelligibility. "Why is it," asks Fredric Jameson, "that our students do not do laboratory work in alchemy? Why is Immanuel Velikosky considered to be an eccentric?" (*The Concept of Postmodernism* viii). The reason is, of course, that neither "alchemy" nor Velikosky's views are recognized as "legitimate" knowledges by the dominant paradigm of sciences because they are not needed for the reproduction of the existing social arrangements.

This social (and not "natural") intelligibility is a necessary part of the life of culture because it is by appeal to these intelligibilities (truths) that a culture explains the world in a manner that is supportive of its values and its world outlook, that is to say, supportive of its existing relations of production: the class structure that is determined by the distribution of wealth in society. The task of explaining the world according to the dominant (social) intelligibility is the task of ideology. Ideology is the way a society represents its existing social arrangements to individuals. It is, in other words, the image that a society gives of itself in order to reproduce itself. The main purpose of these images and representations is to persuade the individual that the way things are is how they ought to be. In its "explanation" of the world and its "justification" of social arrangements, the discourses of ideology produce a set of cultural "obviousnesses" that are extensions and amplifications of the dominant "social" intelligibility. These "obviousnesses" (such as "I think, therefore I am" or that "experience is the final test of truth") operate as the main cognitive frameworks of daily practices and need no "proof." It is, however, necessary for these "obviousnesses," and the "social" intelligibilities that lie behind them, to be beyond the ordinary doubts of individuals and to have the authority of "inevitable," "universal," and "natural" givens. It is to achieve this undoubtable authority of nature for the constructs of culture that the discourse of ideology suppresses the textuality (the ideological mediations) of the dominant intelligibility. By such suppression, the conventions of culture (its values and world outlook, its social institutions and class arrangements) are all represented by ideology as "natural," that is to say, as directly derived from the reality of the empirical world "out there," and are recognized by the cognitive powers of the subject. What is dominant in culture, according the discourse of ideology, is so because it is natural—the only way things can be! The new theory foregrounds the ideological dimensions of the established human sciences, their logocentrism and metaphysical closure. But to the extent that such a foregrounding itself becomes a new metaphysics of textuality without the further understanding of textuality as political mediation ("textuality in ideology"), (post)modern theory and the traditional humanities propose two versions of what is finally the same dominant intelligibility: an apolitical intelligibility achieved through empiricism and cognitivism, in other words, by things and subjects. The narrative that is frequently put forward that, with the arrival of new theory, things have been radically altered thus has to be renarrated and its suppressed narratives displayed. We shall investigate this dominant narrative of "radical" change in Chapter Four.

6

According to the humanist view, the subject appears sometimes to be a "free" subject and sometimes to be "determined," depending on the needs of its argument. Take, for instance, its view of the situation of the author and the reader. For humanism, the actual (rather than the real) engenders the text through the agency of the subject, who is perceived to be, like the text, "full"—an instance of self-presence and plenitude. The subject, in the form of the "author," is the "origin" of the text's meaning, in the sense that meaning in its completeness, totality, and self-sameness exists in the author's mind alone. No other single consciousness has direct access to the full meaning: the subject in the form of the reader can only approximate the complete meaning of the text/consciousness of the author. Though different readers are allowed certain variations in their interpretations of the text (are allowed, in other words, to show their individuality), they must nevertheless recover in their readings a coherent and common core of significance, common enough to ensure that the meaning, in spite of its variations from reader to reader, is stable. A reader whose reading is not informed by this common core is not a genuine reader, but a rude, "disrespectful—to use Abrams's term, "tactless"—one. Though such a reading process is presented as an appreciation of the beauty and humanity of the text, it would seem rather to be an act of ritualized obedience to the text's presumed semantic law and core of truth. Thus the humanist understanding of the reading process makes it an exercise in how to adjust to authority, how to respect its limits and to obey its laws. Humanist ideology's understanding of meaning and text, in other words, is the discourse of obedience to authority.

The humanist subject is the "originator" of meaning, the person who "intuits" things and above all has an intense emotional and physical response to phenomena. Even the authenticity of the reader's reading of a poem is marked not by what he says about the poem, but by the depths of his unspoken response. Yet in spite of being the originary, intuiting, and feeling "individual," the subject is nonetheless a static entity: she is, as we mentioned, "full" in that she is always already determined. That determinedness is the effect of an unchangeable human nature that forms all peoples of the world regardless of their culture, society, and the economic and political coordinates that vary from culture to culture. It is this "essence," this "human nature," that finally determines who we are, in the humanist view.

If the world is comprised of subjects all made of the same "human nature" and essence, they must also be different from one another; for it is only finally in their uniqueness that their status as persons lies. One mark of this uniqueness is the style with which they write. Dickens and George Eliot, Northrop Frye and Wayne Booth are exemplary figures for humanist ideology: they reveal their individuality and difference from one another by writing "differently." In other words, style is a mark of "originality." Deconstructionists, by contrast, all write alike, it is often charged. The claim that style is a marker of separateness is, of course, an ideological characteristic of humanism: the function of the humanist praise of stylistic variation and elegance is in fact to conceal the sameness inscribed within humanist texts. In other words, however superficially different their "styles" may appear to be, nineteenth-century "realist" novelists like Dickens and Eliot and twentieth-century critics like Wayne Booth and Northrop Frye actually occupy the same ideological space in culture: the only thing that hides that sameness is their styles. The "regional" (style) in its heterogeneity occludes the "global" (ideological) homogeneity: style creates an aesthetic separation in order to conceal an ideological sameness.

The (post)modern text, often charged by humanists with exhibiting a boring "sameness" or "repetitiveness" or of having a "stilted" style, is rather an over-coded text that, like a metafictional text, draws attention to its own codedness and verbal constructedness; it is, in Roland Barthes's words, "a mask which points to itself" (*Critical Essays* 98). In the asymptotic zone where it is located, the (post)modern text interrogates itself from inside by indicating its own institutional situationality as a cultural text. It marks its situationality as a highly constructed cultural moment in which what are thought to be the "natural" processes of signification are denaturalized. In order to dramatize that denaturalization, the (post)modern text undertakes a self-denaturalization: it points out that it is a text, an example of writing (being a site of absence and a bearer of traces), not a moment of presence and transparency. Its highly coded language refers to all other languages to which it is linked, to all intertextualities in which it participates, and in which it intends to situate its reader. The (post)modern text is thus "different," not in having a "style" unlike that of other texts: it is different in a much more radical sense. This text does not differ from other texts, but from itself: it is a reversible text and in its reversibility it is an open text, a text whose signifying processes are part of its meaning. On the opening page of *S/Z*, Barthes articulates a concept of "difference" which accounts for the difference between humanist and (post)modern "difference." "This [(post)-modern] difference," Barthes patiently explains, "is not, obviously, some complete, irreducible quality (according to a mythic view of literary creation), it is not what designates the individuality of each text, what names, signs, finishes off each work with a flourish; on the contrary, it is a difference which does not stop and which is articulated upon the infinity of texts, of languages, of systems; a difference of which each text is the return" (3). The difference that marks the text/the subject then is not some humanistic bourgeois essence, but the difference in the process of signification that announces its constructedness, its plurality in the sense of its reversibility. It is in reversibility that closure is disclosed and the conditions of possibility of meaningfulness are interrogated. Unlike the humanist mode of signification, the (post)modern mode does not conceal itself through the effects of obviousness, but marks those obviousnesses as products of the opacity of ideology.

The notion of the full, unitary, and rational subject that is privileged in humanism is contested and demystified in (post)modern theories. In the discourses of (post)modern theory, the subject is regarded to be an effect of ideology, since, as Lacan has put it, the subject is "empty" and this emptiness is filled by means of a set of relationships and (Lacan again) "other voices" (Wilden, *System and Structure* 183) through what Althusser has named Ideological State Apparatuses. These apparatuses (institutions of modern capitalism) constitute the subject through the discourses that are needed for the reproduction of the existing relations of production: family, church, trade unions, media, literature, and especially schools form the individual in a manner which is necessary for the re-production of prevailing social arrangements. Workers (at all levels) must not only be physically available and technically skillful, but —and more importantly—willing to accept their own position in existing social relations: they will have to see dominant class relations not only as the way things are but also as the way they ought to be. This acceptance of and consent to prevailing class relations is actively produced in them through the cultural obvious-nesses that various discourses of ideology form. These discourses offer a philosophical-theological accounting of the world that justifies, explains, and clarifies the world in which the dominant class relations (with their consequent distribution of wealth) are offered as natural and universally given. For the worker, teacher, lawyer, army officer, or doctor to be able to function in society, it is—in other words— not enough to be professionally trained in the technical aspects of a job. Each must also acquire a set of assumptions, attitudes, modes of understanding (subjectivities) that lead to the practices needed for the continuation of the existing social order. The discourses of ideology produce obviousnesses that in their totality propose a theory of life for members of a culture: this theory of life postulates what should be regarded as "the good life," "happiness," "intimacy," "success," and so forth. Different social formations produce different "obviousnesses": that which is obvious in a feudal society is not so obvious in a highly competitive capitalist society.

In his essay, "The Subject of Literature," Terry Eagleton states that one of the most central modes of production in any social formation is the production of the human subject: "Different human societies," he writes, "will of course require greatly different forms of subjectivity to fulfill their ends, and in this sense the production of the subject/subjectivities is just as historically relative and changing as the production of economic goods" (96). The construction of the subject is the effect of various apparatuses and institutions in a society such as family, schooling, and so on, which Eagleton calls, in their entirety, the ensemble of "moral technologies." A moral technology, according to him, "consists of a particular set of techniques and practices for the instilling of specific kinds of values, disciplines, behaviors, and responses in human subjects" (96-97).

The effectivity of ideology in producing cultural obviousnesses that suppress the contradictions in the social order depends, of course, on its success in getting the majority of people to recognize them immediately as obvious. Furthermore, these obviousnesses must be so secure and uncontested that the recognizers not only do not inquire into their constitution but use them as the enabling frames for understanding reality, themselves, and the dominant practices. Cultural obviousnesses, in other words, should work as the grounds upon which a society bases its self-justifications and constructs representations and images of itself that enable it to carry on its life as a community. "Ideology," as Althusser defines it, "is a representation of the imaginary relationship of individuals to their real conditions of existence" (*Lenin and Philosophy* 162). In other words, ideology is a set of discourses, images, myths that establish an imaginary (imaged) relationship between the individual and the world. "Imaginary," it should be stressed, does not mean that this relationship is non-existent (false) since people do indeed live their lives according to these "imaginary" relationships with the world. Althusser adopts this term from Lacan's theories on the formation of the subject. In Lacanian psychoanalysis, the "imaginary" is a mode of relating to the world which is marked by its plenitude and presence. Althusser's view is that ideology is a mode of imaginary relating to the world in this sense: one is situated in a subject-position from which a relationship of presence and fullness is assumed. Thus wifehood and motherhood are subject-positions from which a woman relates to the real conditions of her life in an imaginary manner: in an assumed presence, fullness, and plenitude. The plenitude, in other words, is made possible only if the woman occupies the required subject-positons. It is part of the "imaged/imaginary" mode of relating that it does not allow a full inquiry into the relationships. Ideology attempts to overcome the contradictions of social life under capitalism by privileging certain representations and by suppressing others that threaten its legitimacy.

The mark of the subject's successful inscription in and incorporation into the existing social relations and the ultimate sign that it has obtained unique identity and freedom as a person, is that the recognizer of the cultural obviousnesses responds to the "call" from the Other who addresses him/her in his/her subject-position in the dominant social arrangements. He responds to the Other who "calls" him: teacher, husband, son, wife. Althusser designates this process of calling, which is the sign of the transformation of the individual into a subject (his/her incorporation and insertion into existing social relations), "interpellation." To be constituted as a subject is to be given a consciousness by virtue of which one becomes a free agent and a unique and irreplaceable person (because there is only one "you" that can respond to the call of the Other). The subjectivity and freedom which goes with it, however, as we have implied, are an effect of the person's complicity with the dominant relations of production. In responding to the "call" from the Other (Althusser names this Other as the Subject—with a capital—and exemplifies it in the figure of God, Boss and other symbolic entities which stand for the existing social order), one recognizes in the process the existence of the Caller, who is articulating the social arrangements, and the Caller recognizes the Called back. This double recognition which produces subjectivity is what Althusser calls the "speculary" structure of ideology (180). By means of its speculary composition, ideology, through the Caller (the Subject) turns the subject into a mirror, a reflection of the Subject and thus ensures the subjection of the subject to the Subject, secures the consent of the individual to the dominant obviousnesses of culture. The individual recognizes himself in the mirror (mediation) of the Other; but since the speculary (mediated) nature of this self-recognition is suppressed by ideology, one is given to believe that one is self-constituted: one is a sovereign subject—the notion that informs the humanist view of the individual.

With its essentialist theory of history, its privileging of empiricism as a mode of knowing, and its views of language and text as reflections of the "actual," humanism, like all texts of ideology, participates in the production of the (consenting) subject. The subject produced in humanism is given a position of intelligibility from which the world is seen—as we have argued before—as a battleground between moral forces (good and evil), a picture which is basically the condition of possibility of subjectivities produced in the petty-bourgeoisie, a condition required for their compliance with the existing order.

One of humanism's most frequently deployed strategies for depoliticizing (by anchoring) the world of social practices and subjectivities is to appeal to "natural laws," a move that is favored by some contemporary right-wing theorists, such as Jerry Falwell, who likewise appeals to "immutable laws" in *Listen, America!* (53) to condemn a whole array of anti-patriarchal practices, from new forms of family arrangements (159) to homosexuality and high taxes. "Our founding fathers," Falwell writes, "had profound respect for the law and knew that true liberty is found only in obedience to law because they recognized the fallen nature of man as recorded in the Bible. They understood that they needed law as a guide" (45).

Similar appeals to the "laws of nature" were once used to justify slavery in America,[1] but few texts show as clearly as the following one not only the relationship between the argument from nature and the subjugation of women and slaves but also the ideological and political assumptions involved:

> The right of suffrage is then truly universal when it is extended to all the adult males of the State, without regard to distinctions of property; it can not go beyond this limit and be extended to women, without violating the main principle on which the very being of the State rests for support, which is the subordination of wives to their husbands, of children to their fathers, and of slaves (in every community which has them) to their masters. Women are cared for and protected in their natural rights by the State, and so are children, and so are slaves in those countries in which they chance to form one of the classes of society; but women, children, and slaves are not the State, are not the protectors of society. Their position is one of subordination and

---

1. Seabury, *The Pro-Slavery Argument* (1852); Seabury, *American Slavery Distinguished from the Slavery of English Theorists and Justified by the Law of Nature* (1861); Brownlow and Pryne, *Ought American Slavery to be Perpetuated* (1858); Jenkins, *Pro-Slavery Thought in the Old South* (1935).

dependence; and men—freemen—whether they be "the lords of creation" or not, are in fact the lords and rulers of the political community to which they belong.

And not only *in fact*, but *of right;* for a little reflection will convince us that Nature and right reason point to men as the proper depositories of political power, and restrain two, at least, of the classes above indicated to that mediate relation to the State which, in fact, they hold. (Seabury, *American Slavery* 68-69)

Although frequently not observing them, the dominant class always appeals to laws, since it is their interests that are in any case codified in the laws. Of course the law of nature carries that process one step further: it removes the slightest hint that these laws are "constructed." Here, in its advocacy of the laws of nature, humanism follows the same trajectory of ideas that, as we have already argued, leads to a defense of the fixed *rules* of textuality, subjectivity, and language, as well as history and empiricism. For humanists, thinking empirically is as much a "natural" practice as writing realistic fiction, enforcing the law, and disciplinary knowledge.

The theoretical inquiry that has placed such "natural" practices in question, pointed up their constructedness, and marked the fact that they are not instances of natural givens but sites of the social production of power is (post)modern theory. We therefore turn now to the question: what is (post)modernism?

Part II

. . . But for a Radical Theory

Chapter Three

(Post)Modernism
and Its
Differences

1

The (post)modern has become the common sense of our time and is celebrated by many as the mark of the fundamental break (the achievement of freedom) of our age from modernity and the culture of the Enlightenment and its metanarratives of "totality," "ideology," "critique," "progress," and "opposition." For many radical readers of texts of culture, however, perhaps because of such widespread acceptance, the (post)modern remains "suspect." These readers have, by and large, regarded (post)modernism as the latest cultural frivolity, another discursive device for distracting us from, and thus reducing the effectivity of, political actions to transform contemporary social practices. There are good reasons for this repudiation, since the prevailing readings of (post)modernity derive mostly from two major sets of conservative discourses. On the one hand, there are the discourses of an avant-garde which represents itself as radical but in actuality is, in a rather conventional and predictable manner, merely anti-bourgeois and still complicit in capitalist practices. On the other, there are the philosophical discourses of an equally conservative (post)structuralism that deconstructs the oppressive regime of humanist truth only to reproduce, in more up-to-date fashion, those ideological effects that are so necessary for the unchallenged continuation of corporate capitalism. Thus (post)structuralism produces compelling philosophical discourses that are appropriate for the contemporary emerging high-tech industrial democracies.

These artistic and philosophical discourses have successfully deployed the (post)modern as a structure of limits: they have, in other words, produced the (post)modern as the boundary of radicality beyond which no discourse and practice can go without being rendered unintelligible. It is by naturalizing the dominant conservative (post)modernism as the norm of radicality that Ernesto Laclau and Chantal Mouffe, for example, in *Hegemony and Socialist Strategy* are able to talk about the "dissolution" of the "Jacobin imaginary" (2). However, like all other cultural concepts, "(post)modernism" is not settled or stable, but a shifting and differential cultural site of social struggles: it is, in other words, a contested terrain. Instead of simply dismissing the (post)modern (and conceding it to the conservatives), the radical (Jacobin?) reader must take part in these contestations and offer an "other" understanding of the culture of corporate capitalism that does not simply retreat to a nostalgia for the centered coherence of modernity, but engages the logic of "difference" and at the same time reads difference differently. Such a (post)modernism—which we, following Teresa L. Ebert's "Rewriting the (Post)Modern," shall call *resistance (post)modernism* and distinguish from the conservative reading of the (post)modern that we will designate as *ludic (post)modernism*—will articulate emancipating practices in the (post)modern. In this rearticulation of the (post)modern, such concepts as "totality," "ideology," and "critique" play a key role because they will enable an understanding of the global logic of exploitation underlying the seemingly heterogeneous practices of late capitalism that ludic (post)modernism posits as the only viable sites of the (micro)political. In its reunderstanding of totality (after it has been deconstructed), resistance (post)modernism reactivates the "other" of the dominant (ludic) (post)modernity.

To say what we just said is, of course, to contest one of the founding notions of mainstream (post)modernism, whose popular slogan is that such grand narratives as "critique" and "totality," along with all other logocentric metanarratives of the culture of modernity, have come to an end and that (post)modernity itself is the end (limit) of "totality" and the beginning of "difference." As a preamble to our discussion of ludic (post)modernism in this chapter, which will in turn serve as a context for our critique of its dominant (post)structuralist practices in the rest of the book, we might begin by saying that "(post)modernism" is not autointelligible experience, not a "phenomenon" which can be positivistically "referred to" as "out there." Even though one can mark certain features of the contemporary as "(post)modern" (as we will, in fact, shortly do), the "meaning" of the (post)modern as a cultural experience and as a form of understanding and not merely an aggregate of free-floating traits and lineaments, is the effect of the global frame of intelligibility in which these aspects are articulated. Contrary to what empiricist theory proposes, this frame of intelligibility is neither in the phenomena itself nor, as textualists posit, a merely semiotic and significatory matter, a question of "language." It is rather produced through social struggles over the construction of cultural reality. There are many different and often contesting ways of constructing (post)modernism as a mode of social intelligibility.

Deploying Ebert's terms, we shall name as "ludic (post)modernism" the understanding of (post)modernity that makes sense of it as a problematics of "representation" and, furthermore, conceives "representation" as a rhetorical issue, a matter of signification in which the very process of signification articulates the signified. Knowledge of the "outside"—if one can mark such a zone of being— is, according to ludic theory, traversed by rifts, slippages and alterities that are immanent in signifying practices and, above all, in language. Representation, in other words, is always incommensurate with the represented since it is subject to the law of *différance*. Ludic (post)modernism, therefore, posits the "real" itself as an instance of "simulation" and in no sense the "origin" of the "truth" that can provide a ground for a political project. *Différance*, in ludic (post)modernism, is regarded to be the effect of the unending "playfulness" (thus the term "ludic") of the signifier in signifying practices, which can no longer acquire representational authority by anchoring itself to what Derrida has called in *Of Grammatology* the "transcendental signified" (20).

Contesting the understanding of *différance* as an effect of rhetoric, "resistance (post)modernism," as we shall later elaborate it, articulates difference in the social space of economic exploitation and labor. While "ludic (post)modernism" seeks its own genealogy in Nietzschean texts, "resistance (post)modernism," as we have suggested, is articulated in the writings of Marx.

2

In the popular imagination, (post)modernism has become synonymous with MTV, the architecture of Michael Graves, Madonna, performance art, and futuristic films, phenomena that, by using some of the techniques of the modernist avant-garde, construct a world totally different from the one projected by the earlier avant-garde. In fact for many, the (post)modern is a direct contestation of the modern and, above all, its regime of rationality, its elitism, and its notion of "progress" that locks human history into a linear movement towards a pre-set goal. But the opposition to the modern does not mean that the (post)modern is a total negation or rejection of modernity: the "(post)" in (post)modern ("post" in parentheses) marks the problematic relation between the two. It certainly does not mean "after," since such an understanding of it will take us back to history as "progress" again. We shall have occasion throughout this part of the book to make "(post)" a more nuanced and complex prefix than it is usually understood to be.

Depending on how one reads the "(post)" in (post)modern, (post)modernism can mean two very different understandings of the contemporary. Briefly—and, as we said, we shall come back and re-examine the observations we are going to make here later—if one takes "(post)" in the sense of an "after," one has posited a traditional notion of history based upon "period"—a unique, homogeneous segment of time which in its totality represents the "spirit of an age." Only traditional modernists read (post)modernism in this way; and we have, to a large extent, dealt with their positions and critiqued them in the first part of this book. Those who oppose such a progressive, linear notion of history and believe that history is in itself a problematic issue (since it is only a representation and like all representations not outside the laws of difference), regard "(post)" to be a sign of "reading," interpretation, and "textuality."

For these, (post)modernism would mean the re-reading or text-ualization of modernity. For such readers, there are no "origins," nor are there any originary knowledges that can be said to exist outside the act of interpretation (difference). All knowledges are "fallen" knowledges: as one commentator has recently put it, the deconstructive "experience of undecidability" is the "experience of falling" (Roussel, "The Gesture of Criticism" 147). Thus all knowledges are merely other "interpretations" and not direct, unmediated, non-differential knowledges of the real itself (Lyotard, *Postmodern Condition* 27ff). In this sense, then, there is very little that is, in the traditional sense of the word, "historical" about (post)-modernism. It is, accordingly, a recurring moment in all "periods." The "(post)" in (post)modern marks a subversion of history itself by the operations of language: a demonstration that, as a language construct, history is itself differential and as such cannot serve as a firm ground for the truth of other discourses and practices. In short, (post)modernism is, in this sense, a rebellion against modernist semiotics in which the signifier (word) is held to correspond to the signified (concept) and a declaration of the freedom of the signifier. Putting the modernist view of language under erasure, this (post)-modernism states that the signifier is never exhausted by the signified and its meaning always "exceeds" the conceptual models of the signified. "(Post)" here stands for "excess," for a fracturing of established systems of representation and for the liberation of the (unlawful) overflow of meanings. (Post)modernism is then a regime of excess: the everlasting playfulness of meaning which cannot be contained by any stabilizing concepts. This is the (post)modernism that we have called ludic (post)modernity, a (post)modernity of the playfulness of the signifier (in unending acts of reading).

We, however, take the "(post)" to be neither a marker of linear history (in the manner of modernism) nor simply a hermeneutic practice (the re-reading of modernity in the manner of Lyotard) but rather, as we have already implied, a sign of "resistance." (Post)-modernism, then, in our reading is a resistance to the dominant practices which are, for the most part, residues of the culture and politics of modernity. This resistance, however, is not a merely semiotic resistance, not merely an ideological struggle against what Lyotard calls in *The Postmodern Condition* "cultural policy" (76), but a "class struggle" against the dominant relations of production.

Regardless of the particular reading that we give the "(post)" in (post)modernism, (post)modernism is not simply a collection of facts and data—Madonna, the videos of . . . , the fictions of Barthelme, and punk style. It is rather a historical articulation (not an essential quality) of a set of layered discourses and practices, each with its own history, in political economy, literature, the arts, family structures, sciences, (geo)politics, philosophy, media studies, social policies, schooling, and law. The more common approach to an understanding of the (post)modern has been to "thematize" it and offer a comparative inventory of its "contents," to indicate how, for example, (post)modern architecture or fiction or religion or terrorism varies from the modern or how (post)modern social practices are at odds with those of the modern.[1] Rather than taking

---

1. See Jameson, *The Concept of Postmodernism;* Lyotard, *The*

this path, which eventually will lead to an unproductive positivism, we read the (post)modern as a social frame of intelligibility and a historical move of understanding because the (post)modern, as we have already suggested, does not reside in objects and experiences. Instead its "meaning" lies in the world that it constructs as real and in the "other" world that it suppresses as "unintelligible" (old, regressive, linear). In other words, the (post)modern is the name of a political practice by which social intelligibility is produced. Beyond its specific thematized features (such as the subversion of "plot" in fiction, the collapse of Stalinist states in Eastern Europe, patterns of disarmament, non-continuity in the editing of films, and environmental policies, for instance), it is a way of making sense of late capitalism and its forms of social and cultural truth.

3

By virtue of the inclusions and exclusions of certain features and practices, the theorizing of this frame of intelligibility—the (post)modern—is itself, of course, the site of contestation and social struggle. We now situate our own discourse in this contestation by proposing the (post)modern as a regime of intelligibility which is marked, above all, by "difference" and "self-reflexivity." The (post)modern is reflexive in the sense that it denies the possibility of any metastatement that can be "outside" its own truth. "All totalizations [about (post)modernity] are false" is an instance of a metastatement that proposes a "truth" (the falseness of all totalizations) from which as metatruth, it exempts itself. However, read reflexively, "All totalizations [about (post)modernity] are false" loses its own truth since it is itself an instance of "totalization," and thus, according to its theory of truth, "false." Traditionally, such reflexive statements are dismissed as logical puzzles and treated with amusement as minor epistemological annoyances. The very fact that the truth of the statement is negated by its own implication in that truth is traditionally taken to be a "proof" of its untruth. Although ludic (post)modernism, by a reflexive reading of the

---

Postmodern Condition; Hassan, The Postmodern Turn; Huyssen, After the Great Divide: Modernism, Mass Culture, Postmodernism.

metastatement, reduces it to a statement and includes it in the economy of signification that it attributes to the "other," it does not simply reject it as untruthful. On the contrary, ludic (post)-modernism extends the condition of reflexivity to all texts of culture and, in doing so, denies the possibility of a secure "ground" (metastatement or theory) upon which one can reach a decidable meaning. In other words, although a ludic reflexive reading of "All totalizations [about (post)modernity] are false" deprives it from its commonsensical meaning, it does not dismiss that meaning, but retains it and inscribes it in the same space with its "other." The outcome of such a double inscription of the sentence is that its meaning loses its "decidability" and certainty and thus enters the semantic zone of the "undecidable." In undertaking such a reflexive reading, then, ludic (post)modernism denies the possibility of any secure "foundation" upon which observations about the real can be made, a foundation which is itself not part of the observations and thus subject to the laws of difference.

Whether in the architecture of Robert Venturi, the photography of Ger Dekkers, the paintings of Jasper Johns, the films of Terry Gilliam, or the fictions of John Barth and Ishmael Reed, ludic (post)modern art acts out (post)modern anti-foundationalism in its self-reflexivity. It is an art which is highly self-conscious of its own status as a work of art and as a commodity in consumer society. Not only does it not take seriously the traditional claim of art to the metatruth of representation (the ability of the arts to make a reliable knowledge of "reality" available), but it also turns this claim back upon itself and transforms it into a "joke" about the epistemological pretentiousness of all (modernist) arts and, by extension, all the other discourses of culture, from literature and philosophy to the sciences, psychoanalysis, politics and law.

The fictions of John Barth, for example, emphatically ridicule the very idea of access to a "real" outside of the discourses through which it is produced. By means of an inclusive use of irony, pastiche, parody and other textualizing strategies, Barth problematizes the (modernist) notion of the artist as the knower of the "real":

> Why do you suppose it is, she asked, long participial phrase of the breathless variety characteristic of dialogue attributions in nineteenth-century fiction, that literature people such as we talk like characters in a story? Even supplying the dialogue-tags, she added with wry disgust. Don't put words in her

mouth. The same old story, an old-fashioned one at that. Even if I should fill in the blank with my idle pen? Nothing new about that, to make a fact out of a figure. At least it's good for something. Every story is penned in red ink, breathless variety characteristic of dialogue to make a figure out of a fact. (*Lost in the Funhouse* 107)

By doubling back upon itself reflexively, as in this instance, Barth's fiction denies the truth of its own claim—the possibility that fiction can represent the real without getting in the way of its own representation of truth—and marks itself as a "fact" (truth) made up of a "figure" (rhetoric), and thus includes itself in its own economy of signification. Ludic reflexivity is the hermeneutic move that demonstrates that the "theory" proposed by the text reflexively erases its own claim to truth.

What is "performed" in the (post)modern arts is further problematized in (post)modern "theory," which is itself a complex textual effect blurring what used to be, in the Enlightenment map of knowledge, the distinct "disciplines" of philosophy, psychoanalysis, semiotics, literature, law, the media, and history. The belief in the availability of knowledge in any direct manner is put under erasure in the ludic writings of Derrida, Foucault, Lyotard, Deleuze, Baudrillard, and other conservative thinkers. In their views, representations (philosophy, art, fiction, architecture, dance, the sciences) do not bring us any closer to the "real," but merely "allegorize" the ever-increasing distance between discourse and the real. The more the texts of culture (arts, philosophy, politics, law) attempt to get hold of the real and offer a reliable knowledge of it, the more it recedes in an unending series of textual embeddedness. What defers the presence of knowledge of the real even more is the way that this embeddedness is itself foregrounded in the process of representation. In Barth's fiction, for instance, the instructions to the reader to insert in the text a "long participial phrase of the breathless variety characteristic of dialogue attributions in nineteenth-century fiction" is a textualizing device that points up the gap between the signifier and the signified.

By a reflexive reading of Enlightenment rationality and its idea of reliable knowledge of the real, ludic (post)modernism undermines the very idea of decidable knowledge as "science." In Lyotard's account of (post)modernity in *The Postmodern Condition*, scientific certainty is understood to be constructed by the suppression of non-rational knowledge in "narrative" (25-27). However, unlike narrative knowledge, whose legitimation lies in its very own narration (it *means* because it *does*), scientific knowledge needs an "external" legitimation. Science, in the West, has "legitimated" itself by appealing to two grand narratives of the Enlightenment: the grand narrative of the emancipation of humanity from oppression by scientific knowledge (31) and the grand narrative of "speculation"—the movement, in the fashion Hegel proposes, of the ignorant spirit towards knowledge and self-consciousness (32-37). The reflexive paradox of the Enlightenment idea of science is that while science rejects narrative knowledge as irrational, a species of superstition, it needs to resort to "narrative" for its own legitimation: "Scientific knowledge cannot know and make known that it is the true knowledge without resorting to the other, narrative, kind of knowledge, which from its point of view is no knowledge at all" (29). Under the sign of the (post)modern, however, these metanarratives of "freedom" and "knowledge" which have so far acted as first principles grounding decidable, denotative knowledge (science), lose their credibility ("I define *postmodern* as incredulity towards metanarratives," xxiv) and are displaced by "little narratives," connotative kinds of knowing, that Lyotard calls "paralogy" (60-67). For the question of "truth" as decidable and regulated knowledge, Lyotard substitutes paralogical knowing:

> Postmodern science—by concerning itself with such things as undecidables, the limits of precise control, conflicts characterized by incomplete information, *"fracta,"* catastrophes and pragmatic paradoxes—is theorizing its own evolution as discontinuous, catastrophic, non-rectifiable, paradoxical. . . . It is producing not the known but the unknown. (60)

Ludic (post)modern knowledge (as "unknown") is marked by the "excess" of meaning that is outside the system of representation and, as such, is essentially an "undecidable" form of understanding which is always already self-reflexive and self-included in the economy of signification that it assigns to the "other."

Thus, the (post)modern is, in a radical sense, the inclusion of the "other" in the same and the rupture of the regime of coherent and totalized "identity" and identitarianism. In Lyotard's *Postmodern Condition*, ludic (post)modernism's watchwords become: "Let us wage war on totality; let us be witness to the unrepresentable; let us activate the differences and save the honor of the name" (82).

The ludic deconstruction (reflexive reading) of Enlightenment metanarratives is conducted from within these grand narratives themselves and not from an external ("transcendental") position of a "superior" and "certain" knowledge. Reflexivity, in the first instance, is an immanent critique. The outcome of such immanent reflexive reading is to demonstrate that the ludic (post)modern, in its turning away from the Enlightenment and modernity, is in fact (like all seeming binaries) inscribed in its seeming "opposite." This is one reason why, for example, Lyotard speaks of the (post)modern as a "rewriting" of the modern (*The Differend* 3).

Such an "immanent critique" of modernity makes it clear that ludic deconstruction always takes place from "within" the discourses being deconstructed and is therefore always a part of them and not a simple rejection of them. Also "it makes immaterial," according to Lyotard in *The Differend*, "a periodization of cultural history in terms of 'pre-' and 'post-,' of before and after, and questions the position of the 'now,' the present from which we claim to have a right view over the successive periods of our history" (3). The notion of the historical "period"—as metanarrative of the Enlightenment— is thus discarded as a totalizing concept which presupposes history to be a series of homogeneous eras, each informed by an overarching idea ("the spirit of the times") that shapes its art, politics, sciences, and domestic life. (Post)modern historiography (by means of what Foucault calls "genealogy," which is itself a form of immanent critique) focuses on the specific practices and micromovements of singular events and demonstrates that what is commonsensically thought of as a unified and self-identical "period" is in fact always "different" not merely from other periods, but more importantly, from itself. Ludic (post)modernity, in a reflexive reading, turns out to be not simply the label for a historical period, "after" and thus "outside" the modern, but the name of this "difference" and as such part of the immanent economy of history and a recurring moment throughout history. All "periods," accordingly, have their "(post)-modernity," in the sense of a moment of (self)reflexivity and subversion of their "metanarratives" (first principles) upon which they have constituted themselves. Since there is no limit to this process of doubling back upon first principles in any "period," then the (post)modern is the crisis of metanarratives of modernity that is engendered by their undecidability which is unleashed through their reflexive inclusion in the economy of their own signification.

This notion critical of the idea of "period" is closely related to a theory of history that is perhaps best articulated in the writings of Foucault. Foucault displaces the identity and reliability of the "knowledge" provided by traditional history through his dismantling of what he calls "monumental history" in *Language, Counter-Memory, Practice* (161). This is the kind of history that posits an "origin" for events in order to chain them together in a coherent narrative that represents the "past" as continuing "secretly to animate the present" (146). Instead he argues for a history "without constants" (153): a "genealogical" history that "record[s] the singularity of events outside of any monotonous finality" (139). In this effective history, therefore, an "event" is "the reversal of a relationship of forces . . . the entry of the masked 'other.'" The logic of history is not one of identity—there is no pattern (knowledge) acquired from history because forces in history "are not controlled by destiny or regulative mechanisms, but respond to haphazard conflicts" (154). History, in other words, is other than itself, at odds with itself. Therefore, historical knowledge, like all other knowledges, is more a story about (problems of) knowing than knowing itself: the only knowing is the story of knowing, and nothing outside this story is knowable since history is allowed "to create its own genealogy in the act of cognition" (157).

Our purpose in pointing up the problematization of "period" and "history" in ludic (post)modern theory is to emphasize what we have already stated: (post)modern thought is marked, above all, by its mistrust of "identity," the traditional view that an entity (a word which already assumes "identity") is non-reversible, free from self-contradiction and thus always "self-same" (identical with itself). Behind the logic of "identity," according to Derrida, lies the larger project of Western philosophy which he calls the "metaphysics of presence" or "logocentrism," the need in Western thought to get hold of a secure, self-present and decidable ground (first principles) for the "real." Derrida performs his deconstruction of the "metaphysics of presence" in various discursive regimes by indicating how knowledge (of the real) is constituted by language and by then demonstrating how language is itself marked by "difference." Unlike the traditional idea of difference, the (post)modern notion of difference is, as Heidegger proposed, a reflexive one: thus it is not a difference *between* two self-same and decidable entities, but a difference which is reflexively different from itself, in other words, a difference *within*. Perhaps the most concise way of demonstrating these two notions of difference is to look briefly once again at the opening paragraph of Roland Barthes's *S/Z* (1974).

Rejecting his previous—"structuralist"—semiotics of identity which was devoted to the formulation of a theory of narrative in which one could see "all the world's stories . . . within a single structure" (*S/Z* 3) confirming the identity of a narrative, Barthes in *S/Z* announces the inauguration of a new—"post-structuralist"—project. Unlike the old one, the new project is to mark the "difference" of a narrative and not to totalize it into a universal concept of narrative. However, this difference is not a difference that affirms the identity of each narrative (not a difference *between* one narrative and another one). "This difference," Barthes writes, "is not, obviously, some complete, irreducible quality (according to a mythic view of literary creation), it is not what designates the individuality of each text, what names, signs, finishes off each work with a flourish; on the contrary, it is a difference which does not stop and which is articulated upon the infinity of texts, languages, of systems: a difference of which each text is the return" (3). It is, in other words, a reflexive difference which does not simply produce an "other" outside itself but is itself a site of the recurrence of the "other" and its transgression of the boundaries of the "same."

Although *S/Z* makes the two understandings of "difference" clear and thus marks the (post)modern project in terms of reflexive difference (the difference that, as soon as it is located, differs from itself), it is in the writings of Derrida that the ludic understanding of difference acquires its fullest articulation. Derridean *différance* is a site in which the two sides of (post)modern difference intersect: difference as the effect of language and difference as the other of logocentrism and presence.

As Heidegger writes, difference is primarily a matter of language: "Language speaks. Its speaking bids the dif-ference to come . . ." (*Poetry, Language, Thought* 210). By radicalizing Saussure's idea in the *Course in General Linguistics* that "in language there are only differences *without positive terms*" (120), Derrida argues in *Of Grammatology* that since there is no "transcendental signified" (20), to give this signifier "content" and thus put a stop to its play (by turning it into a decidable signified), the signifier cannot be separated from the signified and thus all language is an endless movement of signifiers referring to other signifiers. What marks a signifier from other signifiers, then, is not a decidable content (with such a content it will become a signified), but its "difference" from them. The "content" of language itself is, in fact, nothing more than this "difference," the difference of one signifier from the others.

Such a view of language also brings about a radical shift in the economy of (the traditional understanding of) signification according to which speech—as the site of the plenitude of meaning—was always given priority over writing. "Spoken words," in the logocentric regime of meaning, as Aristotle states, "are the symbols of mental experience and written words are the symbols of spoken words" (*Of Grammatology* 11). Written words, then, are the translation of a translation and, as such, twice removed from "presence." The "presence" in speech, however, according to Derrida is produced by a violent suppression of "difference" within the spoken words since speech, as he shows in his reading of Saussure, is always already a form of writing (44-65). Derrida's purpose in deconstructing the logocentric relationship between speech and writing is not a simple reversal, but a reflexive reading: the inclusion of speech in the regime of absence that it attributes to its "other" (writing). Both speech and writing, for Derrida, participate in the economy of signification which he calls "arche-writing"—the non-originary origin of "difference" that enables language. Arche-writing does not participate in those modes of "significations that have their source in that of the logos" (10), but is an economy of meaning in which both speech and writing find their reflexive undecidability. Difference, then, is not only the play of the signifiers in their relationship to each other, but also that which enables such a play and furthermore marks the relationship between writing and speech, that is to say, the structural relation of presence and absence. It is here that the full force of Derrida's radical notion of difference surfaces, since in the new economy of difference, presence and absence are both effects of language. There is no presence outside language. Such an inscription of presence in language engenders further "difference," this time in reference and representation.

"Reference" is part of the economy of logocentrism in which language is regarded to be a representation of the real, the plenitude of presence which resides "outside" language. Language, however, is traversed by difference and unable to "represent" presence as such. The "argument"/"theme" of language (the represented) is always already subject to the play of difference of its "tropics." In other words, language represents not the plenitude of the real, but the immanent story of its own difference from itself, the rift between its argument and its tropes. Thus, representation *mirrors* not the world "out there," but "difference" itself: in this speculary relation with itself, "difference" also becomes the allegory of the formation of the (post)modern subject who, in Lacan's narrative, "founds" itself on a differential mirroring relationship.

However, if it were simply the name of the play of signifiers, or that which enabled such a play, or the rift between the tropes and the argument, difference would have been a non-difference, a presence that names the difference. Ludic (post)modern difference, unlike the difference of the Enlightenment, is a reflexive difference, a difference which does not simply name the difference but is included in the economy of signification. In other words, it is a difference which is always already different from itself.

According to ludic (post)modernism, language (as differential representation, slippage and difference) articulates all cultural phenomena and as such constructs them as instances of self-division and non-identity. In ludic writings, the traditional fully self-present subject is transformed into a split subject, who is always already other than itself. It is in Lacanian psychoanalysis that the Cartesian subject of Western thought is deconstructed by theorizing the subject as the speaking subject, who is produced in/by language and marked by gaps and absences as a result of its internal (symbolic) structure of difference. The "difference" is the effect of the slippage of the subject and the negation of its "identity" which it assumes in the "imaginary" by its entrance into the "symbolic." The "imaginary" is the phase in which the child regards itself to be inseparable from its mother and by extension from the world, in which the child is identical with itself and with all that surrounds it. The imaginary is then the moment of presence, plenitude, and security. The Oedipal crisis, which marks the separation of the child from the mother and thus shatters its imaginary plenitude and presence by the intervention of the father and the injunction of the Law of the Father, also marks the child's acquisition of language. Language is paradigmatic of the symbolic order, which is the order of "difference." If the child is to grow up, it must come to know the language of its culture and accept its place in difference, and thus distance itself from the identity of the imaginary.

This knowledge, however, is obtained at the cost of what Lacan calls primary repression, repression of the desire for (the body) of the mother; and it is this repression that forms the unconscious like a language. The desire to regain the imaginary plenitude and identity with the mother never leaves the subject; it is merely repressed. Throughout its life and in all its activities, the subject seeks to reobtain that imaginary plenitude. What it finds is never identical with what it seeks, but a mere substitute for it. This substitute is only metonymically related to the object of desire, which remains forever unobtainable. The subject is formed by this "loss"; and, therefore, the "I" in "I am"—that cultural mark of identity and social intelligibility—is more of a designation of the traces of "loss" than an indication of the fullness of the self. The self is thus really more of a social coding of the "fact" that one is what one is not. The "I," which in social and cultural practices is referred to with certainty, is nothing but the effect of traces of "lack" and "loss" and is therefore void of a secure ground. To his propositions that the subject is the effect of desire and that desire is "lack," Lacan adds that desire, ceaselessly seeking the object of desire—the mother—without success, works like language; it moves from one signifier to another without ever settling on a permanent signified. And since it is the repression of desire that forms the unconscious (the primary repression), Lacan concludes that the unconscious itself is, like a language, differential.

Ludic (post)modernism's understanding of (non)identity at the level of the subject is, as we have already indicated, reproduced at the level of history. It opposes the traditional kind of "monumental history" that is given to recovery of the high points of historical developments and their "maintenance in a perpetual presence," by postulating a secure "origin" for history, the main purpose of which is to smooth the movement of events from one "period" to the next toward a teleological end and to exclude from these events those that contest its "narrative" about the real. Foucault, for example in *Language, Counter-Memory, Practice,* theorizes history "without constants" (153) as instances of discontinuity, conflict, and heterogeneity and thus as marked by gaps, absences, and aporias. Like language and the subject in (post)modern thought, history is not identical to itself. Since it is constituted by conflicts and struggles, then the best way to "write" history is in the form of a "genealogy" that will evade metaphysics and refuse the certainty of absolutes by focussing on the particular conflicts which are in fact configurations of power.

For Foucault, power is always entangled with a mode of knowledge, a regime of truth, which is another way of saying that there is a politics to truth and that truth is always beyond reach. What is privileged as truth is, in fact, a truth-effect legitimated as truth by means of dominant power. ("Truth is . . . the sort of error that cannot be refuted" (144)). Genealogy "must record the singularity of events outside of any monstrous finality," meaning that history does not have an "essence" determining its events towards an inevitable present. An "event," again, is the "reversal of a relationship of forces, the usurpation of power, the appropriation of a vocabulary turned against those who once used it . . . the entry of the masked 'other'" (154). The most significant aspect of Foucault's view of history is his insistence on this lack of logic of determination in history. We wish to repeat that Foucault articulates the point in this manner: "The forces operating in history are not controlled by destiny or regulative mechanisms but respond to haphazard conflicts" (154).

4

In describing the Utah conference (1990) on "Rewriting the (Post)modern: (Post)coloniality/Feminism/Late Capitalism," Teresa L. Ebert writes: "The postmodern is not only the age of performance art and pastiche fiction, but, more important, it is a time of AIDS, changing gender/sex relations and increasing opposition between races and between the 'first' and 'third' worlds—particularly after the end of the Cold War in which terrorism and drugs are replacing communism as the number-one threat in many people's minds."

As we have said, to understand the (post)modern one has to go beyond simply citing such cultural phenomena such as MTV; in fact, what one has to do is ask the question to which Ebert points: what are the effects of ludic notions of self-reflexivity and difference on our understanding of such other dimensions of (post)modernity as race, gender, sexuality, and class? There are a number of ways in which one can contest ludic (post)modernism and its analysis of the contemporary as the site of difference and self-reflexivity. Taking the more traditional (modernist) mode of "debate," one might marshall "arguments" against ludic ideas of difference and self-reflexivity, and show how they are based on "bad" arguments. One might show how, for example, their conclusions are "faulty" because according to (post)modernism's own arguments, they are, like all language constructs, "differential." That is to say, what is offered as argument in defense of "difference" is itself "differential" and, as such, not a reliable knowledge either of difference or of the ludic (post)modernism grounded upon it. In other words, one can read ludic (post)modernism (self)reflexively and show that its argument is "groundless." Such a modernist argument would at most simply mark the (post)modern as incoherent and contradictory. It could thus provide a "logical" counter-argument, which might be appealing to our sense of reason and logic, but still not be able to show the politics of ludic (post)modernism. A more troublesome problem with the modernist approach is this: the very deployment of logical argumentation against (post)modernism would unfortunately legitimate a rather reactionary notion of truth. In such a debate (argument/counter-argument), truth will be implicitly posited as a logical matter, as mainly a question of internal coherence and formal architectonics. Furthermore, such a notion of "truth" (as the result of a debate between contesting parties) regards truth as a matter of private property: the outcome of debate is always a winner who "owns" the truth. None of these consequences of "arguing" against ludic (post)modernism are acceptable to us because, although they may weaken the case of ludic (post)modernism, they also reinscribe into the consideration of these questions some very retrograde and reactionary ideas and practices.

The other, more productive, mode of contesting ludic (post)-modernism is to examine its consequences and effects: what are some of the "truths" produced in ludic (post)modernism and who benefits from them? In other words, we insist that truth is always entangled with politics and that to pursue "truth" in itself (as if it were separable from politics) is to accept the repressive views put forward by both modernism and ludic (post)modernism, which in spite of their ostensible differences still reproduce the same ideological effects needed to perpetuate the dominant social relations of production. Here we shall limit our inquiry into the politics of ludic truth by examining the consequences of the ludic idea of difference for an understanding of the social—the public space in which we conduct our lives, imagine our goals, practice our ideas, earn a living, and "choose" a job.

5

The immediate impact of ludic (post)modernism on social theory has been to render its very subject of inquiry—society—unintelligible. In order to demonstrate this impact, we shall focus here on the work of the well-known theorists, Laclau and Mouffe, who have "read" the social in the light of ludic language theories as a differential construct. As the basis of (post)modern social theory, they posit the "impossibility of society": "The incomplete character of every totality necessarily leads us to abandon, as a terrain of analysis, the premise of 'society' as a sutured and self-defined totality. 'Society' is not a valid object of discourse. There is no single underlying principle fixing—and hence constituting—the whole of the field of differences" (*Hegemony and Socialist Strategy* 111). What Laclau and Mouffe are saying is that "society" cannot serve as the ground for knowledge of the social because its very concept is founded upon the notion of "identity" and as such it is logocentric, that is to say, a "metaphysical fiction." The point to bear in mind here is that the idea of "society" is rejected in ludic theory on *epistemological grounds.* "Society," that is to say, cannot serve as the basis for reliable knowledge, since as a "representation" (we know society only as textuality because there are no unmediated knowledges), it lacks "identity"—all identitarian entities are groundless fictions. In their erasure of "society," Laclau and Mouffe and other postmarxist social theorists such as Paul Hirst, Barry Hindess, and Stanley Aronowitz, rely on some version of Derrida's deconstruction of totality.

In "Structure, Sign, and Play in the Discourses of the Human Sciences," Derrida argues that totalization of the social is impossible, not because it is not empirically feasible and can never be completed, but because "the nature of the field—that is, language and a finite language—excludes totalization. This field is in effect that of *play*, that is to say, a field of infinite substitutions only because it is finite, that is to say, because instead of being an inexhaustible field, as in the classical hypothesis, instead of being too large, there is something missing from it: a center which arrests and grounds the play of substitutions" (in *Writing and Difference* 289). The signifier, in other words, always "exceeds," and is never exhausted by, the signified and systems of representation.

It is on the "foundation" of such a ludic difference that Laclau and Mouffe posit "society" as "impossible" because it cannot be a determined totality but follows the Derridean logic of the "sign." In the absence of any intelligible non-differentiality (totality) or even originary "difference," society is a fractured a-totality: a series of conjunctural sites which are autonomous, auto-intelligible, and make sense without any necessary structural connections with others or any social logic which informs them all. As we shall see later, this notion of society as an ensemble of heterogeneous and autonomous conjunctures provides the "ground" for the ludic theory of politics as essentially a "local" (as opposed to "global") set of practices, practices that aim at "change" on the molecular and capillary level of society rather than at the level of its totality. Like signs, these conjunctural instances, according to ludic theory, have connections with each other, but these connections are more on the order of what Derrida calls the "trace" (a connection through absence) than that of the logic of necessity. There is, so to say, nothing inevitable about their connections other than the impossibility of the inevitable itself. The connections among the various conjunctural sites of society, in short, are merely "rhetorical" and "discursive."

In ludic (post)modernism's social theory, all social practices are "discursive" because any social practice, to have a meaning, has to be a discourse. Since the social is by definition meaningful, it follows according to Laclau that all social practices are discursive: "History and society are an infinite text" ("Populist Rupture and Discourse" 87). The social, in other words, does not exist outside the discursive; and, therefore, contrary to radical theory, one cannot relegate the discursive to the superstructure—that is to say, to a separate level—of the social. Given the ludic assumption that discourses are self-governing because their meaning is the effect of their own immanent laws of signification and is not determined by any "outside" (such as the level of the economy or of class), to say that the connection is discursive is to say that the logic of the social is, like all signifying practices, arbitrary and "aleatory"—as in fact Derrida says in his *Signeponge/Signsponge* (54). In ludic (post)modernism, "society," therefore, is (in Lyotard's terms) an ensemble of "language games" (*Just Gaming* 50-51) that are incommensurate with one another. As the site of reversible differentialities, society is a significatory (discursive) a-totality; a series of autonomous localities each deriving its own logic from its own immanent laws of signification: society, to be more precise, is articulated by the local laws of a set of incommensurable "insides" and not by the universal laws of an "outside," such as those of the domains of class or economics.

Although, as we have pointed out, the rhetoricization of the social is done in the name of the deconstruction of epistemology (to demonstrate the groundlessness of claims to truth and to mark them instead as metaphysical fictions), it is in fact a political practice and a part of what we have called the social struggle over the construction of cultural reality. It is political because what is at stake is not simply the pursuit of truth without the illusion of presence, but something much more immediately economic: the very logic of the social itself, which justifies the present social relations of production (class structure) and the social division of labor and, in doing so, protects the interests of the ruling class. If the social, as ludic (post)modern theory proposes, is subject to the ludic law of rhetorical difference and is nothing more than the effect of the play of the signifier, then it follows that, as we have already stated, there are no necessary connections among various levels and strata of society. The social, like the sign, is, as Laclau argues in "Transformations of Advanced Industrial Societies and the Theory of the Subject," "arbitrary" (41). The most politically important conclusion to be drawn from the "arbitrariness" of the social is that there is no necessary connection between the economic and the ideological.

The discourses of ideology that are assumed to be the immediate sites of the production of social subjectivities, for instance, have no determining relations with class (Mouffe, *Gramsci and Marxist Theory* 168-204). It is, in short, ideology and not class (the social relations of production) that constitutes the subject differentially as a contradictory, split subject, whose diverse discourses are also rhetorically and arbitrarily related and have no necessity (identity) to them. In fact, such ludic postmarxists as Paul Hirst go so far as to deny the existence of such a thing as class: "there is no such thing as 'working class' (that is, a class equivalent to all wage labourers) as a social force in capitalism; nor, indeed, is there a political, ideological, or economic homogeneity of capital" (*On Law and Ideology* 52). The social is an instance of incommensurate heterogeneities. We have chosen the (non)connection between class and ideology not because this is the only site of ludic "arbitrariness," but because it exemplifies, in a more focused fashion than any other case, the class interests of ludic politics.

If subjectivities are produced in the differential discourses of ideology and not in the economics of material practices, then social change—which in ludic discourses is the effect of subjectivities—is the outcome not, as radical theory proposes, of "class struggle," but of ideological struggle. The social will change only when subjectivities have changed. For instance, in order to transform present society, which suffers from the accumulated disregard for the environment, into one which is respectful of nature, what will have to change—according to ludic theory that privileges ideological struggle—is social subjectivities. Instead of subjectivities that are mostly interested in "development," for instance, and thus indifferent to the "environment," ideological struggle will produce new subjectivities which are "sensitive" to the environment and which will consequently, by pressuring for new legislation, change the laws and protect the environment. Thus a social change (from unrestrained capitalist "developmentalism" to a moderating capitalist "environmentalism") is effected. Such a notion of change, however, leaves the economic structure intact and merely reforms its local practices: exploitation, which determines the logic of capitalism and maintains it, does not disappear but simply shifts its site. In fact the shifting of the site of exploitation from the environment at this stage of advanced corporate capitalism is actually necessary for the (post)-modern renovation of capitalism. It is for the sake of renewing capitalism that the environment has been taken up as a cause not only by all major corporations, but also—for the sake of their "ideological struggle"—by all the (upper) middle classes. It is now almost impolite—a breach of middle-class etiquette—to be "insensitive" to the environment.

Ideological struggle is undertaken in the social space that Laclau and Mouffe call "hegemony," a concept they adopt from the Italian Marxist philosopher and revolutionary, Antonio Gramsci, but to which they give a reformist and liberal interpretation. For them, and the postmarxists who follow them, "hegemony" (which in Gramsci is always grounded in class) is simply a bourgeois discursive apparatus for achieving a political coalition of dissimilar elements (as opposed to a class- and economy-based collectivity): hegemony is, in short, an "anomalous relation" (Laclau and Mouffe 50) with "anomalous" acting as the trope of aleatory, arbitrary, non-deterministic, and post-class forms of connection. In such a post-class society, which is composed of a series of heterogeneous localities, hegemony acts as a device to bring groups of dissimilar interests together on the basis of concrete, practical, momentary, ideological (but not economic) interests. The purpose of class-based hegemony, in radical marxism, is to acquire political power for the suppressed class (the proletariat) in order to abolish class society. In hegemony founded upon ideological interests (the environment, abortion, day care . . .), the purpose is to acquire political power, not in order to overthrow class society and its regime of exploitation, but so as to bring about local changes within the already existing class structure. Revolutionary marxist hegemony aims at establishing a socialist society, while the ideology-based hegemony attempts to bring about radical democracy—to extend the range of bourgeois privilege to as many people as possible and thus adjust the present regime to the changing conditions of the time, without ever abolishing the bourgeois political system which is grounded in the extraction of surplus labor.

In a sense, the ludic notion of "difference" in Derrida, Laclau, Mouffe, and others is the trope of a hegemonic, post-class politics: the ludic politics of the signifier which, instead of concerning itself with "class struggle," privileges an "ideological struggle" directed and controlled by the upper (middle) classes who have access to modes of signification—the media, the culture industry, the universities, the publishing networks, and so on. The notion of ideological struggle (and rhetorical difference) has acquired great prominence among the professionals of ideology in ludic (post)-modernism because it is recognized that the new forms needed for deploying capital rely more than ever for their effectivity on the strategic uses of ideology. In fact, ludic (post)modernism rearticulates the very notion of politics and political struggle so as to render "ideological struggle" identical with emancipatory practices by erasing revolutionary "class struggle." The ultimate purpose of ludic politics is to give capitalism "a human face": to change cultural patterns of behavior, lifestyles, and modes of thinking in order to make the exploitative economic relations more tolerable. It is, for example, a mark of social change in ludic politics that after thirty-six years of ideological struggle for change that now, in 1990 in Fort Valley, Georgia, there are "integrated proms" in high schools ("Integrated Proms," *New York Times*, May 14, 1990: A1). The fact that the same state has an unemployment rate for blacks that is twice as high as for whites is almost irrelevant to this ludic idea of social change. Thus it turns out that the erasure of social totality, which is done ostensibly in the name of discrediting metaphysical fictions of presence, is in fact a political strategy with a clear economic goal. By proposing the social as a fractured and dispersed a-totality, with each segment severed from the others, ludic (post)modernism is capable of representing local change as the equivalent of social change, indeed as the only kind of social change that is possible. In the ludic scheme, social change turns out to be a strategy of "reform," which is merely a mode of crisis management. In bringing about local changes on the ideological level, ludic theory justifies the system and helps people to adjust to the limited and limiting horizons of their lives under capitalism. As always, philosophy is what Althusser in *Essays in Self-Criticism* calls "class struggle at the level of theory" (166).

For ludic (post)modernism, radical politics is, therefore, not a matter of providing access for all to the means of production (economic democracy as the foundation of rights) but rather access to the means of signification (free speech and semiotic democracy). In spite of ludic (post)modernism's claim that it deconstructs metaphysical fictions in order to erase such oppressive causal connections as "determinism" and consequently provide a more open form of making the world intelligible, it merely changes the form of "determinism." Instead of an economic determinism that posits the ideological and cultural as an effect of the materiality of modes and relations of production, ludic (post)modernism simply installs a "superstructuralism" that privileges the cultural, the discursive, and the ideological. In ludic superstructuralism (according, for instance, to Baudrillard), it is "exchange value" that determines "use value"; "consumption" that determines "production"; and "simulation" that forms the "original." In other words, the "openness" of ludic (post)modernism is an openness to the erasure of determinism that posits the determining in the "aleatory": in ludic logic, then, the contingent determines the necessary!

Ludic (post)modernism, as we have pointed out, proposes language and its inherent differentiality as the determinant of social intelligibilities; thus radical politics is rearticulated as an intervention in cultural "meaning." The most "radical" form of this intervention, according to ludic deconstruction, "obscures" (renders "undecidable") the established meanings of the old common sense, the bourgeois common sense which is no longer historically relevant to the unimpeded movement of capital. This jettisoning of traditional (humanist) common sense, in the name of ludic "radical politics," in other words, is itself a subtle maneuver to remove from the scene of philosophy those frames of intelligibility that have lost their economic relevance to the relations of capitalist production. Barbara Johnson formulates the major premise of ludic radicalism when she writes in *A World of Difference*, "Nothing could be more comforting to the established order than the requirement that everything be assigned a clear meaning or stand" (30-31). In the writings of Foucault, Derrida, and particularly Lyotard, then, "radical politics" becomes a matter of a local obscuring of the "obviousness" of the dominant common sense, thus problematizing its "certainty" about the real, rather than a global transformation of social arrangements so as to provide access for all to the means of production. Lyotard goes so far in this "obscuring" of meaning as to equate any coherent collective cultural meaning with "cultural policy," and he regards "cultural policy" to be a form of "totalizing" and the effect of its supposedly underlying totalitarianism.

In "anti-totalitarian," democratic ludic politics, "parody," "pastiche," "irony," "pun," and their arche-writing, "laughter," are used as devices through which the connection between the signifier and the signified is deferred and the "obviousness" of "cultural policy" (established meanings) is "obscured." This, by the way, is the main reason for the widespread use of irony (self-reflexivity) in the (post)modern arts. Obscurity is thus thought to produce a radical effect, since it empties the world of ready-made meanings. However, the way this newly emptied world is changed and made to resignify is of political significance.

One consequence is that theorizing social space as a series of disconnected conjunctures also fetishizes "local" (small-scale, concrete, practical) politics. The focus of ideological struggle in ludic politics is always a particular social practice: the situation of prisoners, the problems of a day care system, the question of toxic wastes, and so on. And to repeat: the politics of this politics is that it merely brings about reform, while leaving the global structures of economic exploitation intact. As a result of ideological struggles, the local situation of prisoners may indeed change; but the system of justice—aimed at maintaining and justifying laws of private property—leaves unchanged the conditions under which the prisoner was turned into a criminal in the first place.

6

In what we are calling "resistance (post)modernism," the aim of radical politics is *global*: it works not simply for an ideological intervention and a change of local practices, but for the transformation of the economic structures that bring about those local conditions to begin with. In other words, the goal of resistance (post)modernism is not simply to change the means and relations of signification (to obscure ready-made cultural obviousnesses), but to change the relations of production and end economic exploitation.

After all, a society has a "cultural policy" (no matter how "occluded" some may want to make it) and constructs "obviousnesses" through ideology *for a purpose*; and that purpose is not simply to shape people's "thinking." The purpose is to produce a labor force that acquiesces to the dominant relations of production in which the laborer is himself/herself the object of exploitation. The argument of ludic (post)modernism that an ideological struggle that makes the laborer aware of his situation will terminate his exploitation is, as we have already suggested, more of an accommodation than a termination of dominant practices. In *Capital (I)* Marx addresses the question of a compliant labor force and offers a reason for it which can perhaps serve as the background of our discussion of (post)modern practices in the rest of this book:

> The advance of capitalist production develops a working class which by education, tradition and habit looks upon the requirements of that mode of production as self-evident natural laws. The organization of the capitalist process of production, once it is fully developed, breaks down all resistance. The constant generation of relative surplus population keeps the law of supply and demand of labor, and therefore wages, within narrow limits which correspond to capital's valorization requirements. The silent compulsion of economic relations sets the seal on the domination of the capitalist over the worker. Direct extra-economic force is still of course used, but only in exceptional cases. In the ordinary run of things, the worker can be left to the 'natural laws of production,' i. e., it is possible to rely on his dependence on capital, which springs from the conditions of production themselves, and is guaranteed in perpetuity by them. (899)

The goal of abolishing the "silent compulsion of economic relations" and overthrowing class rule will not be achieved through a local politics conducted in terms of ideological struggles. Such struggles may indeed "reform" the local conditions of the workplace, but will nevertheless leave intact the worker's position in the relations of production. The goal of transforming social relations requires not just an engagement with global economic structures in a single geographical entity; it also requires an approach conducted on an international level. This approach will involve not only economic exploitation, but along with it and as a consequence of it, also the eradication of racism, sexism, and colonialism in their (post)modern forms. In order to help achieve the goals of such an emancipatory politics, resistance (post)modernism theorizes "difference" differently. It moves beyond a simple recognition of difference as a rhetorical slippage of the signifier and argues that the difference that makes a *material* difference is the effect of "labor," focussing on congealed and alienated labor as private property. In other words, the social division of labor and the social contradictions it produces—contradictions that evolve around the extraction of surplus labor and not around language—is the frame of intelligibility that determines the regime of signification and the ensuing "representation" of the real. Language, and all other semiotic processes, are articulated by the division of labor. Difference, in short, is a "materialist" praxis produced through class struggle and not a "rhetorical" effect.

In the following chapters we will engage ludic (post)modernism and, by our critique of its specific practices, mark the various sites for the deployment of resistance (post)modernism and its "difference."

Chapter Four

The Narrative
of Change
and the Change
of Narrative

1

The "truth" produced by (post)modern critical theory has been contested from diverse theoretical positions. One can nevertheless distinguish two major lines of interrogation that we shall designate as "criticism" and "critique."

The "criticism" of (post)modern theory has been located in a cultural space that we have called "modernism" (humanism) and relies on a theory of truth which is based on the epistemological priority of the subject and on supporting theories that privilege community and common sense and regard "experience" as the ultimate guarantee of knowledge. From this perspective, (post)-modern theory has been found wanting in its neglect of the fate of the individual (its anti-subject-ism), its subversion of the intellectual (its anti-cognitivism), and its dismissal of the concrete (its anti-empiricism), among other things.

The "critique" of dominant (ludic) (post)modern theory, on the contrary, is situated in the interstices of a set of discourses that find (post)modern theory to be, in the last instance, a continuation of, rather than an intervention in, the discourses of humanism with their privileging of empiricism and cognitivism, and their desire for intellectual plenitude and presence in knowledge in an apolitical space beyond the mediations of various social practices. Our text is articulated in the space of this political critique.

The common view of contemporary developments in the human sciences is that since 1958 (the year in which Lévi-Strauss's *Structural*

Anthropology was published), there has been a significant change, amounting almost to a paradigm shift, in their modes of inquiry. Prior to this time, it is assumed, the human sciences were mainly engaged in discrete empiricist studies that received their epistemological authority from the then prevailing theory of knowledge and its philosophical ally, "cognitivism." According to this familiar narrative of recent intellectual history, the human sciences have in the last two decades moved away from empirical studies to theoretical investigations that are more concerned with the philosophical grounds of inquiry and their conditions of signification than with the interpretation of individual phenomena. The emergence of the discourse of "theory" (itself an effect of contemporary transdisciplinary inquiries into the domains of history, philosophy, linguistics, law, literature, politics, film and other media studies, semiotics, psychoanalysis, among others) is usually regarded to be a sign of these changes in the knowledge practices of the (post)modern humanities.

However, such a representation of the (post)modern human sciences is an ideological misrecognition and part of the larger political project of contemporary antifoundationalism. According to this new antifoundationalist reading of the (post)modern humanities, expounded in the writings of Derrida, Foucault, Lyotard, Rorty, Fish, and others, the major "problem" with the old humanities was that they were haunted by the Kantian notion of knowledge as epistemological and that, as part of this project, they were preoccupied with securing their theories in an uncontested, self-evident, and self-identical truth. The old human sciences, then, in the language of Derridean deconstructive narratives (i.e. in *Writing and Difference*, *Margins of Philosophy*, or *The Post Card*), were situated in a metaphysical project, the purpose of which was to offer the truth of language (the rhetorical effects of tropes) as the truth of the world and thus to maintain the regime of truth of logocentrism. This "confusion" of "language" with "reality," which Paul de Man in his theory of reading designates as "ideology" (*The Resistance to Theory* 11), is made invisible in the common sense of the humanities by their quiet appeal to such seemingly transdiscursive "foundations" as the (transcendental) "presence" of human consciousness (cognitivism) and to equally presence-ridden evidence obtained from the direct contact of the human senses with the world itself (empiricism).

In support of Derridean narratives, Richard Rorty offers new deconstructive stories of the history of Western philosophy in which the human mind is revealed as having been theorized as the site of presence, as "the mirror of nature"—a theory which enables the entire project of logocentric representation in the West (see *Philosophy and the Mirror of Nature*, *Consequences of Pragmatism*, and *Contingency, Irony and Solidarity*). Rorty's "solution" to the metaphysics of (re)present(ation) and the foundationalism that set limits to the human sciences is to reunderstand "truth" not as an epistemological, but as a pragmatic affair. This idea is articulated in the clearest "picture" of ludic (post)modern human sciences and knowledges available today, Jean-François Lyotard's *The Postmodern Condition*. In this book, Lyotard interrogates the entire "foundationalist" project and argues that its major epistemological strategy, which is the appeal to what he calls "metanarratives" (constructs through which knowledges are "legitimated") has become untenable and that the epistemological bankruptcy of the dominant "metanarratives" (such as the metanarratives of empiricism, the human "cogito," "critique," and the like) has situated (post)modern knowledges in an entirely new domain of "games," that is, of "little narratives" which unlike "grand narratives" are about the regional activities of the individual. In Lyotard's ludic discourses, "narrative," as a mode of knowing, is privileged because, unlike logocentric knowledge, narrative knowledge acquires its truth not from an "outside" (a grand narrative) but from its own immanent laws of signification. In other words, narratives are "legitimated by the simple fact that they do what they do" (*Postmodern Condition* 23). The "test" is *pragmatic*, not *epistemological*.

The new ludic (post)modern human sciences, however, are hardly the antifoundational enterprises which Derrida, Rorty, Lyotard, and their followers claim them to be: the critique of the old humanities in the writings of these thinkers is in fact enabled by appeal to the very notions that they reject in the old regime of truth. To cite one instance, for the (traditionalist, foundationalist) empiricism of the senses, for example, ludic theory substitutes the empiricism of the "trace" (as Derrida has articulated it). Furthermore, for the grand project of Hegelian cognitivism (a "philosophy of the subject"), ludic theory has substituted the equally cognitive project of the resisting "individual" (as articulated by Foucault and others). Lyotard himself actually talks about a "direct" (unmediated) bonding knowledge acquired from narrative and contrasts it with the formal (mediated) knowledges of science that are alienating (*Postmodern*

Condition 25). The ludic (post)modern human sciences are, in short, as much involved in discovering and proposing "founding" concepts as the old ones. To be sure, as we have demonstrated in the first part of this book, their critique of the modernist humanities is both very important and very necessary. It puts in question the common sense of modernism and thus opens up inquiries into the assumptions and presuppositions of modernist knowledges which have assured the status of the "natural" in our daily practices. However, what is "opened up" is then very soon sutured and turned into a new closure, a closure which serves the very necessary political purpose of renewing, reinvigorating and thus maintaining the regime of truth necessary for reproducing the economic relations of late capitalism. If the Hegelian project of a "philosophy of the subject" has become embarrassingly "grand," then the project of the "subject" is reformulated in the "little narratives" of regional negotiations that Lyotard, Foucault, Deleuze and Guattari theorize. If the Cartesian subject(-of-consciousness) is no longer a compelling trope in the age of "simulation," then the subject is rescued through the "body" (see Foucault's *History of Sexuality* and *Power/Knowledge*). The ludic death of the subject, in short, is a (post)modern ritual for its resurrection and reincarnation in an acceptable (post)modern form.

The most urgent question for the human sciences in the contemporary academy has been how to save the subject. Since the old ways have either failed or become historically too cumbersome and ineffective, then new ways had to be found. The bourgeois human sciences cannot function without producing and maintaining a notion of the subject as "free" (whether the subject of history, as in Hegel or the subject of reading, as in Derrida) whose existence is required by the relations of production in the dominant social order. It is only by appeal to the idea of a free, enterprising subject who has autonomy and whose consciousness (cognitivism) or body (empiricism) are said to be guides to truth, that the individual can be (in Althusser's words) "interpellated" into the existing social arrangements, and furthermore so (self)constituted as to freely consent to the "naturalness" and "inevitability" of the dominant social order. In their critique of the metaphysics of presence in the old humanities, the ludic human sciences, then, do indeed manage to dismantle that project, but only in order to reconstruct it in a more up-to-date and historically viable manner. In inquiring into the political effects of Richard Rorty's pragmatism, Cornell West in "After Word" sums up the underlying purpose of ludic antifoundationalism in general: "Rorty's neo-pragmatism is, in part, a self-conscious post-philosophical ideological project to promote the basic practices of bourgeois capitalist societies while discouraging philosophical defenses of them" (267). To a large extent, of course, West is himself situated in the same ludic space: his "opposition" is conducted entirely in the same terms set by Rorty.

The "truth" of the ludic, (post)modern humanities, in short, is not an antifoundational one, but one which might be called (post)foundational. Again, it is "(post)" in the sense that we defined in the previous chapter: it obscures clear meanings by turning the "solemnities" of logocentrism into playful "games." Because what ludic (post)modernists are "radically" against is finally only the solemnities of the bourgeoisie, "foundations," in their program, are not given up, but rather turned into fields of play. In other words, "foundations" have been ritualistically "murdered" in order to be resurrected as "games" suitable for today's dispersed, playful (non-locatable) form of capitalism, which is itself no longer anchored in such traditional solemnities as the state, the family, and the old, solid, unitary self. Understood as "games," foundations do not have the solidity of traditional concepts (which are historically dysfunctional today), but resecure all their effects by means of the "lighter" and more "flexible" local strategies of "little narratives."

By contrast, the resistant (post)modern human sciences go beyond a recognition of the epistemological limits of old foundationalism and, as Marx has done in his readings of Hegel, indicate that "foundations" (of any sort) are in fact not simply epistemological matters. The "foundations" of truth are effects of the struggles of various social groups in any given historical moment—that which is proposed as "foundation" is the conceptual justification for the continuation of the dominant social representations that legitimate the outlook of the ruling class. "Foundations," in other words, are not merely epistemological matters of truth, but are part of the political economy of truth that overdetermines the calculus of power, the regime of exploitation, and the reigning social relations of race, gender, and class.

Resistance (post)modernism, therefore, cannot limit its program to the dismantling of "foundations," either by demonstrating that the epistemological is a species of the tropological (as in Derrida) or, as such traditional Marxists as Stuart Sim in "Lyotard and the Politics of Anti-Foundationalism," have attempted to do, by merely critiquing the "politics of antifoundationalism" in order to go beyond the critique and re-establish a new form of access to nondifferential foundations. For a resistance (post)modernism, the goal of radical critical theory should be an interrogation of "foundations" in order to show (a) that "foundations" are always already inscribed in all philosophical and discursive practices and undertakings, and (b) that they are not a matter of "truth" in the traditional epistemological sense of the word but a site of political contestation in society. The question, then, is not how to "get rid of" foundations (this is the favorite project of such conservative thinkers as Stanley Fish or how to re-establish them in a neo-Engelsian Marxist notion of "science," but how to produce knowledges that are aware of their political constitution and do not represent themselves as the natural bedrock of transdiscursive truth. The "authority" and "justification" of these contestatory knowledges come not from their truth claims, but from their claims to emancipatory effectivity—claims, that is to say, to enable the reorganization of social arrangements along non-exploitative axes. They are "interested" knowledges that do not limit knowledge to truth, but write in knowledge the idea of justice. Furthermore, they do not conceal their own interestedness but, on the contrary, open it up to historical (self)critique. It is not our purpose in this book, however, to develop this line of inquiry, but rather to offer an ideology critique of new theories in the ludic (post)modern human sciences. We wish, furthermore, to make the following point: under the regime of capitalism, bourgeois "research" in the university and in corporations cannot proceed without some form of the empiricism and/or cognitivism that, as we have argued, are exemplary instances of the non-political truth(-as-foundation) promoted by the ludic (post)modern humanities.

By subscribing to empiricism and cognitivism, the dominant contemporary human sciences have theorized cultural reality as basically emanating from two originary foundations: from either the phenomenon itself or from the subject. By doing so, their explanations have segregated social signification from its economic and political conditions. By offering empirical phenomena and/or the subject as the ultimate source of knowledge, the dominant (post)modern humanities have effectively blocked inquiries that attempt to situate the empirical and the cognitive in the historical and economic coordinates in which they acquire their "meaning" and "function." Such an integrative mode of explanation, in which the act of sense-making and production of knowledge is related to the larger historical frames of intelligibility produced by the economic, political, and ideological practices, is rejected by the contemporary human sciences as merely "political" or "ideological" and thus as biased and untruthful—in short, as modes of "non-knowledge."

This equation of the global mode of explanation with the political (i. e., with dogmatism and one-sidedness) and its subsequent rejection as non-explanation is, in dominant theoretical discourses, based on a new privileging of cognitivism and empiricism (the subject and sensory experience) that, ironically, tries to secure their claim to analytical rigor and authority precisely by negating the (old) empiricist/cognitivist modes of inquiry. This double move—both a repudiation and a reinstatement of the empirical and the cognitive—is enabled by a narrative of the intellectual scene of the 1940's and 1950's which constructs that earlier scene as utterly different from the scene of the following (i. e., "theoretical") decades.

2

In the orthodox view of recent changes in the humanities, it is claimed that (post)modern theory has enabled a radical interrogation and displacement of the practices that dominated the human sciences in the 1940's and 1950's. In re-narrating this narrative of the supposedly radical changes brought about by ludic (post)modernism, we take as our exemplary "little narratives" the texts in Quentin Skinner's *The Return of Grand Theory in the Human Sciences* (1985). We choose this inventory of narratives because of the cultural significance of its publication. Not only does this book represent the view that an epistemological break has taken place in the contemporary human sciences, but in addition the book's history and mode of dissemination are also part of the theoretical and political issues that are the concerns of our book.

Our view that it is an integral part of today's ludic (post)modern common sense to say that a revolution has taken place in the humanities in the last two decades is attested by the fact that eight of the ten essays in Skinner's book were originally commissioned for, and delivered as, talks over the BBC Radio 3 for general, educated audiences. After the addition of two other texts, the talks were then presented in book-form to the English-speaking world along with a promotional note claiming that the book portrayed "the most influential developments" in the humanities over the past quarter of a century during which "empiricist assumptions" were "undermined." The fact that the discourses of ludic theory have become part of the general discourses of culture (circulating through radio and paperback books) quite strongly substantiates the affinity we have already noted between the tenets of ludic theory and prevailing common sense and thus poses the question of the relation between the "new truth" of the "radical theory" and the "commonplace truths" of contemporary culture. It is a mark of the closeness of this relationship that the new theory has been received with the kind of enthusiasm that is accorded only to deeply familiar ideas whose very familiarity guarantees their harmlessness to dominant modes of understanding (and living).

In the 1940's and 1950's, the ludic narrative assumes, the prevailing mode of inquiry in the human sciences was rooted in the empiricism and cognitivism that these disciplines had inherited from the past, and that had by then become the common sense of knowledge practices in institutions. Literary critics, for example, interpreted individual texts, while anthropologists prepared descriptive treatises on the eating rituals of distant tribes and political scientists undertook micro-studies of changes in voting habits. At the same time, any attempt to go beyond the concrete and discrete order to account for the general conditions under which the concrete acquired the purported meaning proclaimed by the critic/researcher was looked upon with great suspicion and rejected as abstract and thus irrelevant. In the years immediately following the Second World War, according to the received narrative, theory was attacked from at least three different, but ideologically related, perspectives.

The most widespread practice was to reject theory and theoretical explanation in the name of common sense: the idea was that the concrete reality "speaks for itself" and does not need any general theory to make it clear. The work of Sir Lewis Namier, the leading British historian of the time, exemplifies this anti-theoretical approach. Namier "was not only at his happiest when chronicling the detailed manoevers of individual political actors at the center of political power; he was also a sardonic critic of the belief that any general social theories (or flapdoodle, as he preferred to call them) could possibly be relevant to the explanation of political behaviour or the process of social change" (Skinner 3).

One articulation of the second anti-theoretical thrust was the writings of C. Wright Mills. He attacked theory as a mode of reductive thinking that violated the expansiveness of the speculative imagination; theory, was a "strait-jacket" (Skinner 3). He mocked and rejected what he called "grand theory" not only because it was not readily understandable, but also because it did not deal with genuine problems by examining human affairs in their historical singularity, plenitude, and concreteness. Theory was a systematic refusal to undertake clear observation and an indulgence in willful intellectual distortion.

The most epistemologically powerful attack on theory at this time, according to the narrative of the great shift in the recent human sciences, was the one levelled by scientists or those humanist scholars who took the sciences as their model of research. For them science had, once and for all, put an end to normative and speculative discourses that they identified as "theory." Science was descriptive (scientific theories were "empirical theories," according to Skinner (4)), and value-neutral. If they had any desire to be taken seriously, it was argued, the human sciences should aspire to this descriptivity and give up speculative and theoretical inquiries. In the discourses of scientifically oriented researches, the speculative and theoretical were regarded as a sub-species of the "ideological" (what Lyotard today calls founding "metanarratives"). In this connection, it should be kept in mind that these were the years of the "end-of-ideology" doctrine. At this time, then, rather than speculating and theorizing about politics, the genealogy of power, and dominant values, it was suggested that political science should concern itself, for example, with an empirical study of the "vocabulary" of politics. These, in short, were times in which the "burgeoning of a purely empirical" human sciences seemed assured (Skinner 4).

Of course, the science in whose name speculative and theoretical discourses were rejected was itself the outcome of the "ideologies" of positivism and its accompanying knowledge practices such as empiricism and cognitivism, which in the postwar years had reached the height of their institutional visibility and dominance. At the core of this positivist view of science was the notion of "scientific explanation." Explaining "a puzzling set of facts," as Skinner puts it, "was taken to be a matter of showing that their occurrence can be deduced and hence predicted from known natural or at least statistical laws" (4). The positivism that informs this notion of scientific explanation was reinforced by the urgencies of the war and ultimately justified by rationalist theories of science like those developed by Karl Popper, who—as we indicated in Chapter Two— grounded his theory of science on the idea that what constitutes "scientifically respectable belief" is a belief that successfully passes a "crucial experiment" designed to falsify it. According to Popper in *The Logic of Scientific Discovery*, if a proposition/theory fails the test of falsifiability, that failure is incontestable proof of its falsehood (78-82). The overall impact of Popper's theory on the human sciences was that "piecemeal empirical research in the human sciences was alone commended, while Marxism, psychoanalysis, and all forms of Utopian social philosophy were together consigned to the dustbin of history" (Skinner 5).

In the accounts of the contemporary human sciences, such as the one by Skinner, which postulate a fundamental shift in the modes of inquiry in the recent history of these disciplines, the change of the climate of ideas that finally enabled the move from empirical piecemeal research to "grand theories" (in the words of his book's title) is attributed to the ways in which the grounds of attacks on theory in the 1940's and 1950's were deconstructed by the thinkers of the following decades. In Althusser's theories, for instance, the concept of "common sense," which is the "obvious" underpinning of such commonsensical and humanist attacks on theory as Namier's, is revealed to be a construct of the dominant ideologies, and not an unmediated standard of truth and knowledge. "Imagination," by whose authority Wright Mills had condemned theory and theoretical investigations as a mode of transgression, was deconstructed by Derrida as the last metaphysical construct by whose agency the Western mind recuperated its theological logocentrism. But the major move from empirical research to theoretical work was enabled by dismantling the master notion of "science" and, specifically, the positivist version of scientific explanation.

Positivist scientific practices were put in question by two groups of postwar thinkers. The first group challenged the validity of scientific explanation in the humanities and, instead of this positivist model, offered a hermeneutic approach in which an attempt was made "to recover and interpret the meanings of social actions from the point of view of the agents performing them" (Skinner 6). The hermeneutic explanation is, to a very considerable extent, influenced by the later work of Wittgenstein and its anti-positivist claims that the "understanding of any meaningful episode—whether action or utterance—always involves us in placing it within its appropriate 'form of life'" (Skinner 7). In its modern form, the hermeneutic mode of explanation, however, is based on the work of Gadamer. In his major work, *Truth and Method*, Gadamer argues that the appropriate model for understanding social action is that of interpreting a text, a model "in which we are not in the least concerned with the search for causes or the framing laws, but entirely with the circular process of seeking to understand a whole in terms of its parts, and its parts in terms of the contribution they make to the meaning of the whole" (Skinner 7). The anti-positivist tendencies of Gadamer's model become clearer when he goes on to undermine the traditional goal of interpretation, which before him had been to achieve an objective understanding of an utterance, action, or text. Gadamer doubts that in our quest to understand the unknown and alien forms of life, we can ever hope for more than a fusion of horizons, that is to say, a merely partial knowledge.

An even more powerful critique of science and the scientific mode of explanation was made by those thinkers who not only questioned the validity of scientific explanation for the human sciences, but also for science itself and wondered whether the sciences themselves were truly capable of living up to their own image as paradigms of the rational pursuit of knowledge. The best-known critic of science from this point of view is Thomas Kuhn, whose work we have already mentioned in Chapter Two. In *The Structure of Scientific Revolutions*, Kuhn problematizes—as we have said already—not only "theory" and "fact," but also the "subject" in such a manner as to support the new theories in the human sciences which are, on the whole, anti-humanist in the sense that they deny the epistemological priority of the subject and of man. Since the concept of a self-identical and sovereign subject lies at the very core of cognitivist theories of knowledge, such an interrogation distinguishes the new theories from the old. Our point, however, is that such a rejection of the subject has led not to the eradication of the subject as such, but, as we have already indicated, to an updating of the subject of consciousness as the Foucauldian subject of the body.

According to the ludic narrative of the postwar intellectual scene (rehearsed, among other places, in Skinner's book), Kuhn's radical critique of science and scientific explanation had a great deal of influence on the thinkers in the humanities, who in the light of his deconstruction of the prevailing views undertook more speculative and less empirical inquiries. It was these inquiries that supposedly started a new era in the human sciences: the epoch of theory.

This, then, is the "new" narrative of the emergence of the discourse of theory and theoretical inquiry in the human sciences: a causal narrative whose trajectory of episodes places the publication of Lévi-Strauss's *Structural Anthropology* as the exciting "force" engendering the "complications" of the "rising action" of contestation between "theory" and "empiricism" in the 1940's and 1950's leading to the high moment of "climax" in which empiricism (and positivism) in the human sciences are overcome and the conflicts of opposing paradigms are consequently resolved in the dénouement of "the return of grand theory in the human sciences." Like any dominant narrative, this one too suppresses other narratives that contest its patterning of events and the "reality" that it consequently produces.

There are, of course, "other" narratives of the scene of the humanities. One such counter-narrative—the one we are articulating here—displays ludic (post)modern theory not as the "alterity" that its master narrative depicts, but in fact as the "sameness" that has returned through the story of the "other." This counter-narrative resituates the complications and conflicts (which, in the master story, are presented as marks of opposition between the old and the new) in a narrative of continuity and similarity. The counter-narrative sees the master narrative as a story which needs such complications and conflicts (as those we have just outlined) in order to provide the high drama of self-legitimization for what is actually a rather predictable narrative of the renewal of the old. According to this counter-narrative, the mode of inquiry in the human sciences over the last two decades or so has not changed or, to be more accurate, has changed without transforming any of the fundamental practices of the "old." This non-change has occurred because the "new" practices have remained under the firm control of the hegemonic power of empiricism. Furthermore, the privileged "conflicts" in the master story are seen in the counter-narrative as strategies through which the change from one mode of empiricism to another is represented as a radical epistemological break—a disjunction whose purpose is to offer the old as radically new and thus to guarantee the survival of the empiricist research program by giving it an intellectually rigorous updating.

As we indicated in Part I of this book, rather than being a purely scientific or philosophical issue concerning the reliability of knowledge, empiricism (a mode of foundationalism) is deeply implicated in political and ideological questions. In order to demonstrate the continuity of empiricism in ludic theory, we will focus here not on Derrida's own work—that is the subject of our next chapter—but on the writings of the *Annales* historians, whose work has greatly influenced ludic "localism" in general and Foucault's "genealogy" in particular. The empiricism of the *Annales* school, especially that of Fernand Braudel (who claims to be "by temperament a 'structuralist'" (qtd. in Clark 189)), is indicated not only by the new emphasis its members have placed on the quantifiable. It is even more clear in their ultimate grounding of the theory of history and cultural studies in the "natural" (which is assumed to be open to direct inspection by the human senses) rather than in the "cultural" (which is the product of the mediations of interpretive practices and is thus intelligible only through codes). It is true that the *Annales* historians have declared that their aim is to transcend concrete individual events in order to deal with the larger structures of history. Yet they conceptualize these structures in their work as basically the effect not of discursive and interpretive practices but of "nature" itself.

For instance, regarding their notion of historical time, the empirical division of time into "short," "medium," and "long" durations they seem to regard as a direct reflection of "man's biological, geo-physical and climactic circumstances, of 'man in his intimate relationship to earth which bears and feeds him'" (Clark, "The Annales Historians" 183). The hallmark of their empiricism is that they think knowledge belongs to the object of knowledge itself; and thus they reject traditional history because in using a narrative frame (which is an effect of interpretive activity), traditional history projects formal certainty onto the contingencies of history. They argue that these contingencies, as manifestations of the real, should be captured directly and that one way to do so is to approach them in terms of a three-tier structure of historical time:

1. The time of micro-history; the short-span time of events —the time of the instant and the immediate.
2. The time of *conjunctures*; the time taken by broader movements; an intermediate rate of change.
3. The time of longest duration (*histoire de la longue durée*); where time is almost stationary and the historian needs the perspective of centuries. (Clark 182)

Although a "naturalness" is claimed for these three structures of time (short, intermediate, long), these frames of intelligibility are constructed by interpretive practices. The "real" narrative which emerges from them by no means frees the writing of history from narrativity. In fact the conceptualization of change in terms of these three kinds of temporality in Braudel's work is itself an effect of narration. The effort of these historians to oppose the narrative time of traditional history to the actual time of life and nature itself is finally part of an ideological program to inscribe "presence" which is beyond the reach of the constructedness of culture in historical accounts. Theirs is a desire, in other words, to go beyond the materiality of economics and politics and "found" reality in the last instance on the plenitude of empirical nature itself. The *Annales* school's rejection of what Lyotard would call the imposed meta-narratives of certainty of traditional history is undertaken in fact in order to put aside the authority of culture (social metanarratives) for a new kind of authority founded on the uncontested sovereignty of nature. For these historians, the contingencies of history are, paradoxically enough, a form of certainty, since they are "facts" of history and as such are regarded to have issued directly from the passage of time itself. Locating the interpretive authority in nature itself is part of an ideological move to naturalize authority as such. It is in this space of the natural that Braudel's notion of "realism" comes into being. Although he rejects the traditional conventional metanarratives of representationalism in histories because they are epistemologically naive enough to claim to have portrayed things and events just as they really are, he himself relies on similar metanarratives and "founds" his theory on an empirical notion of realism in order to show "how the world *was* in times past, irrespective of how it was seen by those who lived in it" (Clark 189-190).

In Braudel's *The Mediterranean*, which is a monument to the contemporary empiricist research program in the human sciences and also a supreme example of the kind of empiricism that Foucault legitimates in the name of "genealogy," the ideological imperative of empiricism unveils itself by recuperating and explaining the political and the economic in terms of the natural. In this book, Braudel describes the world of political contestations and economic struggles as narrow, superficial, ephemeral, provisional and capricious—a world of illusion. This is reality as it appears to agents, not reality as it *is*, according to Clark (184). Men and women who inhabit this world are victims of false consciousness; they fail to recognize those forces which are separate from them but which fashion what they do—"just as the destinies of Turks and Christians alike were unknowingly established by common patterns of climate, terrain and vegetation in the Mediterranean region; just as Philip II and his advisers were blind to the way their actions were responses to seismic shifts in its geo-history" (Clark 184). History derives from nature; it is not the product of culture. According to another *Annales* historian, Ladurie, the driving force of history finally lies "in biological phenomena" (qtd. in Clark 186). For Braudel, Ladurie and other practitioners of this kind of history, reality lies outside the significations of culture "in the world of physical objects and relationships—geo-physical formations, patterns of climate, ecological systems, demographic mechanisms, and so on . . . what has interested Braudel is nature rather than culture, 'things' rather than 'words'" (Clark 190).

It is the ideological program of these historians to "found" reality outside of social intelligibility, to posit a reality, in other words, which is itself the site of knowledge and has to be explained in terms of its own "natural" properties and not of its cultural traits. For them, meaning is initiated directly by nature (Clark 192). Intelligibility, which is culture's way of knowing reality, is minimized by Braudel as an explanatory concept, since it is an effect of the economic and political as well as philosophical and theoretical practices of a society. By banishing it, Braudel's model of historiography brackets political understanding and privileges the empirical and the natural. His move legitimates all the dominant ideological practices of contemporary bourgeois society as incontestable, since they can, in his model, be traced back to the bedrock of reality—nature. This "naturalization" of knowledge, attributing it to the object of knowledge, which implies its immutability and inevitability, enables the empiricist paradigm to postulate a closure in history and society that is ideologically required in order for the present practices and relations of production to be reproduced in all sites of culture.

By assuming that knowledge is the effect of an abstraction of essence from object performed by a subject, empiricism posits a self-identical and self-present subject. From its perspective, in fact, knowledge is a "correspondence" between the object and the subject. Such a view of the subject, as the place in which knowledge is created, has close affinity with another idealistic theory of knowledge which is dominant in contemporary ludic theory, that is to say, "cognitivism." If in empiricism the "object" is the foundation of knowledge, in cognitivism, it is the "mind." In fact cognitivism is a form of empiricism of the subject. Both mind and object, in these two theories, are reified as the ultimate grounds of knowing and are perceived as self-evident foundations that are beyond the interpretive practices of culture. Cognitivism regards knowledge to be the effect of the mind and the information processing competencies of a unitary, rational, and intentional subject ("cogito") who is beyond the "interpellation" of ideology and thus outside the reach of history and culture. Cognitivism pervades the dominant notion of knowledge; even empiricism is inscribed by it. In legitimating their proposals about cultural reality as non-contingent "knowledge" both cognitivism and empiricism rely on a set of formal and logical procedures which are used to test the validity of the "truth" thus created. These logical and formal procedures which vary from one knowledge discipline to another, all have one major function which, according to Popper, is to subject knowledge to a "crucial experiment" (a test of falsifiability) to see if the formulated knowledge passes that test. These logical and formal operations, however, are themselves the outcome of cognitive processes: they are constructed by the mind itself and are based on rationalistic premises. Cognitivism and cognitivistic "testing" operations are individualistic, anti-historical and of course formalist and purely logical. Cognitivism, in short, sees knowledge as merely the product of individual acts of reasoning. "By logical inference on the basis of their experience, individual scientists contribute to scientific progress, to the cumulative development of scientific knowledge and its gradually increasing correspondence with the reality it describes" (Barnes, "Thomas Kuhn" 86).

The entire enterprise, clearly, is founded upon the reasoning individual; and the process is threatened if the individual ceases to be rational. The nature and source of this danger, as far as the cognitivist program is concerned, is society. "Social pressures, political passions, economic interests may bias the judgment of the individual so that he irrationally refuses to modify a cherished belief, or to accept a disagreeable one. Over time, these biases may transform thought into political ideology or religious dogma: they must be eliminated or neutralized if the understanding of nature is to be advanced, or a contribution to science be made" (Barnes 86). Knowledge is thus seen as produced in a cultural vacuum by a transcultural, disembodied mind. It is telling that such a view is actually concentrated on a political model, that of a liberal ideology (which values the open-minded, the dispassionate, and above all the fair and the tolerant—in a word, the non-political). Marx's critique of Hegel is in fact a paradigmatic designation and critique of cognitivism: "Hegel," he states in the *Grundrisse*, "fell into the illusion of conceiving the real as the result of thought recapitulating itself within itself, deepening itself within itself, and moving itself from within itself" (198).

Lévi-Strauss's theories are exemplary instances of cognitivism in (post)modern critical theory. In his writings, Lévi-Strauss, "the purveyor of Grand Theory par excellence" "approaches everything in experience as 'matter for' communication codes," whose particular manifestations vary from one domain to another (myth, food customs, marriage laws) and from one society to another (Boon, "Claude Lévi-Strauss" 169). Society, for Lévi-Strauss, is as a whole "a very large machine for establishing communication between human beings." However, the manner in which codes make the real intelligible and thus communicable, is important for him mainly because the laws and rules organizing communication reveal the cognitive structures of the human mind. In its use of binary propositions, for example, in order to establish contrasts and therefore engender differences that produce signification, the human mind seems to work like an algebra of relations, which will eventually unveil not only how a particular culture means, but how meaning is encoded at all. This structure of cognition is unconscious, invariable, and universal: it underlies the operations both of the (primitive) "science of the concrete" as well as of (civilized) abstract thought. Lévi-Strauss's emphasis on the codes of culture and the arbitrariness of meaning distinguishes his work from that of the empiricists with their theory of "inherent" meaning in the (uncoded) "real"—the natural. However, by the very mode of his opposition to the empiricist paradigm, he reveals his own ideological identity with empiricism since for him knowledge ultimately takes place in a space segregated from the materiality of economic and political practices. Knowing, in other words, is the effect of the operation of the human mind by means of formal procedures such as the inventory of codes and the laws of their combination. The codes themselves are, in fact, regarded to be the product of human encoding competence—an assumption that (although Lévi-Strauss denies it) points to built-in subjectivity. Even if this competence is conceptualized as "universal" rather than "individual," one is still left with a theory that conceives of intelligibility (knowledge) as the effect of a disembodied universal cogito. The fact that "codes" make sense only through *practices*, which are social and political undertakings, is undermined.

In its preoccupation with discovering and formalizing the regularities of signification, Lévi-Strauss's work, as Wilden in *Structure and System* has argued (343), legitimates the relations of domination. The "laws" and "rules" of structuration of meaning, for instance, have tended to quietly support the "law and order" ideology of the bourgeois state, on the one hand, and to postulate "stability" and "stasis" as norms in social arrangements, on the other. As a result of this privileging of stability and order (which is the outcome of all modes of cognitivism and its attendant formalism), change is conceived of, in Lévi-Strauss's own words in *The Savage Mind*, as a "disorder introduced from outside." The naturalization of "law and order" in terms of (Western) scientific principles is an ideological alibi for Lévi-Strauss's Eurocentrism (which is hinted at in his concern for a "disorder [coming] from outside"). Interestingly enough, in Lévi-Strauss' more recent statements, the scientific façade drops away: "I have the concern insofar as I mix in practical things, which is very little, to defend a certain number of values which are those of my society and which I consider to be threatened . . . they are threatened by Islamic fundamentalism and the demographic growth of the Third World" (Markham 5).

The universalistic theories of signification that Lévi-Strauss has developed further confirm the existing socio-economic order by backgrounding the daily practices of social life since in these theories quotidian realities are seen as mere mutable "surface" manifestations of a much more fundamental and immutable reality. His universalism (which Paul Ricoeur has called a Kantianism without the transcendental subject) avoids a global explanation of signification in terms of political, ideological and economic practices and remains local and segregative and encourages an almost other-worldly approach to the dailiness of living (to "surface" reality). In doing so, it lends support to ideologies that aim at reproducing the existing social relations.

Both cognitivism and empiricism fulfill the demand of bourgeois epistemologies that require knowing the world as an act that takes place in isolation from political and social practices; both, in other words, segregate knowledge from the discursive activities of culture and in explaining the world represent it as constituted cognitively and empirically, which is to say, non-politically. Knowledge, however, is neither the effect of cognitive processes alone nor the outcome of unchanging objects/facts; rather, as Belsey states "experience of these "facts" is the product of "brains interacting with brains" and is "itself . . . the location of ideology, not the guarantee of truth" ("Letter to the Editor" 1217).

In other words, the subject and his mind are equally the product of historical signifying practices since the subject positions that constitute the subject in a culture are all the effect of the discursive (ideological) practices of that culture. The "successful" theory (the winning "truth") is the one that most completely meets the needs of cultural ideologies in reproducing the dominant relations of production. Contrary to the cognitivist theories that represent knowledge as the outcome of formal procedures (the testing of the knowledge invented by the mind through logical procedures), a discourse acquires the status of knowledge in a culture not because it conforms to certain formal/logical tests, but because it meets cultural requirements for knowledge. The "tests" themselves, as we have already suggested, are in fact theories of knowledge in the sense that they are "assumed" by members of a culture to be markers of truth. By setting up criteria which are internal to knowledge and by measuring scientific "truth" according to them, cognitivist theories attempt to represent truth as a mere matter of logical consistency and internal coherence and thus effectively cut it off from the economic, political, and knowledge practices of society. If internal criteria were the only deciding factors, it is difficult to understand why among a number of competing theories which are usually all internally consistent and logical and thus meet the established criteria, one succeeds in being named as "knowledge" and the rest are dismissed as nonknowledge. Cognitivist theories also fail to explain the changes that take place in these internal criteria themselves: the standards of "truth" vary from one era to another, and unless one accepts that these standards are themselves effects of larger frames of intelligibility of culture which in turn are responses to changing material practices, one will not be able to account for such changefulness.

By setting up internal criteria for judging knowledge practices, cognitivist theories privilege science as an independent activity that has very little to do with a society's social arrangements. It is a testimony to the inevitable inscription of knowledge practices in the economic and political practices of culture that, once examined carefully, the cognitivist theories that on the surface argue for independence of knowledge and its standards of truth, are seen to be in fact deeply involved in the dominant ideological practices and engendering epistemologies that support them.

Cognitivist theories, which set up internal standards of truth *specific* to each knowledge discipline, are, in the last instance, reproducing a political pluralism that conceals relations of domination by representing all elements of power as equal. Cognitivist theories thus operate as the enabling condition of the existing social relations. If each discipline of knowledge has its own standards of truth, it follows, since there are a variety of disciplines in each culture, that truth is, as Derrida says, "plural" (*Spurs* 103). The notion of truth as "plural" has a number of politically significant consequences. For one thing, it reifies and reinforces the democratic pluralism of bourgeois society and fetishizes the sovereign subject. In addition, it prevents a global inquiry into, and understanding of, the space of truth by allowing the co-existence of various versions of truth and by thus blocking any inquiry into the enabling conditions of these various versions of truth. It, furthermore, encourages a mode of eclecticism (pluralism in disguise) that avoids a sustained analysis of the grounds upon which each "truth" is founded. By evading such an inspection, the political conditions of possibility of each truth is veiled (attributed to the internal laws of each discipline) and therefore the "external" factors that determine the "truth" are kept out of sight. The ideological function of such an occlusion is, of course, to prevent exposing the close relation that exists between the truth sanctified by the internal standards of knowledge disciplines and the prevailing social order that needs those versions of truth in order to perpetuate its domination by reproducing the existing social relations. Knowledge, to clarify further, is not the mere effect of cognition, but is conditioned by the politics of cognition: the complex of economic, ideological, legal, political, and other forces that determine what should be regarded as knowledge and situate the subject of consciousness (which is idealistically portrayed as free-standing in cognitivist theories) in a set of cultural coordinates that recognize certain of its activities as "cognitive" and reject others as para- or non-cognitive and thus unveils the historicity of the cogito itself.

In privileging local knowledge (by the authority of cognitivism, which dismisses the integrative mode of knowing as political and thus as non-knowledge), ludic (post)modern theory fulfills its ideological function in the cognitive sphere of (post)modern society.

It is in such maneuvers in the interpretive activities of contemporary theory that one sees the relevance of Althusser's observation that "philosophy is, in the last instance, class struggle at the level of theory" (*Essays in Self-Criticism* 166).

Ludic (post)modern theory achieves this ideological function by reinforcing certain prevailing traits of dominant political practices and philosophies. In his liberationist approach to understanding, for instance, Foucault reifies the individual subject of the bourgeois society of consumption. He does so by denouncing the global mode of knowing as oppressive, since by assuming such a mode of knowledge, one presumes to be speaking for others and such an act amounts to nothing less than a violation of the immanent laws of their being (*Language, Counter-Memory, Practice* 205-217). The effect of such a view of theory is, as we have suggested, to achieve an immunity from interrogation for the underlying logic of late capitalism by keeping the focus of analysis on its many diverse, individual, heterogeneous manifestations. Clearly such a stance recognizes and inscribes pluralism (the variousness of individuals as equal—a move that conceals exploitative relations among them) and endorses liberal humanism (the semiotic right to speak without the economic right to have access to the means of production) that goes with it. In Derrida this pluralism, expressed in a more overt form of cognitivism, becomes even clearer when he declares—as we have pointed out—that "[t]truth is plural" (*Spurs* 103).

Derrida's pluralism is further elaborated and formalized in his deconstructive hermeneutics, which is based on locating an aporia in the text and connecting it to terms of a binary opposition that is finally insurmountable. In positing such unsurpassable oppositions and in refusing to resolve them in a third term (of a dialectic, for instance) ostensibly because such a resolution will lead to a new logocentrist closure, Derrida reifies the plural sites of "truth." As in any political pluralism, he (through, as we shall see in the next chapter, the formalist operation of deconstruction that "reinscribes" the two originally unequally ranked terms of an opposition in a new and supposedly nonhierarchized and even relation) posits the terms involved in opposition as equal and thus conceals the relations of exploitation and subjugation that underlie all modes of pluralism. Having thus been posited as only one among many sites participating in holding power, the dominant power in a pluralistic configuration can continue its hegemonic subjugation without seeming to do so. In the name of obeying the different laws of different beings, by postulating, as we suggested in the last chapter, innumerable sites of power, the localism of ludic theory, therefore, legitimates the dominant political and economic order of late capitalism, which evolves around the notion of enterprising individuals with equal right to compete in the free markets of the world.

The practitioners of the new (ludic) "theoretical" inquiries in the human sciences and their theoreticians and historians share with the old "empiricist" researchers not only the same methodological and epistemological foundationalism but, more important, also the ideological agenda, which is based on localizing the modes of explanation in the human sciences and segregating them from social and political practices. Such a view of knowledge encloses it in a cognitive space which is non-threatening to the dominant powers and safely tames it for strategic use by the ruling order. The changes which have taken place in the human sciences since the 1950's are more *formal* than *(trans)formative*. Ludic (post)modern theory is quite indifferent to the material practices of the world in which it conducts its daily discourses. Gadamer's statement (in his autobiography, *Philosophical Apprenticeship*) that he "basically only read[s] books that are at least two thousand years old," as we see it, is an allegory of the relationship between the new theorists and contemporary culture. That relationship is based on a nostalgic desire for recapturing the lost moments of plenitude by means of apparatuses of knowledge and theories of knowing that are "direct," i. e., that bypass the political mediations produced by knowledge practices) and that inscribe self-presence through the sensory experience of bodily pleasure (*jouissance*). *Jouissance* breaks down subjectivity (the writings of culture on the individual) and sets the subject free from the political economy of the daily. In this moment of transcendence (cognitivism), generated by what Deleuze and Guattari call "intensity" (empirical agitation), the subject moves beyond the social contradictions of capitalism and reaches a monism of being beyond the binaries. The breaking of the binaries constitutes a new mysticism that ludic theory represents as "resistance" to dominant "cultural policy" and names "radical politics." Because this mysticism, the contours of which we described in the last chapter, are rather thoroughly articulated in the final paragraph of Barthes's *The Pleasure of the Text*, we quote it in full:

> *Writing aloud* is not expressive; it leaves expression to the pheno-text, to the regular code of communication; it belongs

to the geno-text, to significance; it is carried not by dramatic inflections, subtle stresses, sympathetic accents, but by the grain of the voice, which is an erotic mixture of timbre and language, and can therefore also be, along with diction, the substance of an art: the art of guiding one's body (whence its importance in Far Eastern theaters). Due allowance being made for the sounds of language, *writing aloud* is not phonological but phonetic; its aim is not the clarity of messages, the theater of emotions; what it searches for (in a perspective of bliss) are the pulsional incidents, the language lined with flesh, a text where we can hear the grain of the throat, the patina of consonants, the voluptuousness of vowels, a whole carnal stereophony: the articulation of the body, of the tongue, not that of meaning, or language. A certain art of singing can give an idea of this vocal writing; but since melody is dead, we may find it more easily today at the cinema. In fact, it suffices that the cinema capture the sound of speech *close up* (this is, in fact, the generalized definition of the "grain" of writing) and make us hear in their materiality, their sensuality, the breath, the gutturals, the fleshiness of the lips, a whole presence of the human muzzle (that the voice, that writing, be as fresh, supple, lubricated, delicately granular and vibrant as an animal's muzzle), to succeed in shifting the signified a great distance and in throwing, so to speak, the anonymous body of the actor into my ear: it granulates, it crackles, it caresses, it grates, it cuts, it comes: that is bliss. (66-67)

The notion (which we are articulating and supporting here) of knowledge as production, as the effect of systems of signification that constitute the subject of consciousness and the object, is of course not unfamiliar to contemporary epistemologies. In fact, one can argue that it is already inscribed in the empiricist and cognitivist paradigms themselves. In empiricism, for example, the idea that knowledge is an abstraction from the object already acknowledges that the object has a "knowledge part" (its real essence). However, the role of the process of knowledge involved here is already designated by empiricists as nothing more than the act of merely separating the inner essence of the object from its inessential parts: knowledge, in other words, as suggested before, is seen to reside in the object itself. The knowledge process does not produce knowledge, but merely unveils (separates out) that which is already knowledge, an essence in the object. In the words of Althusser, who reaches a different conclusion from a similar observation, knowledge here is seen as the function of a "relation inside" the object. In cognitivism, a similar essentialization of knowledge takes place. The difference between empiricism and cognitivism, however, is that in the latter the knowledge process takes place in the mind and not in the object. Yet, as in empiricism, all this knowledge process does (this time in the mind) is to separate "accurate" knowledge from what is clearly "false" and merely "non-knowledge." In other words, all the processes involved in cognitivist theories of knowledge are conceived as being merely instrumental. The logical and formal processes that constitute testing procedures in each knowledge discipline, for example, merely submit various versions of knowledge to rationalist tests to distinguish between true and false knowledge. This is to say that they do not produce knowledge, but merely recognize that which is already produced. But if, as we would argue, a "test" of a "theory" is itself a "theory" of testing, then this cognitivist "testing" is also an act which produces knowledge.

We may sum up by saying that the world/reality that emerges from empiricist and cognitivist theories exists outside the discourses of culture in a pure state of objecthood and cognition. The "there-ness" that empiricism attributes to the world and the "here-ness" that cognitivism inscribes in the world are both, in the last analysis, reifications of the status quo and consequently views of understanding based on the notion that the world is always already constituted (either in the mind or in the equally closural space of the interior of the object). As such it is beyond intervention and negotiation: all one can do, it is assumed in these modes of understanding, is adjust oneself to this pre-existing meaningful world.

Braudel's analysis of social practices in terms of natural, climatological factors and Lévi-Strauss's account of culture in terms of an algebra of the mind are paradigmatic examples of the dominant form of explanation in (post)modern critical theory which privileges the "local" mode of understanding and consequently rejects the "global" explanation as being "totalizing" and by implication totalitarian, that is, oppressive of specific knowledges. This privileging of the "local" mode of accounting for phenomena underlies the writings of most (post)modern theorists. It nevertheless has its clearest manifestations and theoretical articulations in the writings of Foucault and Deleuze and Guattari. By "local," we mean here the mode of inquiry that segregates knowledge from its enabling political, economic and theoretical practices. By "global," we propose the form of explanation that is *relational* and *transdisciplinary* and that produces an account of the "knowledge-effects" of culture by *relating* various cultural series. As we understand it, then, the "global," therefore, is radically different from "totalizing," in that the totalizing form of understanding is, in the last instance, a form of local explanation writ large. Totalizing is the act of generalizing from the law of intelligibility of one phenomena (the operation of the human mind in de/coding, for example, in Lévi-Strauss) to the level of *all* cultural phenomena. Lévi-Strauss and Braudel are usually regarded, by most readers and theorists, as "grand theorists" seeking to offer "total" explanations of culture. But in our theory of knowledge, they are actually "localists," who—by extrapolating from local phenomena—offer "totalized" readings of cultural phenomena and a (dispersive, not integrative) politics of intelligibility situated in multiple and diverse cultural series. Since, in our view, the customary equation of "totalizing" with "globalizing" modes of understanding (even in accounts of the knowledge process itself) is in fact part of the conservative politics of dominant (post)modern critical theory, it is necessary to go on to disentangle the two by focusing on these questions in more detail.

In his reading of Foucault, Mark Philp, treats "globalizing" as a "totalizing" mode of understanding the real. Thus, he makes the typical move of the ludic (post)modern interpreters and regards "theory" itself to be a "totalizing" activity. Accordingly, he describes Foucault essentially as an anti-theorist. "His aim," he suggests, "is to attack great systems, grand theories and vital truths, and to give free play to difference, to local and specific knowledge . . . For Foucault, to act as a grand theorist is to commit the undignified folly of speaking for others—of prescribing to them the law of their being" (Philp, "Michel Foucault" 68). This view of theory as "totalizing" (represented as "globalizing") explanation and thus as an oppressive practice is uncannily similar to the experientialist views (the anti-conceptual attitude that dominated the old humanities) of C. Wright Mills, who is described in *The Return of Grand Theory in the Human Sciences* as one of the arch-anti-theorists of the pre-theoretical era which is behind us, according to the narrative of progress put forth in the book. It was Mills, who in *The Sociological Imagination* (1959), denounced "grand theory" as a "straight jacket" (Skinner 3). This is no accident and indeed, the new theorists bear the unmistakable mark of similarity with the old anti-theorists. This highly significant convergence of the traditional "humanist" notion of "theory" with what might be broadly called ludic (post)modern deconstructive thought is a historically overdetermined practice in the ideology of the dominant social formation (see Zavarzadeh, "Theory as Resistance"). The discursive mutual reinforcement of the humanist and deconstructive positions is a response to the dominant social order that requires the saving of the "subject" through auto-intelligible *experience* in all the human sciences. The traditional humanist project saves the subject (by means of which the existing relations of production are reproduced) through a notion of the sovereign individual, (the empiricity of) his physical existence and (the inviolable cognitivity of) his free consciousness that guarantees "experience" as the site of truth. For its part, the deconstructive project saves the subject by defending its incontestable and irreplaceable freedom and autonomy. The autonomy and freedom of the subject is allegorized in the ludic deconstruction of Derrida and de Man in terms of textual *différance*. Textuality (the configuration of tropes) resists the "totalization" of the concept and thus prevents the imposition of a monolithic meaning on discourses. In other words, the deconstructive project reconstitutes the subject as a subject that achieves auto-intelligible *experience* through the *jouissance* of reaching-in-difference. Such a move marginalizes the notion of concept (theory) by centering the subject in experience (the site of the unique, the molecular, and the nomadic).

This non-totalizing move, fetishized in Paul de Man's "The Resistance to Theory" (1986) is ostensibly a move towards antifoundationalism. However, as we have suggested, the anti-foundationalism of deconstruction, like other modes of ludic (post)modern antifoundationalism, ultimately resecures foundation by placing it in the ludic space of recomposition by collage: (post)foundationalism is a more flexible reacquiring of the notion of foundation, a notion suitable for the age of simulation, nonoriginary reality, and dispersed (transnational) capitalism. What de Man's "resistance," therefore, actually does is to resist the empowering discourses of theory that question the autointelligibility of the experience of *jouissance's* differential reading that displaces the cultural subjectivity of the reader and endows her with a post-political bodily ecstasy: a corporeal subjectivity. Contrary to the narratives of de Man and Derrida, concepts (theory) are not epistemological, but historical, constructs, apparatuses of making sense of daily experience. By erasing concepts, Derrida, de Man, Miller, Lyotard leave the "experience" of *jouissance* as the sole site of truth, formulate truth as a form of "experiential," trace- and absence-marked "sensational" self-reading. However, to quote again Belsey's letter to the *TLS* editor, "experience is itself the location of ideology, not the guarantee of truth" (1217). The ludic erasure of concepts (that actually serve to demystify experience) is, then, a political maneuver that leaves ideology as the sole "reader" of experience: the Derridean and de Manian resistance to theory is, in the last instance, complicit with dominant ideology (Zavarzadeh, "Theory as Resistance").

3

We want to emphasize that the task of a radical resistance (post)modern theory, however, is not merely philosophical (to promote antifoundationalism), but political: its goal is to intervene in the reproduction of exploitative relations of production. To do this, it has to recognize the politics of cognition—including its own— and move beyond the empiricism and cognitivism of the dominant knowledge industry. However, to undertake such a reunderstanding of the role of knowledge, one must first reunderstand theoretical activity itself.

To distinguish (post)modern radical critical theory from ludic theory with more specificity, we shall focus mostly on the idea of theory promoted by deconstruction and its politics. As we have already suggested, deconstruction's "resistance" to theory is based on its own hermeneutic proposal. That proposal holds that as a language construct, theory is ultimately not an instance of "truth," but the site of tropological playfulness. The "argument" or "truth" of theory is thus always already "resisted" by the "textuality" or "literariness" (the configuration of tropes) of its own discourse. The "truth" of theory is therefore seen as a mere "representation" (as not unmediated). As representation it is subject to the laws of representation (language) and is, consequently, a differential construct. The language of theory always resists the ambitions of theory to be truth. Such a resistance to theory is based on the ludic idealistic view of signification, a view that regards "tropes" to be inherently (as empirical objects of knowledge) meaningful to the independent mind of the reader regardless of the frames of historical conventions of intelligibility through which they are read. According to this view, a "metaphor," in other words, is always—pan-historically—a "metaphor" and thus is discursively subversive of the argument of the text in which it occurs. It prevents the "closure" of meaning by displaying its self-difference.

But "tropes" acquire their tropicity (their very intelligibility as metaphor and so on) only within a given, historical, and cultural frame of understanding: metaphors can cease to be metaphors. Furthermore, literal entities are "literal" only by virtue of historically produced reading practices, which in turn are the effect of social relations of production. "Literal" entities can therefore lose their literalness and acquire metaphorical sedimentation. Tropicity, then, is not an inherent empirical attribute of certain linguistic entities, but the historical effect of their *uses*, that is to say, the product of social labor. The question, then, is not whether there are metaphors, but how metaphors mean within a particular historical/social discourse. Sense-fullness (in this case, the sense of a linguistic construct as "metaphor") is the outcome of social and historical assumptions and conventions of cognition—a "theory" of intelligibility. Nothing—neither a metaphor nor anything else—is in itself and "by nature" autointelligible and empirically always already anything. Things become "somethings" when they are used in a culturally senseful way, that is to say, when they are situated in a social location and thus become part of social relations. It is the process of such situating that produces a thing as a "something" (socially). The uses of a linguistic construct make it senseful as "metaphor" and endow it with the "subversive power" that it is said to have in contesting the argument of theory. This contestation is therefore itself historically specific, since it is enabled only within the historically determined frames of understanding in which a particular linguistic entity is designated as a trope and thus seen as an antiargument—an antiargument which, by the way, is a mode of "argument" nonetheless. The force of the trope, in short, is part of its historicity: in a given historical moment the trope is endowed with subversive power, which is seen as a forceful "argument" against the *other* argument offered by those linguistic items of a text which are historically specified as nontropic. Thus, far from being the inherent condition of textuality, *différance* is a socially overdetermined historical effect. Indeed, the "aporias" of the text (that deconstruction foregrounds as a mark of the ceaseless self-difference of the text and its various sites, figure and argument) are historical aporias.

To inquire into these processes of sense-making is to inquire into the ways things (metaphors and other cultural products) make sense and become comprehensible. An understanding of this intelligibility-effect is what we regard to be "theory" (see Zavarzadeh, "Resistance to Theory"). Theory, then, is not, as humanists and deconstructive critics alike conceptualize it, an abstract apparatus of mastery, but an inquiry into intelligibility-effects that are produced by social contradictions. Theory, in other words, is an inquiry into the politics of the "real." It is a result of such an inquiry that readers in a culture become aware of the ways in which signifiers are always so organized that through them the world is produced in that culture in such a manner that its "reality" supports the "reality" of the interests of the dominant classes. Through such a recognition, theory enables readers of texts of a culture to historicize the "reality" of the ruling class that is put forth in culture's texts as the universal reality (of all classes) and thus to engage in social struggle. In our discourse, then, theory is an ally in transformative politics: theory AS resistance, not the resistance to theory, is what distinguishes radical resistance (post)modern theory from ludic theory in the human sciences. In this radical critical theory, figurality and tropicity are historically-specific apparatuses that generate ideological effects in order to reverse social contradictions that cannot be resolved in dominant practices. They function to explain away unresolved social contradictions in the playfulness of the signifier; by means of this understanding of the operations of signification, ludic theory occludes the role of signification in the politics of class struggle.

It is to occult this move—the recognition of the politics of intelligibility in the texts of culture by theory as an interrogation of intelligibility-effects—that the ludic (post)modern theory of (post)structuralism designates "theory" as "totalizing" (a tyrannical, monolithic sealing of meaning) and quietly equates "totalizing" with "totalitarianism" and both with "globalizing." Such a marking of the global mode of understanding effectively prevents the interrogation of the ideology of dominant intelligibility by means of a relational inquiry that points up the working of an underlying logic in signification in all cultural products of late capitalism. Instead of this "global" (i. e., relational) inquiry, (post)structuralism proposes a "regional" and "local" reading of cultural phenomena: each phenomenon is studied in its own terms and in reference to its own immanent laws of intelligibility. This "regionalization" of signification renders the political logic of the dominant understanding of "sense-fullness" immune from inspection and thus reifies the bourgeois regime of truth by positing the "discrete" as the only legitimate site of inquiry for the (post)modern human sciences. It is through this fetishization of the "individual" and the "individualistic" that ludic critical theory converges with the humanist theory of knowledge and signification and both ally themselves in occluding the possibility of radical theory.

The rejection of the global explanation by both the anti-theorists and ludic theorists is a strategy of containment in which they are mutually complicit: both try to represent knowledge as merely a matter of "experience" (empiricism) and "mind" (cognitivism), as something which takes place in isolation from the relational inclusivity of the political conditions of possibility of the meaning of experience and the subject of knowledge.

To see the politics of this segregation of economico-political practices from cognitive behavior more clearly, it might be helpful to observe further that although (post)structuralist thinkers are opposed to "total"/"global" explanations, anti-totalizers such as Foucault, Derrida, Deleuze and Guattari do not hesitate to pronounce "totalizing" conclusions about the nature of signification in culture. Derrida's notion of the phonocentrism that lies behind the logocentric metaphysics of presence marking *all* discourses, Foucault's theory of the capillaries of power that determine *all* discursive formations, Deleuze and Guattari's notion of a "body without organs" and the accompanying allegory of desire as the force of *all* history—these are some instances of ludic totalizing conclusions. "There is no denying," as Skinner puts it in *The Return of Grand Theory*, "that Foucault has articulated a general view about the nature of knowledge, that Wittgenstein presents us with an abstract account of meaning and understanding, that Feyerabend has a preferred an almost Popperian method of judging scientific hypotheses, and even Derrida presupposes the possibility of constructing interpretations when he tells us that our next task should be that of deconstructing them" (13).

In our view, it is in fact the Derridean/Foucauldian mode of explanation that is finally "totalistic" and "totalitarian." By denying *relational* forms of understanding (by which the political, the economic, the ideological and the cognitive-empirical are brought to bear upon each other), these ludic theorists quietly totalize (move from the specific to the general), while ostensibly focusing on the particular.

As we understand it, the global mode of intelligibility foregrounds its global project and, in inquiring into the subject of understanding, takes into account all the social practices (from the economic to the legal to the philosophical) that are involved in the signifying activities of culture that form the object of knowledge. The explanation arrived at in such a fashion is indeed "global," but "global" in the sense of "integrative": it attempts to mix hetero-geneous practices and factors and to thus prevent an absolutist explanation that would be a totalizing and totalitarian form of cognition. If one defines the totalist and the totalitarian as a mode of knowing which, on the basis of regional observations, arrives at a total conclusion that it then willfully represents as an "accounting" of *all* signifying phenomena (which, by their very formation, are traversed by various practices of culture being left out of consideration in drawing this conclusion), then one can see how the seemingly "local" mode of explaining is indeed a concealed form of totalizing and totalitarian logic. After all, deconstruction takes the operation of metaphor in a specific text (a regional observation) as the basis for a theory of tropicity in general (a total conclusion). Ludic theory's objection to what we have called the "global" mode of understanding is that it operates according to preconceptions: that is, before the reader even approaches the text, she has a scheme of analysis—the global—that therefore is oblivious to the specifics of the text in question. In other words, ludic theory holds that the global is abstract to the extend that it coerces the concrete to conform to its pre-established agenda. Yet such an argument is a naive reassertion that the concrete is auto-intelligible: it assumes that the concrete-in-itself means what the analyst says it does. However, as Marx points out in the "Preface" to the first (German) edition of *Capital*, the meaning of the concrete is in the abstract (89-90). Moreover, the ludic rejection of the global is based on the philosophically simple-minded notion that the "local" is somehow less abstract and that the "localist" as reader approaches the text somehow with a less pre-conceived frame of understanding. Ludic theory thus privileges the local on the grounds of the priority of the concrete, but any "local" analysis is already in the first place a theoretical construct and thus has very little to do with the alleged "thisness"/"suchness" of any text. The localist reading is thus determined in advance and, as such, is as "theoretical" as any other form of reading. The political effect of localist analysis is to offer the "experience" of the autonomous individual as autointelligible and thus to occlude the operation of the dominant ideology that silently makes experience meaningful.

To be more "specific," Foucault's understanding of women's oppositional politics in terms of "feminists" who "refuse to surrender their bodies to the established practices of medicine" (Philp 76) or his efforts in the early 1970's to help establish and run prison groups in order to "allow the prisoner the right to be heard" (Philp 77) are examples of the "localist" fetishization of "experience" and the erasure of concepts (theory): these seeming resistances can in fact be revealed as acts of complicity in the structures of patriarchy and systems of economic exploitation coded in laws (Zavarzadeh, *Seeing Films Politically*). In his explanations of them, Foucault privileges (the liberationist) notion of the "recalcitrance of individuals" (in experience/the body) as the grounds of intelligibility of these processes of social signification without investigating the englobing practices that would, as Marx had realized, unveil the romantic mystification engendered by such presuppositions that "there could be an account of what people are like which was prior to any theory about how they come to be that way, and which could thus form an independent starting point for a theory of society" (James, "Louis Althusser" 145).

The *localist* mode of explanation imposes on those who deploy it a nostalgia for interpretive plenitude in signifying activities; while by acknowledging the heterogeneity of signification and the connection between meaning and labor in a culture, the *globalist* frame of knowing is always aware of the otherness of cultural practices that render the localist desire for plenitude an effect of the ruling ideology.

The ludic interpretive ideology (which privileges plenitude in exegesis and seeks it by focusing on what Geertz calls "local knowledge") is closely tied to geo-political factors; it is, in fact, a response to the historical situation in which ludic theory has developed. The new theory has become a dominant force in the Western academy during a time of the growth and development of a new form of capitalism. (Post)modern capitalism, like ludic (post)modern theory, is a de-territorialized and multi-national venture. In the period since the early 1960's, capitalism has left the local markets and ventured overseas, not in its previous form, but in a highly institutionalized fashion. It is worth noting that in this period when a trans-territorial interrogation of international practices is required, the dominant modes of analyzing signifying practices (the new theory) privilege more and more segregative modes of intelligibility (as instances of presence and plenitude). In other words, by turning away from global modes of knowing, ludic theory systematically suppresses those forms of knowing that could explain multi-national capitalism's trans-territoriality and its affiliated phenomena. Instead it promises (as in Foucault) a romantic freedom that can be achieved only by a plenitude of local resistances and knowledges. The local mode of understanding so favored by ludic (post)modern theory is thus a mode of cognition that, by diverting interpretive attention and force from the de-territorialized regime of economy that Ernest Mandel calls "late capitalism," occludes that regime and provides it with a protected space in which its discursive activities can develop outside the reach of "global" theoretical inspection. In privileging local knowledge (by the authority of cognitivism which dismisses the integrative mode of knowing as political and thus non-knowledge), dominant (post)modern theory fulfills its ideological function in the cognitive sphere of contemporary society. From this perspective, ludic theory's maneuvers reveal another moment in which, to repeat Althusser's observation, "philosophy is, in the last instance, class struggle at the level of theory" (*Essays in Self-Criticism* 166). By arguing that each cultural, economic, political phenomenon is a unique, heterogeneous, and concrete "language game" incommensurate with other language games (Lyotard, *The Postmodern Condition* and *The Differend*), "localist" analysis obscures the logic of capital, which in fact connects the seemingly disparate. By foregrounding this logic of exploitation through connecting the seemingly disconnected, the global understanding of the social, by contrast, provides grounds for emancipatory interventions. It is to occlude this very kind of intervention that ludic (post)modernism marks the global as "totalitarian" and thus places it at the extreme (margin) of social practices. (Post)modern localist analysis, we should add here, is of course just one variation on that traditional liberal case-by-case approach to the social that forms the basis of the political eclecticism of capitalism.

Chapter Five

Ludic
Hermeneutics

1

Although ludic (post)modern critical theory has denounced the cognitive and empiricist theories of knowledge in the human sciences, in its own practices and theories it has recuperated them. Such recuperation is a response to the sociopolitical order that requires theories of knowledge that posit knowledge as an unmediated and direct effect of the mind or of experience as a moment of revelation (*parousia*). Thus, by proposing plenitude in knowing as the only mark of truth, such theories of knowledge by-pass the interventions of the political, legal, and economic practices that threaten the purity of the dominant knowledge. The reinstatement of the cognitivist/empiricist theories and practices in ludic (post)modern theory takes place by the agency of various conceptual strategies. In the following interrogation of ludic (post)modern theory, we have focused on one exemplary frame of intelligibility through which the ideological project of ludic (post)modern theory is carried out: the instance of language and its effects: "textuality."

Textuality, as the site of difference of representation and as a model for social knowing, is the master frame of intelligibility in the writings of such hermeneutic critics as Gadamer, who have had a great influence on deconstructive reading practices. The model of comprehension offered by Gadamer loses its "positivity" in Derrida's "radical hermeneutics," according to D. Hoy ("Jacques Derrida" 50), in which the text emerges as the site of *différance*. Since the Derridean project and the ludic notion of textuality it develops is perhaps the most influential model of intelligibility in contemporary critical theory, we shall devote this chapter to deconstruction and to the notion of text in deconstructive hermeneutics. However, before undertaking an exposition and a political critique of the project of deconstruction, it is necessary, as a preface, to briefly outline the traditional project of hermeneutics before Derrida and its ideology in the work of its exemplary twentieth-century figure, Hans-Georg Gadamer.

Gadamer's writings are a productive place to begin an inquiry into textuality as the ludic frame of understanding of all cultural constructs because his notion of text as an empiricist entity knowable through the cognitive processes of the subject of reading and the extension of such a model to understanding all cultural constructs has directly or indirectly influenced most ludic (post)modern human scientists. Gadamer's main point in *Truth and Method* is that "language" is the horizon of our understanding ("experience" as he puts it) of the world (397-414), because "understanding itself has a fundamental connection with language" (457) and at the root of this identity of language and reality lies "reason": "Language is the language of reason" (363). However, it is "in writing" (textuality) that "language gains its true intellectual quality, for when confronted with a written tradition, understanding consciousness acquires its full sovereignty" (352). We can thus best make sense of all forms of reality if we conceive of them as texts. Gadamer's notion of language as the horizon of a hermeneutic ontology and its program for reading the social as text finds its most (positivist) effective articulation in Ricoeur (*Hermeneutics and Human Sciences* 145-164; 197-221), a positivism that Derrida ostensibly "deconstructs" but actually reproduces in his own practice ("there is no outside the text"). Textuality is a mode of cultural understanding, Gadamer explains, in which we are not concerned with the search for determining causes or formulating laws, but entirely with the "circular process of seeking to understand a whole in terms of its parts, and its parts in terms of the contribution they make to the meaning of the whole" (Skinner 7; Gadamer, *Truth and Method* 305-341). In focusing on the hermeneutic circle in the act of understanding, Gadamer limits the factors of intelligibility operative in the process of knowing to the purely empirical and cognitive. The domain of understanding of signification is pluralistically conceptualized as one oscillating between the whole and the segment (both conceived empirically as full totality and partiality) and between the reader and the text (seen as the subject of cognition and as the object of the senses). All of these entities, according to what Gadamer understands as the "laws of being," have equal force in determining meaning. Although related to each other internally, these entities are nevertheless sovereign and free-standing since they have almost nothing to do with the larger cultural and political frames of understanding.

Even when Gadamer allows that understanding is historical (and thus cultural) his final conclusion is that in understanding unfamiliar texts, all we can do is to "merge" and "fuse" our own horizon with those of the alien text. We can never forget ourselves (the subject is the ultimate foundation of knowledge). This appeal to the subject of reading located in a specific place (the historically determined subject position), rather than leading Gadamer to the recognition of social discourses that constitute the self (its various subject positions in culture), drive him instead to reify the self, as a self-justifying and united entity endowed with a unitary consciousness. *Prejudices* are not necessarily unjustified and erroneous, so that they inevitably distort the truth. In fact, the historicity of our existence entails that prejudices, in the literal sense of the word, constitute the initial directedness of our whole ability to experience. Prejudices are biases of our openness to the world. They are simply conditions whereby we experience something—whereby what we encounter says something to us (Gadamer, *Philosophical Hermeneutics 9; Truth and Method* 245-274). Our "prejudices" (the various discourses of culture), rather than being seen as signs of our constructedness, become for Gadamer the bedrock founding elements of subjectivity—a mark of the subject's organic unity. His theory of interpretation then is in a sense the enabling discourse through which the individual subject emerges as the site of knowledge; and we want to stress that it is exactly such a concept of the subject that informs contemporary cognitivism.

Behind Gadamer's subject of cognition, of course, stands Heidegger's transcendental subject who (by the act of interpretation) discovers "poetry" in the texts of the fallen world and thus achieves redemption (Heidegger, *Poetry, Language, Thought*). This discovery is the expression of the experience of the freedom of the subject in pursuing the uncontrollable playfulness of "tropes" in language; and such a theory of the human person provides a powerful resistance against understanding the subject in terms of history. If the notion of cognition as redemption constitutes one ideological pole of Gadamer's hermeneutics, the other is formed by the empiricism that he quietly introduces into his theory of knowledge. In *Truth and Method*, Gadamer is clear about the source of knowledge. "Understanding," he declares, "belongs to the being of that which is understood" (xix). Even if we take "being" here to mean the effective history of the object of knowledge, the fact remains that the acquired knowledge is seen by Gadamer as part of the phenomenon itself and not produced by cultural mediation. As we have already argued, the notion that knowledge is part of the object of knowledge is the central element of foundationalist, empiricist theories. Like other modes of ludic (post)modern theory, Gadamer's hermeneutics is fraught with contradictions and incoherencies that are part of the larger contradictions of late capitalism. Although his theory of understanding rejects general laws and mastering theories and is decidedly anti-methodological because such laws, theories, and methods are, in the last analysis, authoritarian and limit the freedom of signification and the subject, he simultaneously posits the need for authority. In *Philosophical Hermeneutics*, Gadamer writes:

> The unavoidable consequences to which all those observations lead is that the basically emancipatory consciousness must have in mind the dissolution of all authority, all obedience. This means that unconsciously the ultimate guiding image of emancipatory reflection in the social sciences must be an anarchic utopia. Such an image, however, seems to me to select a hermeneutically false consciousness. (42)

The desire for no restraint or interpretive regulation, on the one hand, and the recognition of the need for authority, on the other, is a sign that Gadamer's theory of interpretation participates in the contradictions of bourgeois ideology. This particular contradiction is itself only one manifestation of the larger contradictions of the social and economic regime that, for the reproduction of its relations of production, needs (a) free subjects and (b) the subjugation of the free subject to the authority of the free marketplace. In order to interpellate such a contradictory (free, yet obedient) subject, Gadamer's project of interpretation bears an uncanny resemblance to conservative political economy which needs, on the one hand, "deregulation" of the market (that is, the removal of government intervention) and, on the other hand, at moments of crisis, needs its "interest" to be "protected" by governmental intervention. The "deregulation" of interpretation (which is carried out in a more radical fashion in the writings of Derrida) and yet the ultimate obedience of interpretation to the "laws of meaning" is in fact the informing ideology of Gadamer's theory. (Here "laws of meaning" stand in for the authority of the author/text, both in turn standing in for authority in general.) His notion of interpretation is based on the assumption that the subject, in her rationality, can in the privacy of her consciousness, discover the truth of the text. It also allows for the fact that since each subject is endowed with a different consciousness, there will be variety in the readings of a given text: thus it tolerates differences in interpretation. However—and this is part of its contradictions—it firmly asserts that in spite of all the differences, there is a core truth in the text itself (authority) and that the ultimate goal of interpretation is access to this truth, which is given in the text by another consciousness (the author who stands in for cultural and political authority).

By allowing for individual variation (i.e., interpretive freedom of the subject) but insisting on the central truth of the text, Gadamer reifies the subject as free but at the same time obedient to the authority of the text of the author. The author, needless to say, not only inscribes the idea of the subject in the project of interpretation but also stands for the authority of the social order that is itself organized by the prevailing class. What is taught in such an interpretive project is the proper mode of situating oneself in relation to authority. Gadamer's project of interpretation therefore effectively blocks an interrogation of the concept of the unitary rational subject upon which the notion of authority and obedience is based. In order to undertake such an interrogation, radical critical theory must intervene in the traditional hermeneutic program and pressure "interpretation" into a "critique."

A critique—not to be confused with criticism—is an investigation of the enabling conditions of social discursive practices. In what Seyla Benhabib calls a "defetishizing" move (*Critique, Norm, and Utopia* 105-111), it subjects the grounds of knowledge of the seemingly self-evident discourse to an inspection and reveals that what appears to be natural and universal is actually a situated discourse. It is a construct positioned in the historical coordinates of a cultural institution, even though in blindness to its own situationality, it presents itself as a panhistorical practice. In contrast to Gadamer's interpretive project, the function of radical (post)-modern critique is therefore to demystify "authority," not only that of the author but also that of those whom he/she represents in the symbolic order of culture.

In undertaking a critique rather than an "interpretation," the reader also discovers that the text is not inherently meaningful, but rather that meaning is an effect of the signifying practices and codes with which he is familiar, and that this familiarity is, in turn, determined by education, gender, race, and class constraints. Thus, the critique is not a means through which authoritative meaning is excavated and extracted from the text, but an operation through which the learner realizes that making sense of a text depends on historical frames of intelligibility, that it is therefore collective (transindividual), and that, at any given historical juncture, the available frames of intelligibility (meanings that are "allowable") are closely associated with the economic and political order. Meaning consequently emerges not as the result of certain hegemonic maneuvers between the "whole" and the "part" inside the text, but as a mode of cultural and political behavior. It is in this space of political semantics opened up by critique that the reader further recognizes that there are close affinities between the way she reads a Shakespearean sonnet (the so-called aesthetic experience) and the manner in which she "reads" and understands the events that take place in South Africa/her domestic life. The text, in other words, is de-cognitivized. A critique re-locates "interpretation" in culture and problematizes it by indicating that it is not the outcome of a simple connection between two independent consciousness (author and reader) or between subject and object (reader and text) but a mode of producing significations, of making the world intelligible through material practices.

In Gadamer's scheme of interpretation the individual is free. The only limits to this freedom come in recognition of a higher freedom (i. e., authority), the authority of the text, the author, or what in fact they stand for, that is, market forces. Through his theory of textual interpretation, Gadamer inculcates obedience to authority in the free subject. In theorizing the individual as "free" and yet at the same time subjected to the "authority" of a higher power, whether text, author, or tradition, Gadamer responds to the call of dominant ideology to preserve the notion of the free person who can enter into transactions with other free persons in the free market, but who is at the same time obedient to the values of the free market that legitimize the existing political order. The conflict of these two contradictory notions (freedom and subjection) leads, in his interpretative program, to transcendental resolutions: in reading texts the highest mode of plenitude for the individual consciousness is seen to be one of transcendence, a "going beyond" the contingencies of the social to resolve the contradictions that are not resolvable in capitalist society in the "aesthetic" (*Truth and Method* 91-150). The major role of Gadamer's hermeneutic project is to provide the means for transcending contradictions by initiating the individual into the realm of indeterminate yet ordered reading. Art, music, literature, religion, and most other human sciences are all means by which the individual, through hermeneutic cognition, can purify his worldly and contradictory existence into a contradiction-free moment of lucidity, transparency, and the presence of meaning of the text (Gadamer 95-104). This moment of plenitude is beyond any interrogation: all one can do is hermeneutically "analyze" it in order to appreciate it more deeply. It is important to note here that this injunction against interrogating the transcendental interpretive moment points up the bourgeois anti-intellectualism which prohibits political inspection of the hermeneutic project and rejects intellectual inquiry ("interrogation") as the privileged mode of activity. Gadamer, in short, reaffirms a "levelling" political liberalism by inscribing tolerance and multiple sites of power (reader, text, totality, partiality, author) as seemingly equal and equally involved in the process of analyzing and understanding the meaning of the text. This seeming equality, as we have suggested, is an effect of ideology: underneath the apparent equality of all elements involved in making sense of the text, the authority of a "core" of meaning is ultimately privileged and such a privileging is a disguised fetishizing of what, in late capitalism, is still the "ultimate" authority, the market.

2

In the broadest sense, (Derridean) deconstruction is a mode of careful and slow "reading" that, in order to investigate the constitution of a "meaning effect," subjects the text to a rigorous analysis—that is to say, it de-constructs it. In a deconstructive reading the production of meaning effects is examined by demonstrating the immanent contradictions and aporia of the text and also by marking how the text depends, in its claim to truth, upon metaphysical and transtextual first principles. Some deconstructive readers argue that the text is aware of its own reliance on first principles and in self-reflexive moves inscribed in its margins deconstructs its own a priori logic: it textualizes itself and thus its "meaning" is an "allegory" of its self-reading. Critics such as J. Hillis

Miller, Barbara Johnson, and Jonathan Culler have each narrowed down this general project of deconstructive "reading" and focussed on specific aspects of it that we shall delineate in the following discussion. Here it is necessary, however, to point out that the deconstructive mode of reading is clearly different—both in its "aims" and in the interpretive operation it undertakes—from the traditional, institutionalized forms of reading known as *"explication de texte," "lecture de textes,"* and "close reading."

In both the traditional French and the Anglo-American techniques, the reader "clarifies" the text by showing how all its diverse components work together to produce a coherent, unified, and "full" text. *"Explication de text"* draws upon philology, history, sociology, the author's biography, and formal properties of the text to reveal the text's "truth," and is an avowedly empiricist and positivist enterprise. *"Lecture de textes"* is an immanent form of reading that is more hermeneutical and is deeply influenced by phenomenology and psychoanalysis. "Close reading" is a more interpretive and aesthetic undertaking. "Close reading," which still is the pedagogical mainstay of literary studies in Anglophone universities, aims at illuminating the working of the text by analyzing its various elements (words, connotations, images, and so on) and its different strands and layers, so as to demonstrate that the text is ultimately a unitary, coherent, but ambiguously "meaningful" whole in itself. The "text in itself" is in fact the sole concern of the (New Critical) close reader, so much so as to be regarded often as a "verbal icon" (Wimsatt and Beardsley, 1954). Derridean deconstruction puts in question the theory of the sign and textuality that lies behind traditional close reading. To read deconstructively is to occupy an epistemological space, which is, unlike the position of New Criticism, simultaneously inside/outside the text, or rather in a position that is located in the undecidability of the inside/outside binary. The deconstructive reader cannot "read" from outside (such a reading would be an act of interpretive violence); but the inside is also not a secure site of recognition either. The resolution of this difficulty (a version of Gadamer's hermeneutic circle) is sought (especially by de Man and J. Hillis Miller) through the idea of textual self-reflexivity: the text itself reads itself against itself (from outside its inside and from inside its outside). In other words, the text deconstructs itself and all that the reader does is to be a witness (experiencer) of this self-reflexive analysis of the textual aporia. This theory of reading privileges immanent critique and occludes any interventionist critique of the text. The political consequences of such a move will become clear in the following pages.

Even when the New Critical close reader does not adhere to such an extreme view of meaning as that implied by the term "icon," even when he distances himself from some of the implications of the iconic notion of meaning, or even when he employs other notions of the sign—such as the sign as "symbolic" rather than as "iconic" or "indexical" (Wimsatt and Beardsley x)—he nevertheless adheres to a referential theory of representation that postulates a relationship of equivalence between the signifier and the signified, the "sign" and the "thing"/"idea." Deconstruction, on the contrary, proposes that instead of having a relation of reference and equivalence, the relationship of signifier and signified is marked by excess and difference: the signifier always exceeds the limits of meaning set by the signified and enters a chain of "difference" in signification which is unmasterable. This excess is designated by Derrida's phrase in *Margins of Philosophy*, "expenditure without reserve" (19). This is the unmasterable immanent "difference," which Derrida designates in *Of Grammatology* as *différance*, the "production of differing/deferring" (23). According to Derrida, the "mastery" of meaning, is an illusion which is the condition of possibility of Western metaphysics as reflected in its logocentrism. Before discussing his proposal, however, it is necessary to expand on Derrida's notion of the sign.

As we have already suggested, the empirical theory of language and meaning is rooted in the idea of the referentiality of language, which leads to the belief in the determinacy of meaning and its unmediated availability to human consciousness. In a series of readings of various texts, Derrida demonstrates that, rather than being self-present and determinable, meaning is a constant drift of *différance*, a semantic chase, an unresting referral of one sign to other signs in everlasting deferment. Language is therefore seen as a system of signs acquiring its signification, not by the authority of its reference to a preordained meaning resulting from the positivity of its terms, but by virtue of its differential properties. These properties are the features that distinguish one sign from other signs and thus generate what Saussure calls semiotic "values" that, in turn, produce meanings that are "differential" and not "referential." Such a view of meaning inscribes silence, absence, and alterity into the process of semiosis. Signification and meaning are revealed to be founded on silence ("Inaudible is the difference between two phonemes which alone permits them to be and to operate as such," [Margins of Philosophy 5]) and are implicated in absence. The functioning of a sign not only requires the absence of all other signs from which it is discernible, but more importantly points up the absence of its own signified. A sign, Derrida argues in Margins of Philosophy, is ordinarily "put in the place of the thing itself" (9) and therefore through its alterity, marks the absence of that which it signifies: "The sign represents the present in its absence. It takes the place of the present" (9). In other words, the sign is different from (non-identical to) its signified and in replacing the "thing" defers its presence. This process of difference and deferment is what Derrida calls différance (14). Différance, which is "neither a word nor a concept" (7), is one of the constructs (like the supplement and the pharmakon) through which Derrida deconstructs (without a simple substitution of absence/lack for presence/plenitude) the metaphysical closure of the logocentric, humanistic, and structuralist semiotics, which treats the sign as secondary and provisional in reference to an originary and permanent presence, and unveils the instability of meaning. It is this anti-referential understanding of "meaning" in deconstruction that leads J. Hillis Miller in "The Function of Rhetorical Study in the Present Time" to define deconstruction as "an attempt to interpret as exactly as possible the oscillations in meaning produced by the irreducibly figurative nature of language" (13).

Derrida's deconstruction of the sign also leads to the revision of the meaning and status of writing. In Derridean discourse, writing emerges not as the representation of something that exists outside it ("speech," for example), but as unending and limitless "play," a "play" set in motion by the lack of a grounding authority, the absence of the "transcendental signified" which "at one time or another, would place a reassuring end to the reference from sign to sign" (Of Grammatology 49). Western "logocentrism and metaphysics of presence" (in Derrida's words) are the manifestations of the "exigent, powerful, systematic, and irrepressible desire for such a signified" (49). Another related outcome is that the traditional notion of the text as a full object, as the site of presence and plenitude, is stripped of its covering and disclosed as a tissue of grafts whose operation is a form of dissemination and not of centered signification. Consequently, the reality outside language and other semiotic systems loses its assigned ontological privilege, as do many art forms legitimized by the referential view of the relationship between language and reality. Representation in art and realistic fiction, for instance, are unmasked and their "naturalness" is deconstructed as an effect of signifying systems. As Derrida writes,

> Now if we refer, once again, to the semiological difference, of what does Saussure, in particular, remind us? That 'language [which only consists of differences] is not a function of the speaking subject.' This implies that the subject (in its identity with itself, or eventually in its consciousness of its identity with itself, its self-consciousness) is inscribed in language, is a 'function' of language, becomes a *speaking* subject only by making its speech conform—even in so-called 'creation,' or in so-called 'transgression'—to the system of the rules of language as a system of differences, or at the very least by conforming to the general law of *différance*. . . .
>
> (*Margins of Philosophy* 15)

Since Derrida proposes in *Of Grammatology* (158) that THERE IS NO OUTSIDE THE TEXT (*il n'y a pas de hors-texte*), in the sense that all modes of signification are subject to excess and self-difference, then "meaning" (in all sites of culture) is produced by difference.

The "criticism" of deconstruction (which follows common sense) declares that, after all, deconstruction is a rather "safe" mode of understanding reality, since it only deals with it as "text." However, the Derridean notion that there is nothing outside the text should not be read to mean that the world is reducible to text, but rather that the world is not understandable as a simple instance of self-sameness, self-identity, and plenitude. If, as Derrida puts it in *Dissemination*, "A text is not a text unless it hides from the first comer, from the first glance, the law of its composition and the rules of its game" (63), then the text of the world too is equally self-differential, and the laws of its organization far from "obvious" to common sense. The Real, therefore, is not "substantial" and thus unalterable, but—like a text—"differential" and thus open to unsuspected radical change. This mode of reading has enormous implications, not merely for philosophers, literary critics and theorists, but for all readers, indeed for anyone who is implicated in the production and dissemination of meaningful utterances in culture. To demonstrate the radical implications of Derrida's theory of meaning and to provide an instance for elaborating on other aspects of deconstruction, we now turn to a specific deconstructive reading.

Deconstructive readings reach not only into those "philosophical" spaces open to relatively unimpassioned debate (the spaces, for instance, of the presence/absence, speech/writing hierarchies) but also into spaces where controversies rage today (the spaces, for instance, of the man/woman, white race/Other races, heterosexuality/Other-sexuality hierarchies). To be sure, the separation is artificial: there is at every point a linkage—constantly remarked by Derrida—between the binaries that can be calmly viewed and those that seemingly cannot. By urging such linkages, Derrida presses continually for the pressuring of the entire range of human concerns by speculative thinking, leaving no domain of common sense uncontested. As our exemplary deconstructive reading, then, we choose Freud and his controversial theories of feminine sexuality. We wish to point out that the reading we are about to offer is not only an instance of what a deconstructor might say about Freud, but also an example of how according to deconstructive theory a "reading" comes about. Our text on Freud (our reading) is an effect of Jonathan Culler's text, *On Deconstruction: Theory and Criticism after Structuralism* (167-175), which is itself an effect of the texts of Juliet Mitchell, Luce Irigaray, Sarah Kofman, and others, whose texts are themselves the effects of . . . (that is to say, the series is never-ending; there is no "origin" to this chain of interpretation, a feature of deconstructive reading that puts in question the humanist's notion of "author"/"authority"/"originality" and, thus, the foundation of all "subjectivity" and "presence").

A deconstructive reading of Freud focuses not only on logocentrism, the privileging of speech (in all its "immediacy" and "naturalness") over writing (as an instance of distance and constructedness), but also on phallocentrism, the privileging of man as bearer of the dominant sign (in all its evident potency) over woman (regarded by contrast as "incomplete" in lacking the sign of maleness). Freudian theory both establishes and maintains—through the commonsensical reading—prevailing normative gender roles and sexual practices. The classical deconstructive reader, however, rejects the mere review of the ways in which Freud (as if he were master of his texts) constructs the man/woman hierarchy and instead reunderstands the (composite) Freudian text on gender and sexuality by revealing how it deconstructs itself, that is to say, how it is founded upon logical reversals which undermine its own manifest "intentions." The goal of Freudian theory is to install, as a "scientific" account of the production of gender in culture, these twin narratives:

the castration complex and penis envy, according to which children of both sexes, observing male and female bodies, conclude from physical first impressions that the male child, who has a penis ("presence"), is not only different from, but also superior to, the female child, who lacks such an organ ("absence"). When further anatomical knowledge provides the "evidence" that the female actually possesses her own organ of pleasure (clitoris), that organ is regarded as a residual, vestigial, and much diminished penis. Thus, in the dominant view, female anatomy is read at every turn against "normative" male anatomy and the logic of these narratives reinforces the privileging of man. "Empirical" data is used to reinforce the pride of possession of the male and the "envy" of the female. The deconstructor, however, pressuring the Freudian text, notices that Freud's own argument recognizes something like a greater and self-differing, unmasterable complexity in female sexuality, for woman—it turns out—has two principal (interpreted as male and female) sex organs (clitoris and vagina), not just one like the male, a "fact" which Freud interpreted as suggesting the original "bisexuality" of woman, a condition to be overcome as she "matures" to fit the imperatives of heterosexual life. Thus it is that deconstruction reveals that Freudian theory—in spite of itself—produces a reversal quite inconvenient to prevailing views: what starts as an argument for the "completeness" of the male as possessor of the penis (this supposed completeness guaranteeing his privileged position in the man/woman binary) gives way—it can be argued—to the evidently richer "completeness" of woman, as protowoman. From this reading, man emerges as merely a special case of woman, whose sexuality is much more complex and encompassing.

Such a deconstructive reading involves several interpretive operations that are all contrary to traditional interpretive practices which take as their aim the discovery of a unified meaning in a self-identical and coherent text. However, from this example and others we will provide, it should be understood that, contrary to the view implied by the commonsensical understanding of deconstruction, it is not, in Barbara Johnson's words, a "form of textual vandalism"; it does not attempt to get rid of the text or destroy meaning. "If," to continue with Johnson in her preface to Derrida's *Dissemination*, "anything is destroyed, in a deconstructive reading, it is not meaning but the claim to unequivocal domination of one mode of signifying (i. e., male) over another (i. e., female)" (xiv).

It is in such a context that Johnson offers her more specific "definition" of deconstruction in *Critical Difference* as "the careful teasing out of warring forces of signification within the text" (5) and J. Hillis Miller warns against regarding deconstruction as "nihilism or the denial of meaning in literary texts" ("The Function of Rhetorical Study at the Present Time" 13). In classic deconstructive readings (say, those of early Derrida and de Man), the domination/decidability proposed by traditional textual interpretations is undermined by demonstrating that the text, far from being a self-same, coherent unit "in itself" is the site of reversal, surprise, alterity, excess, and difference. Difference, as we have said, is to be understood here not in the sense of a text being different from other texts (from its "outside") but from itself (from its "inside"), a difference that in fact problematizes the distinction between "outside" and "inside" (*Of Grammatology* 44-65). Deconstruction reveals the text to be a highly reversible and thus unstable and undecidable entity. The undecidability of the text is the effect of the warring forces in its signifying processes in which the "connotation" displaces the "denotation," the "tropological" undermines the "thematic" (the extractable thematic) and thus foregrounds the inability of the text to "represent" anything outside its processes of signification.

When, in de Man's words, "the same grammatical pattern engenders two meanings that are mutually exclusive: the literal meaning asks for the concept (difference) whose existence is denied by the figurative meaning" (*Allegories of Reading* 9), the condition of "undecidability" obtains. Undecidability is the unresolved tension which for de Man and Derrida constitutes the "essence" of the literary (mode of knowing). Although there is a close affinity between "undecidability" and such Romantic notions as Keatsian "negative capability," the latter is, from a deconstructive point of view, merely a mirror image of positivist will to truth, since it proposes the "negative" as the center. Undecidability, as Derrida argues in *Writing and Difference*, is the effect of loss of all centers and centering signifieds (278-279). "To deconstruct a discourse," thus, as Jonathan Culler puts it, "is to show how it undermines the philosophy it asserts, or the hierarchical opposition on which it relies, by identifying in the text the rhetorical operations that produce the supposed ground of argument, the key concept or premise" (*On Deconstruction* 86). No longer regarded as a representation of themes, ideas, things outside itself, the text becomes an extended commentary upon its own textuality and moves towards self-signification, or in Paul de Man's words, becomes an "allegory of reading." There is a radical difference between the text as a narrative of its own textuality (*différance*) and the text as an unproblematic transparent instance of representation in which reality, in its "full plenitude," stands behind the text and guarantees its "truthfulness."

In order to extend the implications of deconstruction, we must more carefully examine several operations in the reading of Freud above. On the whole, one can mark two stages in deconstructive reading which we will name "dehierarchization" and "reinscription." In the first stage, an aggressive reading demonstrates that the "meaningfulness" of the Freudian sexual narrative is the effect of the oppositions it postulates: male/female, presence (of the penis)/absence (of same), for example. Having located the binaries between the terms, the reading then proceeds to indicate how these binaries are in fact metaphysical impositions rather than "natural" oppositions; this is accomplished by a patient and deliberate reading of the text and by a detailed and rigorous teasing out of the presuppositions of the text (castration complex, penis envy . . .) about sexuality—all of this demonstrating how Freud presents these as the actual conditions of women. All aspects of the text, especially its tropological and figural elements, are analyzed in order to show that its assumptions are enabled and naturalized by textual operations, and not an objective "outside." Concepts, which are regarded as embodiments of ideas (truth), are revealed to be the products of textual knots—of metaphors and metonymies, synecdoches and metalepses.

The deconstructive reading demonstrates that the term which is posited as secondary (inferior) is in fact the "difference within" the prior term. The difference within, in other words, is placed in the "outside" so that the "identity" of the prior term is achieved without any fissures and contradictions. Such rigorous reading can show that textual effects and not actuality set up these binaries and that although these binaries are offered as equal and neutral, they are in fact based on, and used to perpetuate, a power relation. The male/female duality, for example, is revealed to be only a repetition of a series of such binaries in the Western metaphysics of presence, of which speech/writing, presence/absence, heterosexual/homosexual, literal/figural, science/literature are well-known instances. These binaries rely on the "obviousnesses" that ideology has circulated about them; and since they are linked to the good/bad dichotomy, the first term of the oppositions is always prior to the second. The function of this hierarchization is to privilege, unobtrusively and by relying on the cultural unconscious, the first term, whose superiority over the second is necessary for the uncontested continuation of "logocentrism": the belief in the possibility of access to full and self-present truth, the logos. In Freud, the logos is the self-same male (the phallus). This metaphysics of presence is ultimately a mode of transcendence, and from its perspective the textual series is regarded as a mere opacity that has to be overcome. A deconstructive reading shows that in fact all that is available to the subject is various modalities of textuality and that the self-present truth is always differed through the differences of these texts. In its dehierarchizing of the binaries, deconstruction, as Jonathan Culler has pointed out in *On Deconstruction*, "appeals to no higher logical principle or superior reason but uses the very principle it deconstructs" (87), so that "the practitioner of deconstruction works within the terms of the system but in order to breach it" (86). This insistence on deconstructive critique as emphatically an immanent critique has significant political consequences that we shall deal with later.

For the traditional empiricist and cognitivist, dehierarchization is the most unsettling and threatening operation in deconstructive reading, for in this stage almost all the accepted norms and procedures of commonsense reading are put under erasure. In fact for most critics, deconstruction is associated mostly with this "dehier-archizing" stage. In his famous essay, "Steven's Rock and Criticism as Cure," J. Hillis Miller describes deconstruction, for the most part, as an operation of dehierarchization:

> Deconstruction as a mode of interpretation works by a careful and circumspect entering of each textual labyrinth. The critic feels his way from figure to figure, from concept to concept, from mythical motif to mythical motif, in a repetition which is in no sense a parody. It employs, nevertheless, the subversive power present in even the most exact and unironical doubling. The deconstructive critic seeks to find, by this process of retracing, the element in the system studied which is alogical, the thread in the text in question which will unravel it all, or the loose stone which will pull down the whole building. (341)

Having located the binaries and dehierarchized them, the Derridean deconstructive reading then proceeds to situate the binary terms in a new relation in which they are not seen as opposed or prioritized, but instead considered to be (equal) versions of an inclusive, generalized prototerm (in Freud, for example, male and female are seen at this stage as both being versions of a new term, protowoman). In other words, the two terms are rewritten and the excluded "difference" is "reinscribed" in the economy of signification in the system. The "difference" *between* the two terms is now thus transferred back and written *in* the two terms. This transference is an element of immanent critique and, as we have suggested before, has significant ideological and political effects, which we shall address below. As we shall argue later on, in the stage of reinscription, the Derridean deconstructive project loses its radicalness and literally becomes an agent of "conservation." Instead of being displaced and transformed, the two terms are merely put under erasure and this immanent "crossing out" takes place in the existing system of social relations and thus acts as a local "reform." The male/female series, for example, is rewritten as male-female, but the gender system is kept intact: the immanent relations of the two terms are "reformed" within the existing social system.

Among the "(non)concepts" (*différance*, hymen, the pharmakon, and so forth) Derrida has introduced to enable these immanent reforms, the one called the supplement—developed from his close reading of Rousseau's texts—especially illuminates the use of his reading strategy in the space of such social and cultural constructs as sexuality. The particular theater of this investigation is the *Confessions*, where Rousseau confides his deeply ambivalent feelings about "that dangerous supplement," masturbation, which following established presuppositions—at least, to begin with—is evidently only rendered intelligible by contrast to its normative opposite, copulation. Rousseau's discussion of the hetero-eroticism/auto-eroticism hierarchy ties it inextricably to those of nature/culture and reality/fantasy, which provide at least part of the argumentative framework for the debate in his text concerning the practice of masturbation (it is "unnatural," mere "fantasy"). The practice is physically dangerous, according to Rousseau, in part because it "cheats Nature and saves up for young men of my temperment [sic] many forms of excess at the expense of their health, strength, and, sometimes, their life" (Derrida, *Of Grammatology*, 150). It is morally dangerous, he believes, because it is highly attractive to "lively imaginations," which enjoy "being able to dispose of the whole sex as they desire, and to make the beauty which tempts them minister to their pleasures, without being obliged to obtain its consent" (151). In such remarks Rousseau musters up self-damning commonsensical arguments to convince himself to give up the practice; but, as Derrida notices, other (far-from-commonsensical) arguments also circulate in Rousseau's text. Of his fantasies of "Mamma," for instance, Rousseau declares: "In a word, between myself and the most passionate lover there was only one, but that an essential, point of distinction, which makes my condition almost unintelligible and inconceivable" (152): though his is a furtive passion, not (at least openly) acknowledged by its object, who appears to be unaware of it, it is as strong an attachment as that of "the most passionate [actual] lover." "Fantasy" thus offers serious competition to "reality." What's more, "fantasy" may in the end be safer than "reality"; for although Rousseau has said that masturbation is dangerous, he also asserts that it is in fact not as dangerous as "cohabitation with women": "Enjoyment! Is such a thing made for man? Ah! If I had ever in my life tasted the delights of love even once in their plenitude, I do not imagine that my frail existence would have been sufficient for them, I would have been dead in the act" (155).

How does Derrida render these contradictions conceivable and comprehensible? What the preceding quotation from Rousseau says, he notes, is that "hetero-eroticism . . . can be lived (effectively, really, as one believes it can be said) only through the ability to reserve within itself its own supplementary protection. In other words, between auto-eroticism and hetero-eroticism, there is not a frontier but an economic distribution" (155), that is, the one is constituted out of the other, each is inextricably dependent upon the other. Hence the relation between the two is a *supplementary* relation, in the meaning (profoundly unsettling to common sense) that Derrida gives to the term. A supplement "harbors within itself two significations" (144): (1) a supplement is something which adds itself, "it is a surplus, a plenitude enriching another plenitude" (144), and (2) at the same time, it "adds only to replace," assuming "the anterior default of a presence" (145). In light of their supplementary relation, what is revealed is the ultimate arbitrariness (in the sense of conventionality) of privileging one form of eroticism over another.

Such an insight contains at least the potential for altering the subject's understanding of his relation to sexuality. If we began our observations by referring to Rousseau's "deeply ambivalent feelings" about sexuality, we must conclude by removing the question altogether from the realm of the personal which is implied by such a reference. For sexual practice is no longer simply a matter of personal or individual choice; the notion of "choice" itself is now seen to be a "fiction" produced by a culture under the imperatives of its particular historico-political conditions. Without pursuing its political consequences, Derrida himself points the way towards this conclusion when he observes that "Rousseau neither wishes to think nor can think that this alteration [the practice of auto-eroticism] does not simply happen to the self, that it is the self's very origin. He must consider it a contingent evil coming from without to affect the integrity of the subject. But he cannot give up what immediately restores to him the other desired presence; no more than one can give up language" (153). In this passage the linked chain of related binaries surfaces. In his account of Rousseau's text, Derrida persistently connects the auto-eroticism/hetero-eroticism binary with the reality/fantasy and speech/writing binaries: if the masturbator is cheating nature by calling forth a mere representation of the love object (an image which is itself a form of inscription or writing), the true lover in the act of copulation has—contrary to common sense—no more direct access to the love object, but—like the masturbator—works also with a representation. It is because there is no direct access to things themselves, but only to representations (marked by *différance*) of them in signification, that supplementarity is always at work. Furthermore, the self cannot be regarded as a haven to which one can simply retreat from the "undesirable" (other) half of the various binaries, but is rather a construct produced by their very operation.

Thus, deconstruction's unweaving of Western philosophical assumptions reaches necessarily into culture's most "private" spaces, where Derrida's disclosures rival those of Freud. If the latter announced that there is more to sexuality than what common sense declares as "obvious," a "more" captured through psychoanalytic retrospection conceived as a plumbing of the self's depths, he also proposed the possibility of mastering psychosexual conflicts, of suspending those disruptions into consciousness of elements from the depths of the unconscious. Which is to say, Freud proposed the possibility of *a cure* for sexual and other dilemmas, the possibility of controlling alterity, by means of "neatening up" the relationship between "reality" and "fantasy." For his part, Derrida aggressively contests the basis on which such a "neatening up," such a "cure" seems possible, much less desirable, and challenges the very notion of the self's depths. For this reason, among others, deconstruction is of considerable value in breaking the hold of common sense on cultural realities, even if its insights can be and have been readily depoliticized and tamed—and turned into a new set of uncontested "obviousnesses"—the clarities of the (post)modern common sense (doxa).

We have so far focused on deconstruction and what are conventionally marked as "non-literary" texts. De Man's discussion of Rilke's poetry in his *Allegories of Reading* supplies an exemplary deconstructive reading of a literary text, *Am Rande der Nacht*, a type of poem familiar, de Man remarks, to the reader "accustomed to Romantic and post-Romantic poetry" (34). By way of inserting his own discourse on Rilke into existing critical discourses, de Man begins his discussion by noting how the latter "account for" Rilke's international popularity by pointing, for one thing, to the poetry's experiential dimensions, its supposedly direct inter-subjective appeal that links the poet's and the reader's experience; for another, to the intellectual/philosophical dimensions of Rilke's themes, especially the ontological one, what is taken to be the poetry's "radical summons to transform our way of being in the world" (24); and, for yet another, to the presumably seamless connection between the poetry's form and its content, its language and its ideas. With the latter, understandably, the deconstructionist's reservations come to the fore, as de Man's commentary illustrates.

Am Rande der Nacht	At the borderline of the night
Meine Stube und diese Weite, wach über nachtendem Land,— ist Eines. Ich bin eine Saite, über rauschende breite Resonanzen gespannt.	My room and this wide space watching over the night of the land are one. I am a string strung over wide, roaring resonances.
Die Dinge sind Geigenleiber, von murrendem Dunkel voll; drin träumt das Weinen der Weiber, drin rührt sich im Schlafe der Groll ganzer Geschlechter . . . Ich soll silbern erzittern: dann wird	Things are hollow violins full of a groaning dark; the laments of women, the ire of generations dream and toss within . . . I must tremble and sing like silver: then

Alles unter mir leben,	All will live under me,
und was in den Dingen irrt,	and what errs in things
wird nach dem Lichte streben,	will strive for the light
das von meinem tanzenden Tone,	that, from my dancing song,
um welchen der Himmel wellt	under the curve of the sky
durch schmale, schmachtende Spalten	through languishing narrow clefts, falls
in die alten	in the ancient depths
Abgründe ohne	without
Ende fällt. . . .	end. . . .

Part of the poem's paradigmatically Romantic quality, as de Man indicates, lies in its focus on the subject/object polarity, on the relation between the speaker's consciousness and the world: if the union the poem establishes appears at first to be merely that between an inner space (the speaker's room) and an outer space (the world), the word "My" attaches the inner one to the subject and urges the linkage of the room's interiority with that of the subject. Whereas many of the Romantic poems to which de Man only very generally refers conclude with the union of subject and object, this poem declares it at the outset. But, de Man argues, the "initial oneness undergoes a transformation . . . which is experienced as a movement of expansion . . . [as] the metamorphosis of an oppressive and constraining inwardness into a liberating outside world" (34). Thus *Am Rande* would appear to repeat, at the level of theme, a quite familiar pattern in Romantic poetry (Wasserman, "The English Romantics"); but de Man's deconstructive reading—alert to (or should one say, open to finding?) the possible gaps between idea and language—does not rest with this (rehearsive) view of the poem. The figures deployed by the poem which—so to speak—"describe" the subject-object union undermine this familiar thematic: "The interiority of the speaking subject is not actively engaged; whatever pathos is mentioned refers to the suffering of others: the woes of women, the ire of historical generations. By a curious reversal, this subjectivity is invested from the start . . . in objects and in things . . . The 'I' of the poem contributes nothing of its own experience, sensations, sufferings, or consciousness. The assimilation of the subject to space . . . implies the loss, the disappearance of the subject as subject. . . . The unity affirmed at the beginning . . . is a negative unity . . . " (36-37).

In de Man's reading, *Am Rande* is then not merely a version of a familiar paradigm (the poem as resolution of the subject-object polarity), not even a version with a new twist. It is the very positivism of such a thematic reading against which de Man works in his tropological reading: "The notion of objects as containers of a subjectivity which is not that of the self that considers them is incomprehensible as long as one tries to understand it from the perspective of the subject. Instead of conceiving of the poem's rhetoric as the instrument of the subject, of the object, or of the relationship between them, it is preferable to reverse the perspective and to conceive of these categories as standing in the service of the language that has produced them" (37). Thus the smooth seam between form and content, language and idea, is rent, their relation posited as a contestatory one, the tropological in fact being given precedence over the conceptual. This mode of reading is radically different from the "motivating" of the text that informs the humanistic interpretation of literary texts.

Deconstruction's interrogation of the ways we make sense of the world is not limited to an examination of the texts of culture in literature, psychoanalysis, philosophy, law and other social texts, but extends to the very principles of intelligibility through which we undertake such sense-making operations. In all the "disciplines" just mentioned, as well as in science, for example, a fundamental frame of intelligibility is the "law of causality," which holds that for every phenomenon (effect) there is a prior phenomenon (cause) to which it is logically and chronologically related. Deconstruction pressures the "law of causality" and reveals its "truth" to be more the effect of tropes than of natural processes. In *The Will to Power*, Nietzsche undertakes such a deconstruction by pointing out that the cause-and-effect relation is in fact the result of a "chronological inversion" and is produced by a trope (metonymy/metalepsis) and not by the operation of actuality itself (265-266).

"Causality," Nietzsche writes, "eludes us; to suppose a direct link between thoughts as logic does—that is the consequence of the crudest and clumsiest observation" (*Will to Power* 264). If we feel pain in a part of our right hand and looking around the room come across a pin, we postulate a relationship between the pain and the pin. In an act of "inversion," we further posit the two in a series of links and conclude: pin . . . "of which we are conscious (pin) is born after an effect from outside has impressed itself upon us, and is subsequently projected as its 'cause'" (265; see also Culler, *On*

Deconstruction 85-89). What, in short, we designate as "cause" and give priority over the "effect" is in fact caused by the effect. Its "cause" is "caused" by the "effect," the relationship between the two is no longer an unproblematic one and the security that the "law of causality" endows upon our sense-making process is no longer available to us.

Deconstructive inquiries than are not limited to philosophical or literary discourses but address all discourses of the human sciences. And, as we suggested at the beginning of this chapter, it is the influence of deconstruction and the mode of understanding that it has inaugurated in the humanities that makes it necessary to devote a great deal of attention to its assumptions, and premises and to their political consequences for the theory of intelligibility in the (post)modern human sciences. In the discourses of deconstruction, philosophy is a form of writing, psychoanalysis establishes its foundational categories by means of textual tropes rather than by the truth of concepts, and law is an indeterminate text whose determinacy is not the representation of the truth of justice, but the processes of signification that are organized according to the economy of social surveillance and control. Furthermore, anthropology, sociology and history take a decidedly "interpretive" and "linguistic" turn by acknowledging their own status as texts. The ludic (post)modern human sciences are no longer "objective" observers of culture but self-aware readers whose reading constitutes a mode of what James Clifford and George Marcus call "writing culture" (1985).

It is such a radical re-understanding of all knowledge practices that has made deconstruction seem to be the exemplary instance of the (post)modern anti-empiricist, anti-cognitivist enterprise in the narrative of the "great change" in the humanities since the Second World War. In its readings of various texts of culture, deconstruction has dislodged the assurance of the commonsensical notion of the real by demonstrating that what is installed as "real" is more an effect of the textual—the differential processes of signification. By virtue of such a dislodging, of course, deconstruction has become an assault on the authority of the seemingly real because for a "solid" reality (the natural given) it has substituted undecidable textuality (the allegories of representation). Deconstruction has further exposed these allegories as the mere effects of the desire for presence, for the assurance of a metaphysics of incontestable foundations achieved through the imposition of closures that enable the continuation of the logocentrism of the dominant regime of truth. In deconstructing the metaphysics of presence, it has put the whole notion of representation in crisis and with it the very enterprise of knowledge itself. If we accept that culture is the ensemble of claims to knowledge, then by interrogating the constitution of knowledges, deconstruction has in a sense placed us in a new relationship with culture itself: a relationship which is different from the familiar one (thus the agony of traditionalists), but not so fundamentally different as to be a radical move (thus the dissatisfaction of those who regard the act of reading as nothing less than a mode of intervention in existing social relations). It is through this double move of producing a local unsettling of established meanings without displacing the global system of oppression and exploitation (in a sense a repetition of its own internal operation in reading through dehierarchization and then reinscription of terms) that deconstruction has worked as an ideological ally of the dominant political regime and supported the existing economic order of explanation and subjugation. It is therefore to a political *critique* of deconstruction that we finally turn.

Chapter Six

Deconstructive Critique,

Ideology Critique,

and Radical

Critique-Al Theory

1

The aim of our book is to articulate a political understanding of contemporary literary and cultural studies by linking the concepts of theory, (post)modernity, and opposition, among others, in a particular way. We began by observing the manner in which Old- and Newhumanists, in the name of defending the cultural understandings they prefer, early on proposed deconstruction to be theory itself and in doing so tried to screen from view "other" theories ultimately more threatening to the academic status quo. We offered sustained interrogations of some of the more important presuppositions (regarding such matters as history, the theory of knowledge, representation, language, textuality and the subject) on which that academic common sense is based. We also noted the manner in which the growing acceptance of deconstruction as itself the new academic lingua franca inevitably changed the discursive strategies the dominant academy needed to continue its occlusion of the political understanding of culture.

One of those strategies was to identify deconstruction not simply as "theory" but more specifically as that theory identified most closely with the discourses of the contemporary moment, that is, as *(post)modern theory* (but which we have designated as ludic theory). At a certain historical point, however, as the lessons of "theory" sank in, it became quite clear to the academy at large that humanism was not itself a-theoretical: it was then no longer plausible for humanists to continue to represent humanism as the non-theoretical "same" and deconstruction as its theoretical "other." This recognition gave rise to another important defensive strategy for trying to place deconstruction and humanism in opposition to each other: that strategy was to argue (as we saw in Skinner's *The Return of Grand Theory in the Human Sciences*) that while both humanism and deconstruction were theoretical, their theoretical moves were held to be fundamentally different. In other words, the articulations of Derrida (the representative of deconstruction), along with the work of other writers of the past two decades (such as Lévi-Strauss, Foucault, Gadamer, Braudel . . .), were promoted by the dominant academy as a crucial part of what amounted to a fundamental change, indeed a "paradigm shift," in the human sciences dating from 1958 (the year when Lévi-Strauss's *Structural Anthropology* was published). On this view, as we have already indicated, before that time, the human sciences produced work—it is said—that involved mostly discrete and local studies based on the assumptions of empiricism and cognitivism, whereas since that time (with Derrida and company) we have witnessed—we are told —the return of theories as (non-empirical, non-cognitive, non-localized) "grand narratives." In other words, the dominant argument posits humanist literary and cultural studies as a part of the pre-1958 theoretical paradigm, while deconstruction is represented as part of an absolutely "other" post-1958 theoretical paradigm.

In order to extend our critique of deconstruction as actually complicit with the humanist status quo, in this chapter we wish to challenge further this dominant narrative of the recent history of the human sciences by revealing the reproduction of empiricism, cognitivism, and immanence in the discourses of deconstruction in particular and of ludic (post)modernism in general. In the process we shall also be pointing to the difference between deconstructive critique, which (because it reproduces humanism's empiricism, cognitivism, localism and experientialism and, at any rate, achieves nothing more than an unsettling of the established meanings of culture) is a kind of rhetorical (not political) theoretical intervention, and ideology critique, which (because it rejects hegemonic presuppositions and by doing so works to oppose and displace the established meanings of culture through intervening in the relations of production and the social formation that produces those meanings/representations) constitutes an oppositional, political practice.

In other words, we are returning here once again to the question of critique-al inquiry and to a more sustained investigation of the differences (which we touched on in Chapter One) between deconstructive critique and political critique. All critics, theorists, and pedagogues in the contemporary academy claim to be engaged in "critical" work, but the word "critical" covers a range of very different practices promoted by the opposing and contesting groups. Humanists of course still tend to think of their work as "critical" in the sense that it involves "criticism," or the evaluation and judgment of the merits of various texts of culture. That is, they still employ "the critical" in the sense exemplified in works like Leavis's famous book, *Revaluations.* In (post)modern theory, however, the term "critical" relates, as we have indicated, to the practice called "critique," which, unlike criticism, must be understood as the investigation of the enabling conditions of the production of meaning in culture. If this practice of "critique," then, is part of the "common ground" shared by (post)modern theorists and critics, then we need to be able to distinguish between deconstructive/(post)structuralist critique" and political "critique."

2

The narrative proposing a great theoretical break in the contemporary human sciences is constructed in part in response to the ideological requirements of the dominant academy that—in order to "keep abreast" of new knowledges—needs both constant "change" in the sense of updating its "moral technologies" (as Eagleton suggests in "The Subject of Literature") and at the same time firm "limits" on change (limits that distinguish responsible and reasonable "change" from uncontrollable transformations which the reigning regime of professionalism in the academy calls "anarchy"). In ideological terms, the academy's professionals embrace certain innocuous theoretical changes so as to represent them as the absolute outer limits of experimentation and innovation in the humanities. They can thus determine the line which separates "responsible" from "irresponsible" change. Inscribed in these limit-setting operations is an "ethical" norm: the moral responsibility of the professional to uphold the research etiquettes and protocols that lead to the construction of those "truths" that support the reproduction of the academy's ruling power/knowledge relations. These "changes" reproduce ideological effects ("subject," "experience," "knowledge") necessary for the reproduction of capitalist relations of production in a philosophical language more compatible with the socioeconomic regime of today's advanced industrial democracies. We can take the history of the "subject" in ludic (post)modern discourses as a highly instructive instance of such maneuvers.

The *early* (post)modern discourses of Foucault, Lacan, Derrida, and Lyotard were all subversive of the traditional Cartesian subject of the humanities. This subject, which was marked, above all, by its autonomous and originary "consciousness" was characterized as a unitary, centered, and unique individual. The "individual" underwritten by Cartesian discourses had served the purposes of liberal market capitalism very well, but it had been found wanting for the more advanced monopoly capitalism and its newer articulations. In other words, unlike early market capitalism, advanced capitalism no longer needed the subject-effect of the traditional, coherent, and centered subject of consciousness. The ludic discourses of early (post)modernism (the Derrida of *Of Grammatology*, the Lacan of *Écrits*, the Foucault of *The Order of Things* and *The Archaeology of Knowledge*) successfully dismantled this Cartesian subject; but the need for a subject-effect did not disappear.

Like early market capitalism, advanced capitalism still depends on the subject-effect as the unique entrepreneur standing for "freedom" of choice and trade. This advanced capitalist subject, however, no longer needs to be burdened by "consciousness" and its insistence on "identity" and "coherence": in order to fulfill late capitalism's own needs as a dispersed, transnational and extraterritorial entity, then, what is required is an equally flexible, dispersed, and nonterritorial subject-effect. Thus the subject of unitary consciousness that had been killed in the early ludic discourses of (post)modern texts is reinvented in an altered guise in the later discourses. Derrida's *Glas*, Foucault's *History of Sexuality*, Lyotard's *The Differend* consequently reproduce the subject-effect, but with attributes more appropriate for dispersed capitalism: here we encounter a subject whose "body," not "consciousness," is its anchoring site and who is characterized by a high degree of tolerance of ambiguity and decenteredness. The new subject renders itself unified and autonomous by undertaking *ethical* (highly undecidable) projects that are "private" and not accountable to any collective norms; and it is, furthermore, not just anti-collectivist, but anti-social. It is the subject of a transcendental pleasure (*jouissance*) that is produced by the transcultural ecstasies of the body (see Zavarzadeh, *Seeing Films Politically*). *Jouissance* breaks the cultural molds of subjectivity by becoming an "other" to the sameness of collectivity. The ludic (post)modern "change" of the subject, then, in a profound sense, is merely a readjustment of the subject to the new economic requirements of advanced capitalism. By deploying the discourses of (post)modern theory, the bourgeois academy naturalizes the "changed" subject as the *new* subject—the hip subject, the avant-garde subject—and in doing so, commodifies the subject and circulates it through the knowledge industry and its supporting culture industry.

We want to stress that, as an apparatus for the production of the ludic subject-effect, the "ethics" of truth promoted today in the bourgeois academy is a strategy of containment: its main function is to render as redundant, partisan, and non-knowledge any interrogation of the "politics" of truth. In the ethics of the new theoretical program, deconstruction is the absolute term of "otherness" beyond which no discourse can go without transgressing the "intelligible" boundaries of knowledge: discourses that cross those boundaries are thought to have entered the domain of non-knowledge (non-intelligibility). Radical political critical theory, whose truths aim not merely at reforming, but trans-forming, the academy are, as far as the "center" of the academy and the culture industry are concerned, such non-knowledges. The enthusiasm with which the deconstructive mode of theoretical inquiry has been received in the academy (and its supporting culture industry) is due in part to the fact that, by renewing the dominant moral technologies, deconstruction offers new ways of displacing politics. Deconstruction, in short, is today's generic mode of innovation and change: what lies on the other side of deconstruction is thought of as chaos, as a kind of immoral extreme, as the "mad" margin. Such a designation of the "political" is itself historical: all bourgeois knowledge discourses realize that although they do not occupy the same *epistemological* space they are nevertheless situated in the same *ideological* space as deconstruction. Along with deconstruction, these other bourgeois discourses legitimize, in their different ways, the dominant order of signification. The established academic research program performs this task by defending "traditional" humanism, while deconstruction does it by "dehierarchizing" the tradition, inspecting it, and then reinscribing it—in a more compelling ludic frame of intelligibility—without making any fundamental change. In Derrida's own words in *Margins of Philosophy* (215), to deconstruct is not to "reject and discard," but to "reinscribe." And notwithstanding the radical claims made for its transformative intervention, "reinscription" is ultimately a device for systems-maintenance and the conservation of the status quo. Neither traditional nor deconstructive discourses radically contest the ruling relations of production: the former "naturalizes" them by appealing to the "native" differences that distinguish various individuals and that thus entitles them to different sites in the social hierarchy, while the latter subjects them to a reformative "play." In the ludic space of playfulness, the social relations of production are posited not as historically necessary but as subject to the laws of the alea: chance and contingency. In ludic deconstruction chance and contingency perform the same ideological role that "native" (i. e., non-logical, random, inscrutable) difference plays in traditional humanistic discourses. Both posit a social field beyond the reach of the logic of necessity and history.

The crisis in cultural studies (the human sciences), of which the contestation between deconstruction and the humanist tradition in the reading of texts of culture is only one instance, is a crisis of interpretation, a crisis in the production of culture's narratives: (post)modern theory has emptied the texts of the world of all inherent "meanings" and recognized the "Actual" as meaningful only within the coordinates of culture, that is to say, when it becomes "Real." In other words, "meaning" has lost its inevitability, naturalness, and authority and has been designated as a construct of texts (of culture), and thus as an open site of cultural and ideological struggle. Since if, as (post)modern theory argues, the Real is a text, then its meaning is not fixed but varies according to the frames of intelligibility the "reader" brings to the act of reading. The results of this view is that urgent questions are raised for cultural studies: what reading strategies should be involved in the process of reading/producing culture's narratives? Through what framework of assumptions and presuppositions should the texts of culture be made intelligible? These frames are the subject of political contestation among social classes since through them the Real of culture is determined in a fashion that legitimates the interests of one class, a particular race or gender, as opposed to the others. Since everyone has a stake in the "intelligibility" of social signs, the "meaning" of the Real, these battles are fought by all social classes in all sites of culture, from the editorials in the local newspaper to the formulations in the physics laboratory of the most abstract scientific "laws."

In the academy, where the struggles are conducted on behalf of various social classes by scientists, scholars, artists, and intellectuals in institutional settings, however, this struggle is often disguised as the disinterested pursuit of knowledge. This view of knowledge as the outcome of disinterested inquiries is a part of the global ideology of the bourgeois university that aims to depoliticize knowledge in order to conceal the struggle for power which is inscribed in its researches that will continue to produce intelligibilities that are needed for the reproduction of the dominant relations of production.

The traditional, empiricist/cognitivist humanities supports the dominant view that knowledge results from disinterested endeavor and derives directly from the actual world through unmediated experience, the evidence for this universal truth of the world being available through common sense to all "reasonable" people. This transpolitical notion of truth is in fact what gives all contesting texts of culture significant ideological use-value, since they help make the political views of the dominant and oppressed and oppositional classes part of the "obviousness" of culture. It is "obvious," from the texts of the dominant humanities, for example, that knowledge is the fruit of disinterested inquiry and that the test of knowledge is the "experience" of the "free" and "sovereign" subject, concepts which are all contested by oppositional theorists.

If the traditional humanities rehearse in a familiar and fairly explicit manner the views defending the dominant regime of truth, they hardly offer the most theoretically informed or most rigorous of such defenses. In fact some of the most sophisticated defenses of the established power/knowledge relations are articulated within discourses seemingly quite opposed to mainstream humanism: this situation is a mark of the power and pervasiveness of the dominant ideology which reproduces itself in almost all discourses of society. One such set of discourses is contemporary deconstruction itself. Even if, as we have argued, deconstructive discourses achieve a certain power by enabling readers of culture's texts to detect and reveal the operation of the metaphysics of presence in the signifying practices of the West, those discourses are basically "regional" undertakings. Although deconstruction puts in question the workings of logocentrism inside the "local" scene of signification, it leaves intact the "global" conditions in terms of which the "local" acquires cultural intelligibility. In her revisionary essay, "Rigorous Unreliability," Barbara Johnson shows deconstruction's systematically limited interrogation of dominant practices: "[D]econstruction," she writes, has tended to remain within the established confines because it "has focused on the ways in which the Western, white male, philosophico-literary tradition subverts itself *from within*" (*A World of Difference* 19). It is not just that, by focusing on texts that question themselves from within their own discourse, deconstruction has limited the *range* of its critique: its emphasis on the "inside" is, as Marx said of Hegel's theoretical enterprise, not "accidental." It is in fact a part of its very "logic" of reading, a logic which is part of the larger political agenda of liberal humanism that proposes "reformism" as the only legitimate mode of social change.

Deconstruction collaborates with this program by putting forth the mode of immanent reading—reading a text in its own terms— as the unique form of ludic anti-metaphysical reading. The ostensible philosophical "reason" for immanent reading is the assumption that by bringing outside (transcendental) terms to the interpretation of the text, the reader in fact imposes a normative closure on it. Since no norm can be justified on absolute epistemological grounds as "truthful," then in selecting any such "external" terms the reader is, in the last analysis, resorting to metaphysics. This desire not to impose closure on the text accounts for why, as Jonathan Culler explains in *On Deconstruction*, "deconstruction appeals to no higher logical principle or superior reason but uses the very principle it deconstructs" (87). The political and ideological consequences of such a reading strategy is that it posits as intelligible the internal ("local") economy of the system within which the terms of the text acquire meaning without ever subjecting that system itself to a global relational interrogation. The outcome of a purely immanent reading is a reification of the text's "own terms," as if these terms were free-standing. The immanent reading of texts of culture in a deconstructive mode finally leads to a discovery of their internal discrepancies, contradictions, aporias and gaps. In short, such a reading is nothing more than a mere "logical" reading that obscures the "politics" of truth by positing "truth" as a matter of internal, formal coherence and not as something constructed by the social relations of production. Derrida himself shows an awareness of the problems of immanent reading; in *Margins of Philosophy* he states:

an opposition of metaphysical concepts . . . is never the face-to-face of two terms, but a hierarchy and an order of subordination. Deconstruction cannot limit itself or proceed immediately to a neutralization, it must, by means of a double gesture, a double science, a double writing, practice an *overturning* of the classical opposition *and* a general *displacement* of the system. It is only on this condition that deconstruction will provide itself the means with which to *intervene* in the field of oppositions that it criticizes, which is a field of nondiscursive forces. Each concept, moreover, belongs to a systematic chain, and itself constitutes a system of predicates. (329)

In *Positions*, he also deals with the problem of immanent reading:

To 'deconstruct' philosophy, thus, would be to think—in the most faithful, interior way—the structured genealogy of philosophy's concepts, but at the same time to determine—from a certain exterior that is unqualifiable or unnameable by philosophy—what this history has been able to dissimulate or forbid, making itself into a history by means of this somewhere motivated repression. (6)

In spite of this theoretical awareness, however, deconstructive readings, as Barbara Johnson has pointed out, have been essentially readings from "within." In fact, Derrida's dilemma about the sufficiency/insufficiency of immanent critique surfaces once again in *Memoires for Paul de Man*, in which he attempts to reunderstand deconstruction by half-approvingly quoting de Man's notion of the operation of deconstructive reading. "Now the word 'deconstruction,'" Derrida writes,

could have been erased in thousands of different ways. I will not speak of my complicated relations with the inscription and erasure of this word. But look at Paul de Man: he begins by saying that finally 'there is no need to deconstruct Rousseau' for the latter has already done so himself. This was another way of saying: there is always already deconstruction at work *in* works, especially in *literary* works. Deconstruction cannot be applied, after the fact and from the outside, as a technical instrument of modernity. Texts deconstruct *themselves* by themselves, it is enough to recall it or to recall them to oneself.

I find myself, *up to a certain point*, rather in agreement with this interpretation that I extend even beyond so-called literary texts—on the condition that we agree on the 'itself' of 'deconstructs itself' and on this self of 'the recalling to oneself.' It is perhaps the reading of this little used word 'itself' ('se') which supports the entire reading of Rousseau, and displaces it from the first to the last texts, from *Blindness and Insight* to *Allegories of Reading*. I myself have often elaborated on this point; the interest of the question is not there. But what is happening then in Paul de Man's work when the word 'deconstruction,' which could have or should have been erased by *itself*, since it only designates the explicitation of a relation of the work to itself, instead of erasing itself inscribes itself more and more, whether it is a question of the number of times it occurs, of the variety or of the prominence of the sentences which give it meaning? I do not have an answer to this question. Always already, as Paul de Man says, there is deconstruction at work in the work of Rousseau, even if Rousseau abstained from saying a word about it, from saying the word. Always already, there is deconstruction at work in the work of Paul de Man, even during the period when he did not speak of it or during the time when he spoke of it in order to say that there was nothing new to say about it. (123-124)

To understand deconstructive reading as a mere reporting, by the reader, of the internal operation of the text—which has already deconstructed itself—is to fetishize, to use Derrida's own words, "a relation of the work to *itself*." In other words, as we have already suggested, the end of such an immanent reading is to display the "logic" of the text as independent of ("outside") the history in which that logic acquires meaning as a signifying practice of culture in designating the "intelligible."

3

Radical critical theory (based on ideology critique) goes beyond (deconstruction's) immanent reading of texts of culture and, in the tradition of Marx's own readings, attempts to relate the internal "logic" of the text to "history." In the "Critique of Hegel's Doctrine of the State," Marx begins with a scrupulous immanent reading of Hegel's text. Having provided an immanent critique, Marx next proceeds to demonstrate how the internal logic of Hegel's text is necessitated by history and how it produces on an abstract level, the needs of ideology. Through his naturalization of "reversal," Hegel turns Idea into a substance and then points to reality (the existing political order) as the embodiment of this substance. "Hegel's task," Marx writes, "is not to discover the truth of empirical existence but to discover the empirical existence of the truth" (in *Early Writings* 98). In other words, having discovered the logic of the text through an interior reading, Marx shows its political outcome: it is through such a reversal that Hegel produces a theory of the state and of civil society, fetishizes private property, and legitimates the Prussian monarchy (75-97, 100-105, 110-114).

The important question for Marx, then, is not the mere discovery of immanent contradictions in the logic of the text. In fact in the "Critique of Hegel's Doctrine of the State," he rejects as "vulgar criticism" the mode of reading that, like deconstruction, "discovers contradictions everywhere" (158). In the same text he states what he regards to be a truly philosophical critique: "Such a critique not only shows up contradictions as existing; it *explains them, it comprehends their genesis, their necessity. It grasps their particular significance*" (158). For Marx, the significance of contradictions and reversals in Hegel's text is their historical necessity: what form of intelligibility does such a reversal posit and thus what modes of political and economic practice does it enable and legitimate? In other words how does the political economy of the text relate to the political economy of culture? It is by historicizing/defetishizing Hegel's logical categories (which Hegel takes as "natural" and "universal" categories of thought) and demonstrating their political constitution that Marx relates Hegel's textual logic to history. He thereby indicates how the "philosophical" views put forth in Hegel's text aim at positing as "intelligible" a form of the state that makes the Prussian monarchy seem inevitable and thus natural. Thus Marx points up the text's contradictions, inconsistencies, and aporias, and shows how these contradictions and aporias are inevitable outcomes of the logic of the text and not, as the young Hegelians insisted, accidental flaws or instances of neglect that can be removed. They are generated rather by Hegel's theory itself, that is to say, by Hegel's "uncritical idealism." This internal logic has a calculus of reversal:

the crux of the matter is that Hegel everywhere makes the
Idea into subject, while the genuine, real Subject, such as
'political sentiment,' is turned into predicate. (65)

However, to leave the reading of the text at this stage of reversal
is to fetishize its "logic." The purpose of radical critique—unlike
that of immanent reading—is not to "explicate" the logical
(non)working of the text but to "implicate" the text and its logic
in history, in the global frames of intelligibility that help to reproduce
the economic, political and ideological reproduction of a particular
social formation. Like the logics of all texts, Hegel's logic here is
constrained by intelligibilities (ideological, political, and economic
practices) "exterior" to the space of his argument. Interventionist
reading/critique must address these constraints and their historical
role in producing the logic of the text: it must investigate what is
taken for granted, what is argued for, what processes are employed.
Through his assumptions, Hegel represents the material practices
of culture, which are subject to historical transformation, as timeless
concepts (ideas) and thus provides a philosophical "justification"
for political conservatism that posits monarchy as the natural form
of political organization that separates the state from civil society
and regards the latter as the sphere of individuality.

The ideological limits of a purely immanent intelligibility given
to the discovery of aporias, logical inconsistencies, and contradictions
are emphasized by Marx in his critique of Proudhon's *Philosophy
of Poverty*. Proudhon, Marx explains, has done for economics what
Hegel has done for religion, law, and so on. Through his "reading"
of political economy, Proudhon has reduced history to mere "logical
categories" (*Collected Works* 38: 90-96). But the logic of a discourse
is not free-standing: "Economic categories are only the theoretical
expressions, the abstractions of social relations of production" (95).
The role of a radical, interventionist critique is to interrogate these
relations and refuse to reify (as deconstruction does) the logic of
the text as the source of global intelligibility in texts of culture.
Proudhon's understanding of political economy first reduces history
to a set of logical categories and, then, in a move uncannily similar
to that of (post)modern deconstruction, sees historical relations as
embodiments of these logical categories.

Marx draws a striking theoretical conclusion from the Hegelian
mode of reading that sheds more light on that reading operation
known today as deconstruction. Towards the end of *Economic and*

Philosophical Manuscripts, Marx summarizes the Hegelian interpretive project with respect to religion. Hegel puts religion in question, or in Marx's own words "supersedes" it, but the project of religion in Hegel's reading remains finally intact, a consequence that is identical with the outcome of readings in Derrida and other deconstructionists:

> Thus, for example, having superseded religion and recognized it as a product of self-alienation, he still finds himself confirmed in *religion as religion*. Here *is* the root of Hegel's *false* positivism or of his merely *apparent* criticism: it is what Feuerbach calls the positing, negating and re-establishing of religion or theology, but it needs to be conceived in a more general way. So reason is at home in unreason. Man, who has realized that in law, politics, etc., he leads an alienated life, leads his true human life in this alienated life as such. Self-affirmation, self-confirmation in *contradiction* with itself and with the knowledge and the nature of the object is therefore true *knowledge* and true *life*.
>
> Therefore there can no longer be any question about a compromise on Hegel's part with religion, the state, etc., since this untruth is the untruth of his principle. If I *know* religion as *alienated* human self-consciousness, then what I know in it as religion is not my self-consciousness but my alienated self-consciousness confirmed in it. Thus I know that the self-consciousness which belongs to the essence of my own self is confirmed not in *religion* but in the *destruction* and *supersession* of religion.
>
> In Hegel, therefore, the negation of the negation is not the confirmation of true being through the negation of apparent being. It is the confirmation of apparent being or self-estranged being in its negation, or the negation of this apparent being as an objective being residing outside man and independent of him and its transformation into the subject.
>
> *The act of superseding* therefore plays a special role in which negation and preservation (affirmation) are brought together.
>
> (*Economic and Philosophic Manuscripts of 1844* 393)

At the beginning of this chapter we referred to such American deconstructionists as J. Hillis Miller and Paul de Man who situate

the "reader" of the text inside the text and thus propose deconstructive reading as a mere reporting by the reader who is "within"
the economy of the text of the process of self-deconstruction of the
text by the text itself. To use deconstructive reading as part of a
radical (post)modern critique one has to reunderstand the relationship
between the "reader" and the text: the reader in such a radical
critique is not so unproblematically always situated *within the text,
but has a historical and changing relation with it*. Having inquired
into the text immanently, the reader then must place the immanent
laws of textual signification in the global series of intelligibility
produced by the material practices of culture.

The radical critique of texts of culture, however, does not end
with the two stages that we have so far discussed, namely, the stage
of "immanent reading" (situating the internal operation of the logic
of the text in its systematic economy) and the stage of "historicizing"
(articulating the logic of the textual system with the political
economy of intelligibility in culture and the historical and material
practices that engender it and that it legitimates). If one limits the
"reading" of texts of culture to these two operations, one has still
worked within the given (the given of the text, the given of history)
and accepted the given as immutable reality. The radical purpose
of an interventionist critique is to produce change. It is in this sense
that radical critique is truly (and not merely on a cognitive level,
as in the case of deconstruction and the new pragmatism) an
antifoundationalist undertaking: it regards the knowledge
assumptions and epistemological presuppositions to be constructed
categories through which a culture produces the historically
necessary discourses and other practices to come to terms with its
material conditions. Radical critique then is an antifoundationalist
practice that aims at surfacing the ideological closures of the cultural
text in order to intervene in them and bring about change.

The stage of intervention by radical critique is perhaps best
exemplified in Marx's own texts. In *Capital* the trajectory of Marxian
critique moves along from "immanent critique" to "historicizing
critique" and finally to what Seyla Benhabib, in *Critique, Norm and
Utopia*, calls "crises diagnosis" (109). Marx's critique in *Capital* of
bourgeois political economy not only points up the self-contradictions
of the dominant categories in bourgeois political economy but also
historicizes these categories. He undertakes, in other words, to do
what he said Proudhon had, for ideological reasons, to do. In
displaying through his "immanent reading" the aporias and self-

cancelling of categories of bourgeois political economy, Marx shows how these inconsistencies are in fact a symptom of a historical crisis of ideology in the text. In his "historicizing" of this internal crisis, he effectively demonstrates that the crisis of the text is inextricable from the crisis of the system of economy that it attempts to "justify." The "crisis," however, should not be simply situated and seen as a given but (and here is where the role of interventionist radical critique comes in) used as the basis of pointing towards a re-organization of relations of production in the future. In other words, Marx's critique (which starts with the given of the text of political economy and with the frames of existing social relations which set the limits of the text) finally, through interrogating the given, moves beyond it. This moving "beyond" towards a view of "other" social arrangements, however, is not—as we indicated in Chapter One—to propose the kind of disembodied, idealistic utopia that Marx himself attacked in the *Communist Manifesto*, but is what might be called an "immanent utopia" (Benhabib 35).

Radical critique begins with an interior reading, but moves towards displaying, in the contradictions and aporias of the text surfaced by an internal inquiry, the crisis of ideology and the social relations that the discourses of ideology justify and thus finally points toward the "immanent utopia" in such a crisis, toward the transformation of the *existent* into the *possible*. By confining itself to an immanent reading of texts of culture, deconstructive critique remains essentially a conservative and retrograde ideological practice. All modes of inquiry that posit intelligibility exclusively "inside" the texts of culture reproduce the very structure of signification/domination that they intend to account for. This is why, at the beginning of our excursus into critique, we suggested that a reading that remains a merely immanent reading is part of a larger political (hegemonic) program that only reproduces existing structures through an internal shift and re-formation of the regional/internal elements. This regionalization of the global is in fact inscribed in the various forms of contemporary deconstruction: what is "dehierarchized" at one stage of deconstructive reading is "reinscribed" at a later stage. The interrogation of the reinstated terms does not amount to anything more than a repairing of the terms that have been ideologically damaged by the pressures of the political and economic series. Deconstruction, in short, is the critical operation of crisis management in late capitalist cultural studies: those terms which must be preserved if the dominant regime of truth is to survive but which history has put under economic and political pressure, are re-formed in the double move of deconstruction so that they can start a new life as viable concepts.

Deconstruction's most radical undertaking at the moment of its appearance on the discursive horizons of the West was its critique of "structuralism." Derrida's own text, "Structure, Sign, and Play in the Discourses of the Human Sciences" (in *Writing and Difference* 278-293) by which the dominant mode of inquiry of the day was displaced as metaphysical, proceeded by means of a critique which was itself based on an equally metaphysical assumption: namely that "structure" is the effect of the internal operations of a given system of signification. According to Derrida, the prevailing concept of structure was an instance of metaphysical thinking since it was given a "center" or referred to a "point of presence, a fixed origin" (278). The function of such centering, Derrida argued, was to limit the "play of structure." His proposal was to de-center the "structure" of "structuralism" and thus, by depriving it of an anchoring center, open it up to the slippage in the process of structuration itself. The notion that he critiques and places under erasure and the one he reinscribes, however, are both fundamentally the same: the damaged notion of "structure" is revived and endowed with a new ("reinscribed") life. Both Lévi-Strauss's notion of structure and Derrida's are effects of formal properties placed in operation by the cognitive processes of the subject of the structure. However, as Marx has shown in *Capital*, structure is the theoretical reproduction of the dominant social relations. In order to protect the empiricism and cognitivism of the prevailing human sciences that require a formal notion of structure to (mis)recognize the reigning social relations, Derrida's deconstruction replaces one concept with another (in a move that Marx, referring to Hegel, calls an "apparent criticism"). "Structure" as a cognitive, formal construct is pressured. This de-socialization of structure and its exile to the cognitive interior of the system is almost paradigmatic of all deconstructive operations. Because it limits its critique to the "local" aspects of the economy of the sign, deconstruction fails to situate the "global" operation of power in the dominant economic metaphysics and thus is unable to empower those who have suffered most from the ruling metaphysics. In actuality it has done quite the opposite: it has rigorously inhibited the "global" inquiries that might point up the structure of domination and the logic of exploitation that underlies the seemingly heterogeneous "local" discourses of culture.

By focussing on the "regional," deconstruction has offered isolated readings of texts of culture (from literature and philosophy to films and texts of history, sexuality and nationhood) that are exemplary instances of cognitive plenitude and articulations of a self-delighting bourgeois academic fantasy that finds no other cultural outlet under the existing social order but in the spaces of regional readings. To support and legitimate this kind of regional reading, the current intelligibilities designate such a reading as a mark of hermeneutic "imagination." We would argue, however, that what deserves to be called imagination does not accept the confines of the boundaries set by ruling discourses but instead contests them. In regional readings the boundaries are fetishized and, perhaps ironically, that very operation which is celebrated by ludic (post)modernism as "de-territorializing" ends up in a more oppressive neo-territorialization. The regionalism legitimated in ludic deconstructive readings is finally a strategy of containment: a discursive apparatus that protects forms of intelligibility that the ruling regime of truth needs. As we have already suggested, these intelligibilities (which rely on empiricism, the fetishization of "experience," and cognitivism, the reification of "consciousness") posit the "individual" (whose participation, as an "independent agent," is needed in the economic regime of late capitalism) as either a "free person" (in the old academy) or an "autonomous subject" (in the renovated academy).

4

In ludic theory's regionalizing of the discourses of culture in order to "save the subject," one of the most effective knowledge strategies has been the deployment of "rhetoric." In the (post)modern academy, almost all the human sciences have taken what might be called a "rhetorical turn," from literature, religion, and philosophy to history, anthropology, sociology, and law. The rhetorical turn in the humanities has successfully diverted inquiries from the politics of intelligibility to the tropics of knowledge. The constitution of the free subject, for example, is now, under the pressure of Lacan's rhetorical psychoanalysis, purely a matter of local rhetorical investigation rather than the place of global inquiries that will demonstrate not merely "how" the subject is produced but more urgently, "why." The Lacanian subject is foremost the subject of "desire"; but instead of an understanding of "desire" in the global political economy of desiring, Lacanianism posits "desire" as a floating entity: as a "lack" and a "lack" itself made intelligible in terms of a network of never-ending metonymies and metaphors, understood as devices of substitution for that which will never be "found." The politics of this rhetoricization of the subject is thus pushed to the background. What is furthermore occluded is the ideology of such a theoretical move that articulates the subject (as an instance of everlasting desire) in terms suited to the logic of late capitalist consumer society.

The rhetorical turn, as we have suggested, is the general move in all the new humanities and each "discipline" has made its own "unique" contribution to the furthering of ludic rhetoric of/as intelligibility. However, new literary studies have played a major role in developing the theory of deconstructive rhetoric and the works of Paul de Man are exemplary instances of the ludic reunderstanding of rhetoric, not merely (as traditionally understood) as part of the study of literature, but in fact as the underlying grid of intelligibility in all human sciences. De Man's theorizing of (post)modern rhetoric in "The Resistance to Theory" is highly instructive both for its illuminations (his unusually incisive readings of larger features of the theoretical terrain) and its limitations (his defensive maneuvers to reassert the claim of cognitivity in the guise of rhetoric as the still central element of humanistic study). He insists upon the separation of contemporary literary theory from philosophy (and in particular, from its subdiscourse of aesthetics), arguing that "literary theory is a relatively autonomous version of questions that also surface, in a different context, in philosophy, though not necessarily in a clearer and more rigorous form" (*The Resistance to Theory* 8) and that although literary theory "may now well have become a legitimate concern of philosophy," it cannot "be assimilated to it" (8).

Long regarded as an acceptable adjunct to literary history and criticism, literary theory has—according to de Man—only become threateningly problematic since the introduction of linguistic terminology into its enterprise: "The assumption that there can be a science of language which is not necessarily a logic leads to the development of a terminology which is not necessarily aesthetic" (8)—which is to say that current literary theory finds its ground in the study of language, not in the study of (separable) ideas, in the study of signs and signification rather than in "an established pattern of meaning" (9). Literariness, he argues, is no longer to be approached as a matter of aesthetics, but as a consequence of the "autonomous potential of language" (10). Furthermore, "Literature involves the voiding, rather than the affirmation, of aesthetic categories" (10). "Literature," which in de Man's texts is a synechdochic substitution for "rhetoric" and "aesthetics," stands in for "theory" in general— any mode of globalization. His statement therefore is in fact the manifesto of the New Theory: rhetoric is the discourse of the "voiding" of all global inquiries that put in question the political legitimacy of free-standing regional zones of intelligibility.

With the conceptual and implicitly political roots of the conflict between contemporary literary theorists and their opponents (philosophers, literary historians and critics) now exposed, de Man makes a second move which is crucial in the (post)modern rhetorical turn in the humanities. The outcome of this second move is to further theorize his primary binaries ("literariness"/"aesthetics") by grounding them in the contestation between the desire to "master" (grammar) and the inescapable condition of unmasterability in the form of textual "undecidability" (rhetoric). The matter, he proposes, cannot be understood as merely a struggle between disciplines and professional camps: he now relocates the theoretical problematic precisely in the theoretical enterprise itself, where it is not so much a question of the inevitable recuperations practiced by theorists (although he mentions these) but a feature inherent in language itself. Here de Man's commitment to rhetoric as the ludic discourse of "voiding" comes to the fore. He argues that the advent of current theory involves not merely the introduction of linguistic terminology to theoretical problems, but also a productive, if still troublesome, encroachment of grammar (supported by its affiliate, logic) upon the domain of rhetoric. He proposes that perhaps the greatest advance in recent theory has been the effort of semiotics to assimilate rhetorical categories to grammatical ones, that is, to codify what up until then had remained "undecidable." De Man understands "undecidability" itself as the effect of tropicity—a mode of excess that resists systems of representation. Whatever its achievements, however, such an effort as that of semiotics is bound to fail, according to de Man, because texts "contain" rhetorical elements that—as opposed to grammatical ones—are inherently undecidable. As an exemplary instance, de Man offers the unresolvable conflict between two equally acceptable and supportable meanings for the title of Keats's *The Fall of Hyperion*.

In de Man's view, resistance to theory, can come either from "outside" (the resistance of traditional scholars, for example) or from the "inside" (from the conditions of possibility of theory as textual construct). He does not take the external resistance very seriously but focuses on the resistance from inside. This resistance manifests itself on several levels, as the resistance of tropics to thematics, of literariness to aesthetics, of rhetoric to grammar. It is the resistance from inside that he theorizes as the resistance of rhetoric to (global) theory and considers the ineluctable subject of inquiry in all studies in the humanities. The notion of rhetoric as a "voiding" of the global understanding in the humanities developed here by de Man has influenced the wide-spread turn to rhetoric in ludic (post)modern culture studies. Ludic (post)modern culture studies, with its commitment to rhetoric, is best described as "textual studies" because it is concerned with the mechanics of signification, whereas "cultural studies," particularly as developed in Britain under the influence of the Birmingham School, is concerned with the politics of the production and maintenance of subjectivities, that is to say, with language as a social praxis and not merely a formal system of differences. Although it takes the materiality of signification into account, "cultural studies," in its focus on the politics of the production of subjectivities rather than on textual operations, understands "politics" as access to the material base of power/knowledge/resources, not merely as access to rhetoric and signification.

De Man's text, which has played so important a role in the development of textual studies, ends in fact with a defense of the new understanding of rhetoric—rhetoric as the primary matrix of theoretical understanding itself. In "The Resistance to Theory," he develops this idea by a series of "poetic" repetitions which sweep the reader towards his conclusion that rhetoric is the very domain of undecidability. He finally crowns the rhetorician as the supreme reader among readers, as the one who can untangle and present but not decide between, the available alternative meanings of a text.

De Man's lengthy and elaborate reading of "resistance to theory" as an immanent critique of theory by its own tropics is an exemplary instance of the deployment of immanent critique for reinforcing the status quo. His notion of "resistance," as we have already indicated, is in fact a "defense" of the dominant ideology: by positing theory as immanently torn by its own aporia, de Man in effect erases the notion of "concept": the purpose of "The Resistance to Theory," in other words, is not a simple exploration of the truth of theory, but a complex political act of displacing concept. It is concept (theory) which is resisted by the tropes of the discourse. What makes de Man's resistance to concept (as a totalitarian closure) more plausible, of course, is his deployment of the Hegelian idea of concept as the proximation of (in fact, the essence of) truth. But concepts are not "essences"; they are historical constructs. Thus to resist concepts is, in the last instance, to render *experience* immune from interrogation by regarding it as transconceptual. In de Man's essay, a text is made sense of not by theory (concepts) but by the recognition of the aleatory movements of tropes. The erasure of concepts, in other words, is part of the current political struggle over the very logic of the social. The question it poses is this: is the social (as the dominant academy argues, on behalf of the ruling class) the effect of *alea*—"haphazard conflicts" (as Foucault puts it in *Language, Counter-Memory, Practice* 154), or is it the effect of "class struggle"? By positing the "resistance to theory" as the resistance of tropes, de Man renders unintelligible the idea of "class struggle" (which is based on a concept-bound, systematic, theoretical analysis) by instituting the logic of the alea and of contingent "experience."

That de Man relies ultimately on traditional empiricism and a conventional notion of knowledge (as the independent act of cognition by the unitary subject) becomes clear in his assumption about the diversity of meanings in a text. He thinks that these meanings are formal properties of the text itself and the effect of rhetorical features which constitute the text. Here we would like to observe that the very act of recognizing the diversity of meanings and their incompatibility (the final undecidability of the text as de Man suggests in *Allegories of Reading*) is itself a *historical* act. After all, a particular configuration in the text is designated as "meaning" (i. e., as being intelligible) not in a semiotic void but in reference to the global frames of understanding of the Real in culture. The "readable" and "unreadable" are both historical effects: many instances of the "unreadable" and the "undecidable," such as innovative texts like *Finnegans Wake* and *Project for a Revolution in New York*, have been rendered readable and decidable. In order to propose a text as undecidable, the reader or theorist will still always have to assume the norms of decidability (i. e., intelligibility) in her culture. "Undecidability" in de Man's theory is, of course, an ahistorical effect of the immanent laws of language itself, a move that erases history and, as de Man's wartime journalism shows, prepares the way for a neofascist regime of "meaning."

Rhetoricism produces the *undecidable* by certain reading practices, but these practices are all historically *decided*: undecidability is then always already the effect of this decidability in the sense that the reader marks as undecidable texts as such by using those texts in a manner "permitted" by the reading strategies made available to her by her culture. This availability is itself the outcome of the highly complex process of social construction of her subjectivity in terms of her gender, class, and race and her relations to the state (marriage laws, property codes, and so on). To locate undecidability (or decidability) in the text itself as a language effect, rather than to understand it as an effect produced by the historical frames of global intelligibility in a society, is part of the political agenda of the new rhetoric. That agenda is to regionalize intelligibility and thus to situate the text in a rhetorical presence and plenitude unentangled with the political, economic, and ideological practices of the social formation in which the text is used (read).

In her book, *A World of Difference*, Barbara Johnson brings new rigor to de Man's defense of this program of intelligibility as locality by offering an overtly political argument for "undecidability." She writes:

> If undecidability is politically suspect, it is so not only to the left, but also to the right. Nothing could be more comforting to the established order than the requirement that everything be assigned a clear meaning or stand. It is precisely because the established order leaves no room for un-neutralized (*i. e.*, unestheticized) ambiguity that it seems urgent to meet decisiveness with decisiveness. But for that same reason it also seems urgent not to. (30-31)

In a traditional manner, Johnson, however, situates the oppositional subjectivities of the readers who resist "undecidability" within the domain of discourses of "decidability." In other words, she equates the oppositional act of putting "undecidability" in question with a defense of "readability," "clarity," and "decidability." This philosophically naive and politically simple-minded binarization comes from a notion of knowledge as the either/or of freestanding cognition and from a fetishized empiricism that prevents her from realizing that the question at stake is not formulable in terms of the simple undecidable/decidable binary. The question rather is the *constitution of the (un)decidable* through its uses in culture. For example, is the undecidable, as de Man believes, a textual effect (see *Allegories of Reading* 10) and thus the inescapable condition of the human situation as the subject of rhetoric? Or is it the outcome of class struggle and social contestation? What de Man and Johnson suggest is that texts are inherently "undecidable" and as such have political consequences about which the reading subject can do nothing. On the contrary, we insist that texts can be *produced* as "undecidable" by the intervention of oppositional readers, who through their adversarial practices (in reading texts of culture) make unavailable the dominant frames of intelligibility within which certain readings are always already and unproblematically "decided." The question that Johnson, for ideological reasons, misrecognizes is not whether texts are decidable or undecidable, but how decidability and undecidability are produced: rhetorically or politically? Here we find displayed, perhaps more clearly than in other places, the contestation between the "political" and the "rhetorical" in (post)modern theory.

The desire of right-wing conservative readers (like Jerry Falwell, who, among other things, is author of *Listen, America!*) for stability of meaning is the semiotic expression of the desire for social stability and for bracketing the class struggle and social conflictuality over the ownership of the means of production. De Man's and Johnson's desire for "undecidability," manifested by their situating intelligibility in the rhetoric of the regional sites of texts (and their thus removing discourse and knowledge from politics and economics), leads them to make a move that is as stabilizing and decidable as Falwell's. Their moves are, in other words, as decided or undecidable as Falwell's own decidability: both want a symbolic order which is not subject to the laws of history and its (un)decidability, which is an outcome of class struggle. Falwell articulates the class interests of the petty-bourgeoisie while de Man and Johnson defend the class interests of the (upper) middle classes. All of them represent their "readings" of texts of culture as universal—as the way all texts should be read by all subjects of reading. The seeming opposition between the "difference" and "radicalness" of the one and the "conservativeness" of the other fades when one considers the consequences of their theories of meaning. De Manian "undecidability" produces, for the relations of production, the same ideological effects that Falwell produces: the difference is the way they mobilize different classes and recruit them for the dominant ideology. It is not the de Mans, the Johnsons, the Falwells, but the oppositional subjectivities of adversarial readers that have always argued for the "undecidability" of meaning in culture and furthermore indicated that undecidablility is the effect of class struggle: the contestation over the meanings of signs of culture which make "readable" (intelligible) the interests of one class as the universal interest of all classes. "Undecidability," in other words, is not an inherent quality of texts, but a mark of ideological crisis in the text brought about by the oppositional practices of culture. As we have already argued, the crisis in the text is the effect of the de-securing of cultural intelligibilities. It is in these moments of crisis (undecidability) that adversarial readers intervene in texts of culture by pointing up the "immanent utopia" surfacing through the decentered decidability, by pointing to the dislodging of the existent and the emergence of the possible. In other words, in a radical critique, the meanings of culture are rendered undecidable by overthrowing the semiotic regime that supports the dominant social order.

De Man is, of course, not the only ludic theorist to place intelligibility in a purely cognitive space. His writings are in fact very much associated with the texts of Derrida. We have already analyzed Derrida's texts as a mode of deconstructive reading which locates binaries and by locating aporias in them (the effects of the tropics of discourse), dehierarchizes them, and then reinscribes the dehierarchized terms. Derrida believes that dehierarchization ends the domination of one term by the other (speech over writing, male over female, literal over figurative); but although his reading practice does displace the dominant term, it does not intervene in the economy of the system. This economy is not a formalist construct, but in the last analysis the articulation of a relation of ownership in society. Thus in Derrida's reading practices the systematic function of the binaries is not changed and their relations to the global frames of knowledge/power/exploitation remain undisturbed. The notion of system (concept), as we have already suggested, is erased in ludic reading and replaced by the local, the heterogeneous, and the nomadic. The relation of the two terms has changed, but only *within* the system as it is. The internal formal relation between male and female may be changed (as we implied in our summary of a deconstructive reading of Freud's theory of female sexuality) and both now may be seen as effects of a prototerm; but the dominant social system of "gender," for example, remains intact. Through the immunity thus granted to it, the entire system of patriarchy and its supporting economic system is given a new lease on life. In the wake of deconstructive reading practices, it now becomes a "self-reflexive" patriarchy, aware of the problematic of sexuality and in a better position to shore up the defenses of the heterosexual system. Terms which were opposed before now become complementary (supplementary, in Derrida's sense), without the economy of the power between the gender system and the larger cultural series having changed. Ludic (post)modern theory substitutes the dehierarchization of terms in a succession of regions for the interrogation and dismantling of the dominant global frames. Deconstruction not only needs to regionalize signification but, like mainstream humanism, uses such regionalizing to legitimate pluralism as the support for existing power relations.

The ideological function of deconstructive dehierarchization is to establish a form of "equality" between terms within the system and thus reinforce what is essentially a form of pluralism. In this pluralism the domination of one term over the other is not negated (because Derrida refuses the resolution of the binary opposition in a third term) but is merely put in quotation marks by resituating the two terms and representing this new arrangement as one based in dispersed regional sites of equal power. Such a "pluralist" view of signification reproduces the political pluralism that conceals the relation of domination by representing the elements of power as sovereign, individual, and equal, each element operating within its own "truth." It follows that if each is true in "its own terms" and if (as is the case) there are a variety of terms, then truth, as Derrida says, is "plural" (*Spurs* 103). The notion of the plurality of truth not only reifies and reinforces the pluralism of the bourgeois political order and fetishizes the sovereign subject, it also prevents a global interrogation of the space of truth by allowing the unquestioned and evasive co-existence of various versions of truth and thus encouraging a mode of pragmatic eclecticism (cognitive pluralism) that avoids a sustained interrogation of the political assumptions upon which each "truth" is founded. When such inspection is evaded, the political conditions of possibility of each truth (that is, both the "external" factors that determine, and the internal standards that certify, each truth) are veiled. Ideologically such occultation prevents the exposure of the close relation between the truths sanctified by the internal standards of a system and the prevailing political order which needs diverse versions of truth (that is, the imaginary free individual) to reproduce existing social relations and thus perpetuate its dominion.

Derrida achieves his deconstruction of the hierarchy and reinscribes what he represents as "dehierarchized" terms through a new kind of "reading" that like "close reading" takes the text as its unit of cognition. In this respect he, like Gadamer and almost all traditional humanist interpreters of texts, conceives of the text as an empirical given (not as a set of material relationships); and like all empiricists, he assumes that knowledge derives from this empirical entity itself. Of course, Derrida's is not a "vulgar empiricism": but what might be called (using one of his own terms) an empiricism of the "trace," the weaving of the signifying vestiges of difference into the tissue of a text, which he thematizes as a "farbric of grafts" that configures the cognitive processes of the subject. It is such an empiricism that enables and is enabled by Derrida's empiricism of the subject, whose consciousness is the space of textual knowledge.

As a "fabric of grafts," textuality is for Derrida the network of difference into which the sign enters and thus inaugurates the (unending) process of dissemination. It is an undetermined and undeterminable move of difference, differing, and subversion of centered signification. As the site of *différance*, textuality is the master frame of intelligibility in Derrida's writings; and it is through such theorizing of textuality that he posits intelligibility to be the effect of cognitivism. It is cognitive because intelligibility is achieved through the hermeneutic self-reflexivity of the subject of interpretation and as the outcome of the empiricism of the trace through an exegetical enterprise that regards the text as the locus of meaning.

5

The general pattern of the maneuver through which textuality is used as a frame of intelligibility to produce the notion of the real that is supportive of the dominant ideologies requires us to propose, as Gadamer does, that social actions should be understood as a form of textuality (Skinner, 7). The nature of this knowledge (of the social) is, like the text, indeterminate; such knowledge has only the status deconstruction assigns to a "signified" (the "meaning" of the "social"). As the model of intelligibility of the social analytic, the text posits the social as arbitrary (the effect of the laws of the alea), that is to say, as having no determining "cause" and no origin or telos. Among those modes of social philosophy most influenced by this deconstructive social analytic, one of the most significant is postmarxism, as we indicated in section 5 of Chapter Three above. Here we would like to elaborate further on those earlier observations.

In his essay, "Transformations of Advanced Industrial Societies and the Theory of the Subject," Laclau begins by defining the social as "that which is always already there, as a possibility and as a terrain for the constitution of differences" (39). Such a definition of the social enables Laclau to dispense immediately with the need for a social analytic in which the social can be "explained" in terms of any relation of determination—a logic, in other words, that will enable the analyst to account for asymmetrical relations of power. He is quite explicit on this. The question is not that of explaining "exploitative" relations (this being a concern of Marxism that has been left behind), but that of "identifying the social with an infinite play of differences in relation to which there is no privileged point of entry" (39). The similarity of this notion of the social with Roland Barthes's idea of the plural text is clear. The notion of a social analytic that does not account for relations of exploitation through a social calculus of power but is merely interested in the trajectory of "difference" allows Laclau to reject the concept of class conflicts and finally to erase the very idea of "society" ("as a founding totality of its discrete process") as an "impossible object" (40). He also dispenses with the notions of the social as having an "origin" and a "telos." The elision of "origin" is, of course, the familiar move in deconstruction for cancelling "history." Without an "origin" the phenomenon (whether social, economic, ideological) is "always already" there and will "always already" be there and as such exists in an *eternity* of ludic difference ("textuality"). We would like to point out that this elision of origin amounts, in fact, to the recuperation of "presence." It is a move similar to the one we suggested is found in the death and rebirth of the subject in ludic (post)modern theory, and is a mark of the neotranscendentalism revived in deconstruction and in its social analytics.

Having posited the social as an instance of "difference" (rather than conflict), Laclau is thus able to dispense completely with any logic that attempts to account for unequal relations in society. The suspension of such a logic, however, creates difficulty in accounting for the "unification" that characterizes the social. Laclau's solution to this problem is to introduce a ludic relation of connotation to explain social "relatedness," instead of employing relations of determination and thus producing a social analytic that can account for exploitation. The ideological function of making sense of the social in terms of connotations (as suggested in our previous parallel between Laclau and Roland Barthes) is to "rhetoricize" the social: to read the social in terms of a set of connotative conventions or as he puts it, a "connotative logic," rather than in terms of historical practices. This logic proposes the "unification" in the social not as "identity" (Derrida's association of "identity" with logocentrism lies behind Laclau's theory), but as an instance of ludic difference. Laclau states:

> [t]his unification does not presuppose any identity but, instead, its starting point is the recognition of the differences between the connoted elements. And this, of course, is the specific characteristic of the sign: a type of relationship between elements in which each of the elements points towards the rest without this relationship being pre-determined by the nature of any of them.
>
> To conceive social relations as articulations of differences is to conceive them as signifying relations. And the two principles of the linguistic sign established by Saussure— the arbitrariness—are also valid for all the signifying systems on the basis of which social relations are constituted. As Saussure puts it: 'If the mechanism of language were entirely rational it would be possible to study it in itself; but since it is nothing more than the partial correction of a system that is naturally chaotic, we adopt the perspective imposed by the nature of language itself and we study this mechanism as a limitation of the arbitrary' (*Cours de linguistique générale* 182-183). Something similar can be said of social relations which, far from constituting the expression of an underlying necessity, exist only as partial efforts of construction and rationalization of an experience which by definition transcends them. This impossibility of referring the social order to a transcendent principle is what establishes the discursive nature of the social. (40-41)

Appealing to Derrida's notion in *Writing and Difference* that "the absence of a transcendental signified extends the domain and the play of signification infinitely" (280), Laclau arrives at his most ideologically significant conclusion, which is "ultimately the arbitrary character of social relations" ("Transformations of Advanced Industrial Societies" 41). Therefore in the deconstructive social analytic of postmarxism, "no social linkage can be constituted except as an overdetermination of differences" (44). "Exploitation," the asymmetry of "power" as the logic of the social is therefore, according to Laclau, part of the "transcendental signified" and as such should be placed under erasure. Such a notion of the social as textual difference foregrounds the role that deconstructive theory has played in providing the late capitalist regime of truth with a philosophical justification, that is, in managing its crisis of legitimacy. The social as textual and the textual as *difference* allows for history to be seen as the textualization of difference and the social itself as an instance of the playfulness of the sign. The political consequence is that the social is seen not as constructed by the conflicts generated by class struggle, but as produced by "difference," a non-conflictual "variousness" (pluralism). By removing con-flictuality and class struggle as contestation over the economic order of the social formation, *rhetoric* rather than *economics* becomes the term that explains history.

The model of text assumed here is that which is made popular through Roland Barthes's notion of the "writerly text." As a writerly text, the social is plural, reversible, and finally and most significantly "undecidable." As a writerly text, the social is knowable only through the cognitive self-reflexivity of the "process" of the "pleasure" of the split subject, rather than through its "product" (effect), the exploitation of the labor of one class by another. Since texts (as models of reality) are proved empirically—by close reading and a lexia-by-lexia semiotic meditation—to be indeterminate and since furthermore their indeterminacy is set up as an occasion for *jouissance* and the arousal of desire, then the Real itself (which is now regarded as a mode of textuality) should also be approached aesthetically. "The aesthetic dimension," writes Laclau in "Building the New Left," "the dimension of desire that is fulfilled in the aesthetic experience, is fundamental to the configuration of a world" (22). The apotheosis of "process," "openness," and "non-closure" of the writerly text/the Real is in fact a legitimation of political liberalism and its most valued term, "pluralism." It is through tolerant pluralism (which is the ethics of acquiescence, rather than the politics of conflict) of the Real in its existing form that the dominant order reproduces itself. It is a mark of the success of the dominant textualist ideologies that any act of oppositional intervention is represented in culture as a totalitarian act of violence (intolerance) and thus a sign of the mis-reading of the opulence, plurality, and indeterminacy of the undecidable social.

One significant consequence of the deconstructive social analytic is that the social is like the deconstructed text. The text, as we have seen, in deconstructive problematics, does not "refer" to any entity other than its own processes of signification and is an instance of slippage of representation. It is, in other words, a self-allegory of its own dissemination; and, as such, it contains the "true knowledge" about itself in itself and is, therefore, auto-intelligible. Like the deconstructed text, the deconstructed social too has no other center than itself and, as such, is also auto-intelligible: it contains within itself the true knowledge about itself: knowledge of the impossibility of (social) knowledge. The social, in other words, is intelligible in its own terms as a ludic empirical entity and is not in need of a "conceptual" analytic to make sense of it. Deconstructive textuality, which begins as an argument for "mediation" thus ends up as an analytic of autonomy and autointelligibility: as the ethics of ludic transparency! History, the site of concepts through which different classes grapple with social contradictions, is itself erased in the interest of an "always already" that makes sense in its "own" immanent terms.

In Derridean deconstruction, as in any empiricist paradigm, knowledge belongs to the object (the text) itself, which is assumed to be the site of a set of determining properties such as "literariness" or "philosophicality." Derridian deconstruction claims that texts do not have a representational meaning and therefore cannot be self-identical: a philosophical text, for instance, is said to be ultimately self-divided as a form of writing and fiction and as a literary text, to be equally heterogeneous and thus non-literary since it is involved in the inevitable movement of the metaphorical towards the literal. Nevertheless, such a claim is based on pregiven empirical categories such as the literary, the philosophical, and the like. In deconstructing a philosophical text, Derrida demonstrates how it "behaves" like a literary text, which means that it transgresses its traditional boundaries and enters the "forbidden" domains of what culture makes intelligible as the literary. Without positing a pre-given, non-differential intelligibility called the "literary," the Derridian deconstruction of the "philosophical" cannot take place. The existence of the "literary" as an empirical category with a set of well-textualized properties is not only assumed in the deconstructive operation, but is fully and clearly articulated and "thematized—in fact positively "proven"—in the works of such deconstructors as de Man.

In *Blindness and Insight*, de Man locates "rhetoric" in the literariness and defines the "literary" in quite traditional and empirical manner: "We are ... calling the 'literary,' in the full sense of the term, any text that implicitly or explicitly signifies its own rhetorical mode and prefigures its own misunderstanding as the correlative of its rhetorical nature; that is, of its 'rhetoricity'" (136). "Rhetoricity" becomes here the foundation of the new definition of literature, a new quality through which literature is essentialized. Such an essentialization is very much in accord with humanist views of literature which deconstruction supposedly displaces—at least according to the narrative by which a great shift is supposed to have taken place with the coming of the (post)modern humanities. In fact deconstruction is a rather sophisticated reproduction of dominant values. A radical theory must not only decenter such an essentialization, but rigorously work to demonstrate that literature is in itself a historical construct, the effect of global frames of intelligibility that designate certain texts of culture as literary in order to preserve in that space a private place for the circulation of required values and assumptions about the Real through the operations of the "aesthetic."

6

Radical critical theories have problematized such traditional notions as that there is a distinct category of texts which can be called "literary," and through such a problematization, they have moved towards a transgressive transdisciplinarity in which the texts of culture are interrogated in relation to the politics of knowing and the power/knowledge/exploitation relations of society. The established view of literary texts as "by nature" different from other modes of writing culture (such as anthropology, psychoanalysis, biology, history, politics, and popular discourses) is based on two major arguments. The first is that literature is a discourse marked by such inherent formal properties as metaphoric density, narrative technique and syntax all governed by unique laws and structures. However, efforts to distinguish literary discourse from other discourses by its use of metaphor, sound, imagery, and narrative devices are dispelled by the fact that there are more metaphors, for instance, in one page of *Sports Illustrated* than in a story by Hemingway. The second argument assumes that literary texts, unlike texts by physicists and biologists, for instance, serve no practical purpose. This criterion too fails to separate the literary from the non-literary, since many texts now read almost exclusively as "literature" one had such "practical" purposes as recording historical events (Gibbon, for instance). Furthermore, to take the inverse, texts that are composed as "literary" are often read as "practical," for instance, as anthropological and sociological data: for example, the texts of Updike are read by some French critics as research "documents" in the archives of American class behavior. As Terry Eagleton has persuasively argued (in "The Subject of Literature"), literary texts do have very clear pragmatic uses in culture because they produce the required subjectivities necessitated by the material operations of that culture. Radical critical theory brackets the received distinctions between such categories as the "literary" and the "non-literary" as themselves merely the "effects" of reading practices which are in turn historically shaped. In fact some contemporary texts, such as Mailer's *Armies of the Night* or Michael Herr's *Dispatches*, dramatize these theoretical questions: readers wonder whether they are "literary works" or "journalistic reportage." The answer seems to lie not in locating some "given" quality and a set of formal properties in the texts themselves, but in the way they are made intelligible by the dominant theories of knowledge (Ebert and Zavarzadeh, "Literary Studies as Cultural Studies"). As Eagleton again remarks in summing up contemporary debates over the concept of literature, "literature, in the sense of a set of works of assured and unalterable value, distinguished by certain shared inherent properties, does not exist" (*Literary Theory* 11).

In radical theory, "literature" is not "essentially" the discourse of "voiding," as de Man thinks, but a discourse which is historically specific and socially determined. Any text can be "literary" if the historical forces shaping the reading practices of social class allow it to be subjected to certain kinds of reading operations (see Bennett, *Outside Literature*). These operations aim at answering not only merely the conventional question of *what* a text means, but also the questions of *how* and, more importantly, *why* it means. Traditionally the "how" is taken as a sign of the non-pragmaticality of literary discourse: it is not the "what" (the practical" that matters in reading literature but the "how" (its aesthetic and rhetorical impact). Radical theory takes the "how" to be not so much the signifier of an aesthetic effect, but the sign of the *materiality* of signification: the specific ways in which the "meaning effect" is enabled by the dominant signifying processes, social contradictions, and ideology that situate the reader in historically constituted positions of intelligibility (that is, subject positions) in terms of which the text "makes sense"—*why* a text means what it is assumed to mean. The why, in short, is the marking of the political economy of reading.

This radical re-understanding of literature as the effect of operations that foreground its historical materiality, its social constructedness, and the historical situation in which the text has become meaningful (why) has placed the study of the texts of culture on an entirely new ground. If there are no inherent properties to set literature apart from other modes of cultural writing, then the function of "reading" ("literary studies") is no longer the effort to guard an established and closed canon of texts (Leavis's "Great Tradition") by imparting special skills and attitudes, but becomes instead the transformation of literary studies itself so that it can address the problems of textuality and the political economy of representation in culture. From the perspective of radical critical theory, the function of literary studies is to inquire into the ways "meaning" is produced and disseminated in all texts of culture. The "literary" is thus not so much the name of a class of texts or qualities as it is the mark of the political economy of signification itself. All texts of culture, from the scientific to the popular, from the written book to rock video, are open to material-ist reading—materialist not in the narrow (post)structuralist sense (the materiality of the word) but in the sense of the relations of production (what we call political economy). Such a reunderstanding of the "literary" (moving it beyond deconstruction's "rhetorical" understanding and connecting it with the relations of productions) will not only decenter the traditional notion of literature as a set of rhetorical objects but will also put in question de Man's idea of literature/the rhetorical as "essentially" the discourse of "voiding," and thus display rhetoric as an apparatus of class struggle.

From such a perspective we can acquire a new grasp of deconstruction's project. If, as de Man claims, rhetoric is the discourse of voiding, then the act of voiding does not take place in a political vacuum: it voids those intelligibilities that stand in the way of the hegemonic rule of a particular class. The discourses that, for example,

Derrida, de Man, Lyotard, Deleuze have tended to void are those discourses that posit history, the social, and the economic as central, material discourses of culture. In other words, rhetoric is, like all other cultural texts, the effects of its uses: it thus may in fact "void" and "affirm" at the same time. The reading operation Derrida deploys in order to "void," by the very economy of signification, "affirms" nevertheless: it affirms the discourse of "textuality" as difference, as an unending series of differings. It thus undercuts the "certainty" of the historical agent in undertaking practices that are antagonistic to the class that uses deconstruction to "affirm" its values (values, that is, which support that class's regime of truth). To theorize rhetoric as in "essence" the discourse of "voiding," therefore, is itself a political act, an act of affirmation. The "rhetorical turn" in the ludic (post)modern human sciences, is, by the same token, a historical turn: it is an attempt to cancel those class intelligibilities theorized in the sciences of man which are no longer effective modes of legitimation of the ruling regime of truth and are thus unable to offer sustained and forceful support to the dominant economic organization of society.

The old empirical anthropology is, at this historical moment, too "weak" a theoretical support for the hegemonic powers of the West: the new "poetic" anthropology is historically a much more effective and sophisticated mode of inquiry into those truths that are favorable to the reproduction of existing social relations on a global scale. The old empirical anthropology and the new interpretive anthropology, in other words, are both discourses of history and, as such, are the effects of their uses. There uses have been at the service of the dominant academy, which, on behalf of the reigning social order, has attempted to offer new, up-to-date, and fresh legitimations to the existing exploitative economic relations. The old and the new are thus both strategies of containment and both attempt, in various manners, to save the most necessary entity in the perpetuation of the dominant social order: the free individual. In undertaking such a project, they both need to posit an empirical/cognitivist intelligibility that is located within the object of knowledge and within the interiority of consciousness of the subject of knowledge.

Derrida's rejection of the traditional "decidability" of meaning and his introduction instead of the concept of "dissemination" as a mode of "undecidable" signification in texts combines this empiricism and cognitivism with his ideology of liberal pluralism.

"Dissemination" is, in the last analysis, an exemplification of his contention that "Truth is plural" (*Writing and Difference* 103). Dissemination rejects an interpretive model (like Gadamer's) that is based on a central authority determining the meaning of a text in favor of scattered sites of signification (each with its own local "law of being") in the processes of textual semiosis. Derrida's rejection of a controlled semiosis in favor of dissemination is an ideological move that he makes in order to dismantle the last remnants of Western feudalism which survive in late capitalism and manifest themselves as efforts to establish a central authority over the processes of signification in the texts of culture. Instead of this central authority (centered signification), the Derridean notion of dissemination installs a post-feudal, bourgeois (democratic) idea of signification which allows for different sites of a text to be equally involved in engendering the "meaning" of that text. Such a pluralistic mode of "free" signification ("dissemination") based on the presumed "equality" of various semiotic nodes of the text, each acting in the production of meaning "according to its own law," quietly legit-imized the *laissez faire* ethics and the economic organization that it articulates: the free competition in the market among (plural) sovereign individuals. It thus posits a mode of intelligibility that privileges the enterprising, free individual as the center of all meaningful activities of culture. Derrida does not then remove "authority" from the science of texts; he merely provides a new avenue for its continued domination. His pluralistic model of dissemination allows the authority to remain in place in such a manner that its domination is seen as the outcome of the consent of equal, rational, and free persons, that is, as the effect of "voluntarism." We hardly need to add that Derrida's theory of "dissemination" regionalizes meaning in different sites in the text and thus blocks any move towards a global and integrative understanding of meaning in relation to cultural and political frames of signification. Dissemination further enhances the idea of the undecidability of the Real. "Insofar as textual undecidabilility precludes raising questions about truth, and thus truth in normative, social and political matters, it perpetuates the status quo" (Hoy, "Jacques Derrida" 60). It should be noted, however, that although Derrida has opposed global and integrative modes of explanation, he does not hesitate to declare "totalizing" conclusions such as the total theory about meaning as dissemination or "rhetoric" as the discourse of "voiding."

The traditional hermeneutic enterprise is based on the assumption that texts are "readable"—that they are, by and large, reliable constructs that have a "meaning," although this meaning is problematic because of the situationality of both the text and the reader. In Derridean "deconstruction," which can be viewed as a form of "radical hermeneutics" (Hoy 50), the legibility/readability of the text is put in question. The "meaning" of the text, consequently, becomes not merely relative (as Gadamer has argued) but in a radical sense of the word "undecidable." The "undecidability" of the meaning of a text in Derrida's writings, it should be further clarified, is the outcome of his critique of the traditional theories of representation. These theories were on the whole mentalist in the sense that questions of representation were focused on the notion of whether or not the mind (that is, its ideas) represented reality appropriately. After the mentalist theories were displaced by linguistic theories, the question was reformulated as the ability of language to represent reality (the problem of "reference"). In language-based theories of representation the questions centers around the ability of a text to represent reality outside itself, since any claim to truth is based on the assumption that the text (writing) "represents" reality (either the reality of the text—an "argument" in a philosophical text, for instance—or a reality which exists outside the text). It is the belief in the ability of language to do so that lies behind hermeneutic theories of interpretation and other humanist modes of understanding that regard the text as "readable." Derrida's rejection of "representation" as a ground of meaning is based on the idea that the text is a rhetorical construct whose tropic structure constantly undermines its mimetic desires and thus renders it "unreadable." The subversion of the representational in the text by its tropic structure is, for Derrida, an indication not only that texts fail to achieve their stated purpose (have a "literal," "representational" meaning) but also that they in fact work against themselves and demonstrate the impossibility of the very self-coherence upon which their claim to representation is founded.

In our view, all theories of the text are, in the last instance, theories of the subject. In our interrogation of humanist theories of the text, we argued that such theories are finally aimed at the production and maintenance of the "moral" subject—the subject position in which the class interests of the petty-bourgeoise are most securely established. In his *The Ethics of Criticism* Tobin Siebers has recently updated humanist "moral"/"ethical" readings of the texts of culture to take into account some of the moves of contemporary theory. Although Siebers tries at the outset to distinguish his own understanding of ethics from the "undecidable" deconstructive "ethics" promoted, for example, by Hillis Miller in *The Ethics of Reading*, he nevertheless makes it clear that, whatever their differences, both humanist and (post)structuralist versions of "ethics" "do not reflect the same ends" as political understandings of culture (1). Like humanist textuality, the deconstructive textuality of Derrida, Deleuze, Lyotard, de Man, and Miller also produces—via a different route that we have been examining in this book—an apolitical and ahistorical subject which is the ludic subject of "ethics." The return to "ethics" in (post)structuralist theory is part of a move to erase the idea of the "polis" and inscribe the space of the "community" as the authentic site of the social. Ludic ethics, as represented by its most articulate theorist, Foucault, lies in the domain of interpersonal relations rather than in the space of "collectivity" (politics and the city). Through ethical norms, the social conflicts in the city are reduced to interpersonal conversations in the community (see "Ethics of Care for the Self"). Undecidable "ethics" has also become an important discourse of the ludic feminism that dominates academic and intellectual circles in America: Alice Jardine, for instance, produces it by giving a reverse reading to Lawrence Kohlberg's theory of moral stages. Whereas humanist Kohlberg situates women in the "in-between" Stage Three of his model of moral development (thus rendering them morally "incomplete" as compared to men, some of whom go on to reach the "ultimate" moral state), Jardine reunderstands Kohlberg's paradigm in terms of the undecidable "logic of the in-between" ("Opaque Texts and Transparent Contexts" 104) 'and thus situates the Stage Three position (which, from Kohlberg's viewpoint, is "deficient") as in effect "desire-able."

In contrast to humanist and ludic theory, the task of radical critical theory is to change the dominant social relations of production. To do this, it should first intervene in the construction of hegemonic cultural meanings that erase social contradictions from the scene of the social and produce a ludic political imaginary free of class antagonism for the subject in late capitalism. Such an intervention requires that radical theory not only go beyond humanist common sense but also beyond ludic undecidability. This going "beyond" will involve, among other things, both the reconceptualization of the subject not merely as the speaking subject of an ahistorical symbolic order but as the contradictory subject of class, race, gender, sexuality, state . . . as well as the reunderstanding of subjects as social agents who "make their own history, but . . . not . . . just as they please": "they do not make it under circumstances chosen by themselves, but under circumstances directly encountered, given and transmitted from the past" (Marx, *The Eighteenth Brumaire of Louis Bonaparte* 15).

However, it is just such a going "beyond" (revolutionary practice) that is prohibited in almost all the discourses of contemporary literary and cultural theory. The discourse of humanism posits deconstruction as the absolute "other" beyond which the reader should not venture. Derrida, Lyotard, Foucault, and other (post)structuralists are, of course, highly critical of such a going "beyond." For Derrida, for instance, a going "beyond"—striving for a "post" state—is merely an expression of desire for/an illusion of "progress," a wish to get ever closer to truth ("presence"). It is, of course, quite instructive that Derrida's injunction against a going "beyond" has not deterred him from undertaking a rather "violent" move beyond himself. In recent pronouncements about his non-opposition to presence, such as "Some Questions and Responses," he has revealed a side of his work that accepts the telepathic and the mystical as a mode of true knowing. In this he has indeed gone "beyond" and in a manner similar to that of Kristiva, Sollers, and other *Tel Quel* intellectuals of his generation who have embraced mysticism as the region of unbounded knowledge and libidinal freedom: a region free from the torture of the political. (This move, incidentally, once more reveals the proximity/identity of Derrida's readings with those of the mainstream humanist interpretation of cultural signs.) In her essay, "The Differends of Man," Avital Ronell writes that the mystical tendency in Derrida is part of his Jewish heritage and that people like Habermas who attack his mysticism are therefore anti-semitic. This reading of Derrida's mysticism is part of the current larger cultural move to erase concept and to fetishize experience (it offers Jewishness as the "experience" of the transcendental). Sartre, of course, in *Anti-Semite and Jew* offers a radically different reading of Jewishness—as passionate rationality (see also Zavarzadeh, *Pun(k)deconstruction*).

The going "beyond" of radical critical theory is undertaken not to acquire transdiscursive (mystical) pleasure, nor to foster the illusion that cultural meanings are somehow authorized by a panhistorical truth. Its "beyond" or "post" is not so much the site of some proximate to an ahistorical truth as it is the space of opposition to the reigning truth which is fraught with social contradictions. As we have indicated, the meanings of culture are the effects of social and class struggles, and it is to account for and then support these struggles to inscribe oppositional and revolutionary meanings in the texts of culture that radical critical theory should undertake a going "beyond" the discourses of both humanistic and ludic theory.

7

We started the discourses of this book abruptly, and we shall also end them abruptly, that is to say, without offering any "affirmative" view, any blue-print of how things should be. The demand to articulate what "should be," as Marx implied in his own refusal to provide detailed plans for the future and in his critique of "utopian" thinking, only serves (in the benign guise of guiding change) to erase history and thus to postpone any revolutionary transformation. However, as is shown in Marx's practice of critique —which is itself the articulation of a radical commitment to transformation—the "affirmative" is always inscribed in "negation," that is to say, in the critique of what exists.

Without accepting the philosophical and political implications of the Hegelian twist that Adorno and Marcuse bring to "negative dialectics," we nevertheless believe that Marcuse's notion of "affirmative culture" set forth in *Negations* (88-133) does, to some extent, mark the "positivistic" idea of the social underlying the "affirmative" and capture the ideological imperatives in the call from the dominant for an "affirmative" discourse. By projecting an "ideal" state, the "affirmative" brackets the "factual world of the daily struggle for existence" (95) and by doing so, renders the social contradictions of capitalism immune to critique. The "affirmative" (the privileged discourse of the hegemonic ludic academy, as we have already noted in arguing even the ultimately "affirmative" character of deconstruction), in other words, is a mode of deferring —it says: "Not now; it is not practical today; maybe later." In the "promise" (for happiness) that is inscribed in the "affirmative," the existing is legitimated as that which cannot, at the present time, be changed. The "later," of course, will never be "practical"—it will never actually materialize in the promise of the "affirmative"—and the practical (what exists) will conserve its hegemonic rule as the only possible form of social truth.

In short, the "affirmative," by focusing on what is to come, ignores what actually is and thereby relegates the existing to a space outside critique. In the last analysis, the pervasive rejection of critique (derived from seeing it as a negation founded on a merely illusory—not "solid—social truth) and the consequent insistence of the dominant that unless its critics offer an "affirmative" blue-print for the future, their critique of the present cannot be seen as valid, only reproduces the hegemonic pluralism that allows multiple "realities" to co-exist without ever attempting to relate them together so as to indicate how they are not equal and how the inequality of some is the direct result of the domination of others. The hegemonic, in other words, demands the "affirmative" and eagerly provides a site for its discourses in the current discourses of the social so that the "affirmative" can have a life *parallel* to that of the dominant and can thus serve as a discourse in which the pressures of social contradictions are safely released. What the "affirmative" therefore affirms—by way of concealing class conflicts—is in fact the existing relations of production in late capitalism. It diverts attention from the "now" and thus, by affirming the bourgeois imaginary, provides an escape to the "after." Critique, by contrast, marks the contradictions of the social and relates the situation of the exploited to that of the exploiting: it offers a global understanding in which the dominant and the dominated, the now and the later, are all related to the underlying logic of the social division of labor. As long as the pluralism of the dominant prevails, there will always be "affirmative" discourses parallel to the existing ones which, through the promise of transcendence structured by this parallelism, help to preserve the existing hegemonic discourses. We believe that social transformation (which is the main goal of theory) will not take place as long as the existing is allowed to be (along with "affirmative" others) one of the parallel "alternative" social realities. The negation of the existing, then, is the condition of possibility of change, and critique is the inaugural act for this displacement (negation) of the existing. The radically "affirmative" is the effect of critique—*is written in the critique*—and is not separate, parallel, a substitute for it. This is the meaning of Marx's recommendation (to which we referred in our "Foreward" and to which we return finally once again) not to offer the world a "doctrinaire . . . new principle . . . [as the] truth" but to "develop new principles" out of the existing ones (Marx and Engels, *Collected Works* 3: 142). This we regard to be the difference between a materialist and an idealist cultural theory.

Works Cited

Abrams, M. H. et al., eds. *The Norton Anthology of English Literature.* 5th ed. New York: Norton, 1986.
_____. *Doing Things With Words: Essays in Criticism and Critical Theory.* Ed. M. Fischer. New York: Norton, 1989.
Adams, H. "The Dizziness of Freedom, or Why I Read William Blake." *College English* 48.5 (1986): 431-443.
Alter, R. *The Pleasure of Reading in an Ideological Age.* New York: Simon and Schuster, 1989.
Alterman, E. "Not So Great." *The Nation* November 19, 1990: 584-585.
Althusser, L. *Lenin and Philosophy.* Trans. B. Brewster. New York: Monthly Review Press, 1971.
_____. *Essays in Self-Criticism.* Trans. G. Lock. London: New Left Books, 1986.
_____ and E. Balibar. *Reading Capital.* Trans. B. Brewster. London: New Left Books, 1970.
Altieri, C. *Act and Quality.* Amherst, MA: University of Massachusetts Press, 1981.
American Studies Association. "Creativity in Difference: The Culture of Gender, Race, Ethnicity, and Class." Videocassette Order Form. *American Studies Association Newsletter* 11.4 (December 1988): 9.
Arac, J. *Critical Genealogies: Historical Situations for Postmodern Literary Studies.* New York: Columbia University Press, 1989.
Atlas, J. "The Battle of the Books." *New York Times Magazine* June 5, 1988: 24ff.
_____. "What Is Fukuyama Saying?" *New York Times Magazine* October 22, 1989: 38ff.
Barnes, B. "Thomas Kuhn." In Q. Skinner, ed., *The Return of Grand Theory in the Human Sciences.* London and New York: Cambridge University Press, 1985. 83-100.
Barth, J. *Lost in the Funhouse.* New York: Doubleday, 1988.
Barthes, R. *Elements of Semiology.* Trans. A. Lavers and C. Smith. Boston: Beacon Press, 1968.
_____. *Critical Essays.* Trans. R. Howard. Evanston: Northwestern University Press, 1972.

_____. *The Pleasures of the Text*. Trans. R. Miller. New York: Hill and Wang, 1975.

_____. *S/Z*. Trans. R. Miller. New York: Hill and Wang, 1976.

Belsey, C. *Critical Practice*. London and New York: Metheun, 1980.

_____. "Letter to the Editor." *Times Literary Supplement* November 4, 1983: 1217.

Benhabib, S. *Critique, Norm and Utopia: A Study of the Foundations of Critical Theory*. New York: Columbia, 1986.

Bennett, T. *Outside Literature*. New York: Routledge, 1990.

Benveniste, E. *Problems of General Linguistics*. Trans. M. E. Meek. Coral Gables, FL: University of Florida Press, 1971.

Berkhofer, R. "Poetics and Politics in and of a New American Studies." American Studies Association Convention. Miami Beach. October 21, 1988.

Black, J. ed. *Radical Lawyers*. New York: Avon Books. 1971.

Blonsky, M. ed. *On Signs*. Baltimore, MD: Johns Hopkins University Press, 1985.

Blumenthal, S. "Bushwhacked! From the White House, a Thousand Points of Light." *GQ* January 1991: 100ff.

Boon, J. J. "Claude Levi Strauss." In Q. Skinner, ed., *The Return of Grand Theory in the Human Sciences*. London and New York: Cambridge University Press, 1985. 159-176.

Boyle, J. "The Politics of Reason: Critical Legal Theory and Local Social Thought." *University of Pennsylvania Law Review* 133 (1985): 685-780.

Brinton, C. *Anatomy of Revolution*. New York: Vintage Books, 1957.

Brownlow, W. G. and A. Pryne. *Ought American Slavery to be Perpetuated*. 1858; rpt. Miami: Mnemosyne Publishing, 1969.

Bruner, J. *Actual Minds, Possible Worlds*. Cambridge: Harvard University Press, 1986.

Clark, S. "The Annales Historians." In Q. Skinner, ed., *The Return of Grand Theory in the Human Sciences*. London and New York: Cambridge University Press, 1985. 177-198.

Clifford, J. and G. E. Marcus, eds. *Writing Culture*. Berkeley: University of California Press, 1985.

Conklin, H. E. "Hanunoo Color Terms." *Southern Journal of Anthropology* 11 (1955): 339-344.

Coward, R. and J. Ellis. *Language and Materialism*. London: Routledge and Kegan Paul, 1977.

Crews, F. *Skeptical Engagements*. New York, Oxford University Press, 1986.

"Critical Times at Harvard." *Harvard Magazine* 88.4 (March-April 1986): 67.

Culler, J. *The Pursuit of Signs*. Ithaca, NY: Cornell University Press, 1981.

_____. *On Deconstruction: Theory and Criticism after Structuralism*. Ithaca, NY: Cornell University Press, 1982.

Dalton, C. "An Essay in the Deconstruction of Contract Doctrine." *Yale Law Journal* 94 (1985): 997-1114.

De Man, Paul. *Allegories of Reading*. New Haven, CT: Yale University Press, 1977.

_____. *The Resistance to Theory*. Minneapolis: University of Minnesota Press. 1986.

Derrida, J. *Of Grammatology*. Trans. G. C. Spivak. Baltimore: Johns Hopkins University Press, 1976.

_____. *Spurs: Nietzsche's Styles*. Trans. B. Harlow. Chicago: University of Chicago Press, 1978.

_____. *Writing and Difference*. Trans. A. Bass. Chicago: University of Chicago Press, 1978.

_____. *Dissemination*. Trans. B. Johnson. Chicago: University of Chicago Press, 1981.

_____. *Positions*. Trans. A. Bass. Chicago: University of Chicago Press, 1981.

_____. *Margins of Philosophy*. Trans. A. Bass. Chicago: University of Chicago Press, 1982.

_____. "Sending: On Representation." *Social Research* 49 (1982): 284-326.

_____. *Signeponge/Signspong*. Trans. R. Rand. New York: Columbia University Press, 1984.

_____. *The Post Card*. Trans. A. Bass. Chicago: University of Chicago Press, 1987.

_____. "Some Questions and Responses." In N. Fabb et al., eds., *The Linguistic of Writing: Arguments between Language and Literature*. New York: Metheun, 1987. 252-264.

_____. *Limited Inc*. Evanston, IL: Northwestern University Press: 1988.

Dreyfus, H. L. and P. Rabinow. *Michel Foucault: Beyond Structuralism and Hermeneutics*. 2nd ed. Chicago: University of Chicago Press, 1983.

Eagleton, T. *Literary Theory: An Introduction*. Minneapolis: University of Minnesota Press, 1983.

_____. "The Subject of Literature." *Cultural Critique* 2 (1985-86): 95-104.

_____. "Marxism and the Future of Criticism." In E. Wood, ed., *Writing and Future*. London and New York: Routledge, 1990. 177-180.

_____. *The Ideology of the Aesthetic*. Oxford: Blackwell, 1990.

Ebert, T. "Rewriting the (Post)modern: Resistance (Post)Modernism." Paper delivered at the conference Rewriting the (Post)Modern: (Post)Colonialism, Feminism, and Late Capitalism. University of Utah, March 30-31, 1990.

_____ and M. Zavarzadeh. "Literary Studies as Cultural Studies," forthcoming.

Eco, U. "How Culture Conditions the Colours We See." In M. Blonsky, ed., *On Signs*. Baltimore: Johns Hopkins Press, 1985. 158-175.

Eliot, C. N. ed. *The Harvard Classics*. 2nd ed. 50 Vols. New York: Collier, 1917.

Ellis, J. *Against Deconstruction*. Princeton: Princeton University Press, 1989.

Fabb, N. et al. *The Linguistics of Writing: Arguments between Language and Literature.* New York: Metheun, 1987.

Falwell, J. *Listen, America!* New York: Bantam Books, 1981.

Felperin, H. *Beyond Deconstruction: The Uses and Abuses of Literary Theory.* Oxford: Clarendon Press, 1985.

Fish, S. "Reply." *PMLA* 104 (1989): 219-221.

_____. *Doing What Comes Naturally.* Durham: Duke University Press, 1990.

Fiske, J. *Reading Popular Culture.* Boston: Unwin, Hyman, 1989.

_____. *Understanding Popular Culture.* Boston: Unwin, Hyman, 1989.

Foucault, M. *The Archaeology of Knowledge.* Trans. A. M. Sheridan Smith. New York: Pantheon, 1972.

_____. *The Order of Things.* New York: Vintage Books, 1973.

_____. *Language, Counter-Memory, Practice: Selected Essays.* Ed. D. F. Bouchard. Ithaca, NY: Cornell University Press, 1977.

_____. "Politics and the Study of Discourse." *Ideology and Consciousness* 3 (1978): 3-26.

_____. *The History of Sexuality. Volume 1: An Introduction.* Trans. R. Hurley. New York: Vintage Books. 1980.

_____. *Power/Knowledge.* Ed. C. Gordon. New York: Pantheon, 1980.

_____. "The Ethics of Care for the Self." In "The Final Foucault: Studies on Michel Foucault's Last Works." *Philosophy and Social Criticism* 2/3 (1987): 112-32.

Fowler, R. et al. *Language and Control.* London: Routledge and Kegan Paul, 1979.

Frege, G. "On Sense and Reference." In F. Zabeeth, et al., *Readings in Semiotics.* Urbana: University of Illinois Press, 1974.

Fukuyama, F. "The End of History." *National Interest* Summer 1989: 3-18.

Furet, F. *Interpreting the French Revolution.* Trans. E. Foster. New York: Cambridge University Press, 1981.

_____. *Marx and the French Revolution.* Trans. D. K. Furet. Chicago: University of Chicago Press, 1989.

Gadamer, H. G. *Philosophical Hermeneutics.* Trans. D. Linge. Berkeley: University of California Press, 1976.

_____. *Truth and Method.* New York: Crossroad, 1984.

Gardner, H. *In Defense of the Imagination.* Cambridge: Harvard University Press, 1984.

Graff, G. "Fear and Trembling at Yale." *American Scholar* 46 (1976-1977): 467-478.

_____. *Literature Against Itself.* Chicago: University of Chicago Press, 1979.

_____. "Editor's Forward." In J. Derrida, *Limited Inc.* Evanston, IL: Northwestern University Press, 1988.

_____. "Response to Papers: 'The Cultural Wars and the Classroom.'" Modern Language Association Convention. Washington, D.C. December 29, 1989.

_____ and R. Gibbons, et al. *Criticism in the University.* Evanston, IL: Northwestern University Press, 1985.

Habermas, J. *The Philosophical Discourse of Modernity.* Trans. F. Lawrence. Cambridge: MIT Press, 1983.

Hanninen, S. and L. Paldan. *Rethinking Ideology: A Marxist Debate.* Berlin: Argument-Verlag, 1983.

Harlow, B. *Resistance Literature.* New York and London: Metheun, 1987.

Hassan, I. *The Postmodern Turn.* Columbus: Ohio State Press, 1987.

Hegel, G. W. F. *The Philosophy of History.* Trans. J. Sibree. New York: Dover, 1956.

_____. *Reason in History.* Trans. R. S. Hartman. Indianapolis: Bobbs-Merrill, 1974.

_____. *The Phenomenology of the Spirit.* Trans. A. V. Miller. New York: Oxford University Press, 1977.

Heidegger, M. *Poetry, Language, Thought.* Trans. A. H. Hofstadter. New York: Harper & Row, 1975.

Hirst, P. *On Law and Ideology.* Atlantic Highlands, NJ: Humanities Press, 1979.

Hjelmslev, L. *Prolegomena to a Theory of Language.* Trans. F. J. Whitfield. Madison: University of Wisconsin Press, 1961.

Hodge, R., G. Kress and G. Jones. "The Ideology of Middle Management." In Fowler et al., *Language and Control.* London: Routledge and Kegan Paul, 1979. 81-93.

Hoy, D. "Jacques Derrida." In Q. Skinner, ed., *The Return of Grand Theory in the Human Sciences.* London and New York: Cambridge University Press, 1985. 41-64.

Huyssen, A. *After the Great Divide: Modernism, Mass Culture, Postmodernism.* Bloomington: Indiana University Press, 1986.

"Integrated Proms." *New York Times* May 14, 1990: A-1.

Iser, W. *The Act of Reading: A Theory of Aesthetic Response.* Baltimore: Johns Hopkins University Press, 1978.

James, S. "Louis Althusser." In Q. Skinner, ed., *The Return of Grand Theory in the Human Sciences.* London and New York: Cambridge University Press, 1985. 141-157.

Jameson, F. "Foreword." In J.-F. Lyotard, *The Postmodern Condition.* Minneapolis: University of Minnesota Press, 1984.

_____. *The Concept of Postmodernism.* Durham: University of North Carolina Press, 1990.

Jardine, A. "Opaque Texts and Transparent Contexts: The Political Difference of Julia Kristeva." In N. K. Miller, *The Poetics of Gender.* New York: Columbia University Press, 1986. 96-116.

Jenkins, W. S. *Pro-Slavery Thought in the Old South.* Chapel Hill: University of North Carolina Press, 1935; rpt. Gloucester, MA: Peter Smith, 1960.

Johnson, B. *The Critical Difference.* Baltimore: Johns Hopkins Press, 1980.

_____. *A World of Difference.* Baltimore: Johns Hopkins Press, 1987.

Kaufmann, D. "The Profession of Theory." *PMLA* 105 (1990): 519-530.

Kavanagh, T. *The Limits of Theory.* Stanford: Stanford University Press, 1989.

Kennedy, D. *Legal Education and the Reproduction of Hierarchy.* Cambridge, MA: Afar, 1983.

_____. "The Political Significance of the Structure of Law School Curriculum." *Seton Hall Law Review* 14.1 (1983): 1-16.

Kermode, F. *An Appetite for Poetry.* Cambridge: Harvard University Press, 1989.

Kirby, D. ed. *The Politics of Law.* New York: Pantheon, 1982.

Knapp, S and W. B. Michaels. "Against Theory." In W. T. J. Mitchell., *Against Theory.* Chicago: University of Chicago Press, 1985.

Kronik, John W. "Editor's Column." *PMLA* 106 (1991): 200-204.

Kuhn, T. *The Structure of Scientific Revolutions.* Chicago: University of Chicago Press, 1970.

Lacan, J. *Speech and Language in Psychoanalysis.* Baltimore: Johns Hopkins University Press, 1968.

_____. *Écrits: A Selection.* Trans. A. Sheridan. New York: Norton, 1977.

Laclau, E. "Populist Rupture and Discourse." *Screen Education* 34 (1980): 87-93.

_____. "Transformations of Advanced Industrial Societies and the Theory of the Subject." In S. Hanninen and L. Paldan, *Rethinking Ideology: A Marxist Debate.* Berlin: Argument-Verlag, 1983.

_____. "Building a New Left." *Strategies* 1 (1988): 10-28.

_____ and C. Mouffe. "Recasting Marxism: Hegemony and New Political Movements." *Socialist Review* 66 (1982): 91-113.

_____. *Hegemony and Socialist Strategy.* London: Verso, 1985.

Lecourt, D. *Marxism and Epistemology.* London: New Left Books, 1975.

Lerner, L. *Reconstructing Literature.* Totowa, NJ: Barnes and Noble, 1983.

Lévi-Strauss, C. *The Savage Mind.* Chicago: University of Chicago Press, 1966.

Lyons, J. *Introduction to Theoretical Linguistics.* London: Cambridge University Press, 1968.

Lyotard, J.-F. *The Postmodern Condition.* Minneapolis: University of Minnesota Press, 1984.

_____. *The Differend.* Trans. G. Van Dan Abbeele. Minneapolis: University of Minnesota Press, 1988.

_____. "Sensus Communis." *Paragraph* 11 (1988): 1-23.

_____ and J.-L. Thébaud. *Just Gaming.* Trans. W. Godzich. Minneapolis: University of Minnesota Press, 1985.

Machèrey, P. *A Theory of Literary Production.* Trans. G. Wall. London: Routledge and Kegan Paul, 1978.

Maddocks, M. "Save Us, Batman, It's the P-M Word." *World Monitor* November 1989: 11-12.

Marcuse, H. *Negations.* Trans. J. J. Shapiro. Boston: Beacon Press, 1969.

Markham, J. M. "A French Thinker Who Declines a Guru Mantle." *New York Times* December 21, 1987: A-5.

Marx, K. *The Eighteenth Brumaire of Louis Bonaparte*. New York: International Publishers, 1963.

_____. *Grundrisse*. Trans. M. Nicolaus. New York: Vintage Books, 1973.

_____. *Economic and Philosophic Manuscripts of 1844*. Moscow: Progress Publishers, 1974.

_____. *Early Writings*. Trans. R. Livingstone and G. Benton. New York, Vintage Books, 1975.

_____. *Capital I*. Trans. B. Fowkes. New York: Vintage Books, 1977.

_____ and F. Engels. *Collected Works*. Vol. 3. New York: International Publishers, 1975.

_____. *Collected Works*. Vol. 5. New York: International Publishers, 1976.

_____. *Collected Works*. Vol. 38. New York: International Publishers, 1982.

Megill, A. *Prophets of Extremity: Nietzsche, Heidegger, Foucault, Derrida*. Berkeley: University of California Press, 1985.

Miller, J. H. "Steven's Rock and Criticism as Cure." *Georgia Review* 30 (1976): 5-31.

_____. "The Function of Rhetorical Study at the Present Time." *ADE Bulletin* 62 (September/November 1979): 12-16.

_____. *The Ethics of Reading*. New York: Columbia University Press, 1987.

Miller, N. K. *The Poetics of Gender*. New York: Columbia University Press, 1986.

Mitchell, W. J. T. "Critical Inquiry and the Ideology of Pluralism." *Critical Inquiry* 8 (1982): 609-618.

_____. *Against Theory: Literary Studies and the New Pragmatism*. Chicago: University of Chicago Press, 1985.

Morton, D. "Texts of Limits, the Limits of Texts, and the Containment of Politics in Contemporary Critical Theory." *diacritics* 20.1 (1990): 57-75.

_____. "Class Wars at the Limits and the Containment of Politics." In J. Berlin and M. Vivion, eds., *Critical Cultural Studies and English Studies*, forthcoming.

Mouffe, C. "Hegemony and Ideology in Gramsci," *Gramsci and Marxist Theory*. London: Routledge and Kegan Paul, 1979.

Nietzsche, F. *The Will to Power*. Trans. W. Kaufmann. New York: Vintage, 1968.

Norris, C. "Suspended Sentences: Textual Theory and the Law," *The Contest of Faculties*. London and New York: Metheun, 1985.

Outhwaite, W. "Hans-Georg Gadamer." In Q. Skinner, ed., *The Return of Grand Theory in the Human Sciences*. London and New York: Cambridge University Press, 1985. 21-39.

Peller, G. "The Metaphysics of American Law." *California Law Review* 73 (1985): 1151-1290.

Penley, C., E. Lyon, L. Spigel and J. Bergstrom, eds. *Close Encounters: Film,*

Feminism, and Science Fiction. Minneapolis: University of Minnesota Press, 1991.

Philp, M. "Michel Foucault." In Q. Skinner, ed., *The Return of Grand Theory in the Human Sciences.* London and New York: Cambridge University Press, 1985. 65-81.

Podhoretz, N. *Making It.* New York: Random House, 1967.

———. *Breaking Ranks: A Political Memoir.* New York: Harper and Row, 1979.

Popper, K. *The Logic of Scientific Discovery.* London: 1959.

Prieto, L. *Pertinence et pratique.* Paris: Minuit, 1975.

Radhakrishnan, R. "Toward an Effective Intellectual: Foucault and Gramsci." In B. Robbins, *Intellectuals: Aesthetics, Politics, Academics.* Minneapolis: University of Minneapolis Press, 1990.

Rajchman, J. and C. West, eds. *Post-Anaytic Philosophy.* New York: Columbia University Press, 1985.

"Revolution Brought Cruel Justice." *Oregon State University Center for the Humanities Newsletter* Fall 1990: 1, 6.

Ricoeur, P. *Hermeneutics and the Human Sciences.* Ed. and trans. J. B. Thompson. Cambridge: Cambridge University Press, 1983.

Robbins, B. ed. *Intellectuals: Aesthetics, Politics, Academics.* Minneapolis: University of Minneapolis Press, 1990.

Ronell, Avital. "The Differends of Man." *diacritics* 19.3 (Fall-Winter 1990): 64-75.

Rooney, E. *Seductive Reasoning: Pluralism as the Problematic of Contemporary Literary Theory.* Ithaca: Cornell University Press, 1989.

Rorty, R. *Philosophy and the Mirror of Nature.* Princeton: Princeton University Press, 1979.

———. *Consequences of Pragamatism.* Minneapolis: University of Minnesota Press, 1982.

———. "Solidarity or Objectivity?" In J. Rajchman and C. West, eds., *Post-Anaytic Philosophy.* New York: Columbia University Press, 1985. 3-19

———. *Contingency, Irony, and Solidarity.* New York: Cambridge University Press, 1989.

———. "Foucault/Dewey/Nietzsche." *Raritan* 9.4 (1990): 1-8.

Roussel, R. "The Gesture of Criticism." In T. Kavanagh, ed., *The Limits of Theory.* Stanford, CA: Stanford University Press, 1989. 139-167.

Sartre, J.-P. *Anti-Semite and Jew.* New York: Schocken, 1965.

Saussure, F. de. *Course in General Linguistics.* Trans. W. Baskin. New York: McGraw-Hill, 1966.

Seabury, S. *The Pro-Slavery Argument.* Charleston, SC: Walker, Richards & Company, 1852.

———. *American Slavery Distinguished from the Slavery of English Theorists and Justified by the Law of Nature.* New York: Mason Brothers, 1861.

Sebeok, T. ed. *How Animals Communicate.* Bloomington: Indiana University Press, 1977.

_____ and J. Umiker-Sebeok, eds. *Speaking of Apes.* New York: Plenum Press, 1980.

Shaw, P. *The War Against the Intellect: Episodes in the Decline of Discourse.* Iowa City: University of Iowa Press, 1989.

Siebers, T. *The Ethics of Criticism.* Ithaca: Cornell University Press, 1988.

Sim, S. "Lyotard and the Politics of Anti-Foundationalism." *Radical Philosopher* 44 (1986): 8-13.

Skinner, Q. ed. *The Return of Grand Theory in the Human Sciences.* London and New York: Cambridge University Press, 1985. 159-176.

Spivak, G. C. "Criticism, Feminism, and the Institution." In B. Robbins, *Intellectuals: Aesthetics, Politics, Academics.* Minneapolis: University of Minneapolis Press, 1990. 153-171.

_____. "Gayatri Spivak on the Politics of the Subaltern. Interview by Howard Winant." *Socialist Review* 90.3 (1990): 81-97.

Steiner, G. *Real Presences.* Chicago: University of Chicago Press, 1989.

Ulmer, G. "The Puncept in Grammatology." In J. Culler, ed., *On Puns.* Oxford: Blackwell, 1988.

Volshinov, V. N. [M. Bakhtin]. *Marxism and the Philosophy of Language.* Trans. L. Matejka and I. R. Titunik. Cambridge: Harvard University Press, 1986.

Wasserman, E. R. "The English Romantics: The Grounds of Knowledge." *Studies in Romanticism* 3 (1964): 17-34.

Watt, C. "Bottom's Children: The Fallacies of Structuralist, Post-Structuralist, and Deconstructionist Literary Theory." In L. Lerner, *Reconstructing Literature.* Totowa, NJ: Barnes and Noble, 1983.

Wellek, R. *The Attack on Literature and Other Essays.* Chapel Hill: University of North Carolina Press, 1982.

West, C. "After Word." In J. Rajchman and C. West, eds., *Post-Anaytic Philosophy.* New York: Columbia University Press, 1985. 259-275.

Wimsatt, W. K. and M. C. Beardsley. *The Verbal Icon.* Lexington, KY: University of Kentucky Press, 1954.

Wilden, A. *System and Structure.* 2nd ed. London: Tavistock, 1980.

Wood, E. ed. *Writing and Future.* London and New York: Routledge, 1990.

Zabeeth, F. et al. *Readings in Semantics.* Urbana: University of Illinois Press, 1974.

Zavarzadeh, M. "Theory as Resistance." *Rethinking Marxism* 2.1 (1989): 50-70.

_____. *Seeing Films Politically.* Albany: State University of New York Press, 1991.

_____. *Pun(k)deconstruction and the Ludic Political Imaginary.* Forthcoming.

_____ and D. Morton. "(Post)Modern Critical Theory and the Articulations of Critical Pedagogies." *College Literature* 17.2/3 (1990): 51-63.

Index